POTENTIAL ON THE PERIPHERY

POTENTIAL ON THE PERIPHERY

College Access from the Ground Up

OMARI SCOTT SIMMONS

FOREWORD BY
DAMON T. HEWITT

RUTGERS UNIVERSITY PRESS
New Brunswick, Camden, and Newark, New Jersey, and London

Library of Congress Cataloging-in-Publication Data

Names: Simmons, Omari Scott, author.
Title: Potential on the periphery : college access from the ground up /
    Omari Scott Simmons.
Description: New Brunswick, New Jersey : Rutgers University Press, 2018. |
    Includes bibliographical references and index.
Identifiers: LCCN 2018018794| ISBN 9780813592886 (cloth) |
    ISBN 9780813592879 (pbk.)
Subjects: LCSH: College attendance—Social aspects—United States. |
    Minorities—Education (Higher)—United States. | People with social
    disabilities—Education (Higher)—United States. | Counseling in higher
    education—United States. | Academic achievement—United States. |
    Mentoring in education—United States. | Simmons Memorial Foundation.
Classification: LCC LC148.2 .S55 2018 | DDC 378.1/6913—dc23
    LC record available at https://lccn.loc.gov/2018018794

A British Cataloging-in-Publication record for this book is available from the
British Library.

⊖ The paper used in this publication meets the requirements of the American National
Standard for Information Sciences—Permanence of Paper for Printed Library
Materials, ANSI Z39.48-1992.

www.rutgersuniversitypress.org

Manufactured in the United States of America

CONTENTS

FOREWORD

Narratives are powerful. They are not merely stories about objective facts or what we know. Narratives are about what we *believe*. They help us to interpret facts, to make meaning of the world. They influence how we think and how we see each other and, when internalized, how we see ourselves. They can define limitations and boundaries or create new possibilities. In a more sinister way, narratives can be vehicles of oppression, justifying perverse outcomes, assigning responsibility and blame.

Narratives are societal phenomena in which we are all complicit; they touch us all, but none of us alone can control them. They can take on a life of their own. Toni Morrison observed their organic nature when she accepted her 1993 Nobel prize in literature: "Narrative is radical, creating us at the very moment it is being created."

The context of access to higher education has its own powerful narratives— stories of fairness and unfairness, opportunity and disadvantage. They inform whether we conceive of higher education as a privilege or a right. They define for us who deserves opportunity, who has the skills and intellect to succeed—quite simply, who belongs and who does not.

Many subconsciously rely on dominant narratives to justify inequitable outcomes along lines of race and class. Warped conceptions of merit, oblivious to privilege and the structural challenges many aspiring students face, are advanced to explain decades-long patterns of exclusion and suggest that mediocrity is the inevitable result of living in poverty. These narratives are related to the dominant narratives about young people of color—false and deficit-based but persistent narratives about their alleged intellectual inferiority, their so-called anti-intellectualism, and the presumed rarity of talent among them. These narratives are part of what sustains opportunity and affordability gaps, what brings more police to their schools than college counselors, as if expressing the natural order. Worse yet, young people can succumb to them, sometimes even erecting psychic barriers to their own success that can feel just as powerful as the structural obstacles they already face.

Buttressed by false narratives, higher education is less a great equalizer and more an agent of social stratification. According to researchers Anthony Carnevale and Jeff Strohl, more African American and Hispanic students are attending college than ever before, but their access is not equal: the vast majority of white freshmen enroll in more selective colleges, which have greater resources and higher success rates across their student bodies, while African American and Hispanic students typically enroll in two-year colleges, nonselective four-year institutions, and for-profit and online schools, which are often underresourced and not otherwise poised to help students transcend poverty and socially imposed racial isolation. This stratification has lifelong and long-term intergenerational consequences for vulnerable students as well as the nation's educational, health, and labor market outcomes.

Breaking these patterns and shifting the narratives that define college access and future success are important work that too few take on due to the complexity, scale, and seeming intractability of the problem. Meeting this challenge will require a great playbook. In *Potential on the Periphery: College Access from the Ground Up*, Omari Scott Simmons gives us that playbook, born out of his own personal and professional experiences and those of the countless young people he has helped to scale incredible heights through the work of the Simmons Memorial Foundation. He addresses both systemic and individual dimensions, ranging from policy and regulatory solutions to structural barriers to college access to immediate and tangible interventions designed to remediate their ramifications in the lives of specific young people and their families. This mix of perspective, urgency, and purpose beautifully illustrates the kind of personal fortitude and political will needed to make change.

At its core, *Potential on the Periphery* reminds us that although changing narratives about college access will take generations, the work begins with individuals, and it can start now. It is a participatory endeavor, requiring each of us to put aside what we think we know and to wrestle with what we believe is possible.

Damon T. Hewitt

Senior Advisor, Open Society Foundations, Director of the Executives' Alliance for Boys and Men of Color, former Director of the Education Practice Group at the NAACP Legal Defense and Educational Fund, and SMF Advisory Board Member and Volunteer

POTENTIAL ON THE PERIPHERY

INTRODUCTION

Education is all a matter of building bridges.

—Ralph Ellison[1]

Despite undeniable advances in higher education attainment across demographic groups over the course of history, the United States still has two higher education systems—one serving the privileged and the other the vulnerable.[2] Higher education is connected to such socioeconomic benefits as higher wages, lower unemployment rates, lower crime rates, and less public spending on social support programs.[3] It also yields political benefits, such as higher rates of volunteerism and voting. Thus, it remains the most important step toward economic, social, and political empowerment, especially for students of limited economic means: racial minorities and immigrants; residents of remote, sparsely populated rural towns or impoverished urban centers; and those whose parents did not attend college.

However, these students are often unaware that deciding whether and where to attend college will have a critical impact on their lives.[4] They and their families do not receive the necessary counseling, and although hundreds of college guidebooks target ambitious parents and students with so-called winning application strategies, few directly address the needs and concerns of vulnerable students. In public high schools nationwide, every counselor serves approximately 470 students. In larger school districts, the ratio can rise to more than 700 students per counselor. These statistics underscore the dearth of meaningful college counseling available to large numbers of vulnerable students. Such deficits and oversights explain why, for many capable students, lack of mobility is less a function of merit than of privilege. For far too many, the notion of equality through education remains a false hope, and the descent into a permanent underclass is a sobering reality, dimming opportunity, achievement, and the American Dream.[5] Instead of tearing down distinctions, current educational policies and practices reinforce them.[6]

Moving beyond this unacceptable status quo requires more than simply leading students into a dense forest—the college-admissions process—and leaving them to fend for themselves. Policy makers generally employ two approaches to promote college access for vulnerable students. The first focuses on K–12 academic preparation to close achievement gaps that have a downstream impact on college access. The second allows colleges and universities discretion in diversity admissions and providing financial aid to needy students. These approaches fail to build an adequate bridge between high school and college because their effectiveness hinges on a single act—submitting an application for college admission. This single act should not be taken for granted. A third approach, transitional assistance between high school and postsecondary education, deserves greater attention from policy makers and practitioners. This critical component, requiring robust college access interventions, profoundly impacts the entire education continuum for vulnerable students.

The stratified status quo is often justified in terms of "merit" and "academic ability" since college admission ostensibly employs fair and legitimate criteria.[7] This acquiescence ignores a fact clear to most social scientists: class and parental educational attainment are the primary determinants of college attendance.[8] Fears that expanding access to some will deprive others, especially in preconceived, deterministic terms of worthiness, are shortsighted. In reality, depriving vulnerable students, including those of low socioeconomic status, of education deprives all of society of "a potential cadre of leaders and many competent citizens."[9] Ideological debates pitting individual liberty versus equal opportunity create a false dichotomy. Glenn Loury describes romanticized notions of individual merit: in a free society, each individual will rise to the level justified by his or her competence.[10] This perspective, he observes, "conflicts with the observation that no one travels that road entirely alone."[11]

The case for advancing higher education attainment among vulnerable students is not merely a question of economic necessity; it is firmly rooted in our nation's commitment to participatory democracy and equity.[12] Income disparities have reached their highest levels since the Gilded Age, and the higher education system mirrors our stratified society.[13] Nationwide, 48 percent of public school students are low income.[14] The majority of students in seventeen states are low income, and thirteen of these states are in the South.[15] Extensive wealth gaps among demographic subgroups reveal an even bleaker outlook. The Great Recession only exacerbated inequality.[16]

The racial and ethnic makeup of the nation's students is also shifting. A stroll through the hallways of many public schools nationwide shows that of our total fifty million students, the proportion who are students of color, especially Hispanics, is growing rapidly.[17] By 2042, the United States will be a "majority minority" country, and certain states will cross the threshold sooner.[18] Public schools in the South and West already enroll a majority of minority students.[19] These trends underscore the present and future importance of expanding higher education access for underserved groups.

As a high school student in rural southern Delaware during the late 1980s and early 1990s, I noticed a troubling pattern. Many talented students of color, students of low socioeconomic status, and students who would be the first in their family to attend college did not convert their K–12 academic achievement into higher education outcomes matching their potential. Instead, too many of these high-achieving students failed to attend college. If they did pursue higher education, they attended community colleges or less selective four-year colleges with lower degree completion rates. Many adopted a short-term perspective, viewing high school graduation as the pinnacle of their lifetime achievement and the end of their formal education. Some were deterred from college or certain college environments by the immediate price tag, ignoring the long-term educational and economic benefits. The future brought uncertainty and limited options: taking a job at a poultry plant, working on a farm, waiting tables, signing up for military service, living in a double-wide trailer, maybe serving time in jail. Harsh realities—generations of political impotence, limited educational attainment, modest economic means, and broken families—confronted them.

Unfortunately, the ability to assemble a strong college application often correlates with social class.[20] The complex college admissions process advantages wealthy and middle-class students who have a college-educated parent, access to quality K–12 schooling and elite social networks, and access to quality college-admissions counseling and standardized test preparation.[21] Additionally, legacy admission practices persist at both private and public institutions. Especially for selective and elite colleges, the admissions process is a high-stakes enterprise where parents seek any edge in the competition for coveted seats, often paying thousands of dollars to help secure a favorable result.[22]

In stark contrast, the vulnerable students I encountered over two decades ago as a high school student in southern Delaware—students of color, with low socioeconomic status, or from families without college experience—received little or no guidance from their schools, families, and community on the college selection and planning process. Their approach to college was often ad hoc, relying on a combination of serendipity and imperfect information. The thought of attending the University of Delaware, the state's flagship campus less than 70 miles north in Newark, Delaware, was intimidating. Attending an out-of-state, selective private university seemed like traveling to a foreign country.

This state of affairs led my father and me to start a grassroots nonprofit over twenty years ago, the Simmons Memorial Foundation (SMF). Since then, I have thought deeply about addressing the layered obstacles that limit higher education attainment for vulnerable students. First among them is the absence of an adequate bridge between high school achievement and commensurate higher education outcomes.

Today's higher education discourse is often cynical and preoccupied with "student dysfunction" while de-emphasizing deep structural and environmental challenges. Pundits, politicians, and even some academics defend rigid ideological positions rather than student needs and dismiss the insights of those who work directly with youth. Commitments to libertarianism, individualism, and market fundamentalism have become popular stances among lawmakers and citizens who indiscriminately invoke the market's "invisible hand" to right wrongs, such as acute inequity.[23] Realistically, interventions by government and civil society are often needed to guide the invisible hand to protect vulnerable members of society.

My nonprofit experience with SMF offers a unique lens on higher education opportunity in America. Student success stories, the important role of college access organizations, and the social-structural realities vulnerable students encounter are noticeably absent from current education debates. Consequently, the nation's policy framework as implemented by schools and communities has critical holes that must be filled. The absence of an adequate K–16 bridge between high school and college leaves a gaping hole. Today, a wide body of research; organizations such as the National Association for College Admission Counseling, the National College Access Network, and the College Board; and Obama administration initiatives have finally brought more attention to college access for vulnerable students.[24] Yet the current state of political turmoil and uncertainty threatens even these modest efforts.

The following chapters provide a unique perspective on the impact of SMF, a small, nonprofit college access organization supporting vulnerable students as they transition to, and persist through, college. This book draws heavily upon in-depth interviews of former SMF program participants, who offer candid insights on college access. SMF is one of thousands of civil society organizations across the country that, with limited resources, address college access needs from the ground up. For vulnerable students, these organizational experiences, in the aggregate, reflect the important complementary, "gap-filling" role civil society, particularly college access organizations, can play in transforming the higher education narrative. The microsuccesses of SMF and other college access organizations can inform the macro-policy framework.

The book illustrates how SMF's programmatic interventions heighten students' higher education aspirations and trajectories. It strongly suggests how certain interventions can help high-achieving students from rural areas and inner cities attend selective higher education institutions when they otherwise would not. Furthermore, it indicates that we cannot assume vulnerable students who are engaged in a rigorous secondary school curriculum—advanced placement, International Baccalaureate, and honors—will enter selective higher education environments in the absence of targeted interventions. There are simply too many variables. Our nation's high schools and postsecondary institutions are, at present, ill-equipped to address the complex college access challenges for vulnerable students. As the following chapters reveal, SMF's programming does more than simply help students identify and overcome these variables to secure admission to college; it cultivates college survival skills, encourages informed decision making, and serves as an expanded social support network. The value of such interventions extends well beyond the college admissions decision.

The ensuing chapters explore these challenges and provide poignant examples of how, with organizational interventions, courageous students surmount obstacles, alter trajectories, and transform their own narratives.

ROADMAP

The chapters proceed as follows:

Chapter 1. "Origins" provides background on SMF's origins in rural Delaware and current operations in North Carolina. It describes the obstacles to college access that students confront and SMF's attempts to address them.

Chapter 2. "The SMF College Access Program" describes current program features and the geopolitical environment and provides greater context for the ensuing student interviews. It summarizes interviewee demographic information, with a brief note on methodology.

Chapter 3. "Challenges in College Access" looks through the lens of student interview findings and academic insights to describe the multilayered obstacles that conspire to thwart vulnerable student higher education achievement. Specifically, this chapter analyzes the diverse challenges students face with respect to three key areas: the high school level, college affordability, and the college level and beyond.

Chapter 4. "The Role of SMF Intervention" illustrates how SMF's interventions address college access challenges in the three key areas. It includes an extensive analysis of interviews exploring how SMF programming works to level the college access landscape for vulnerable students. It captures student perspectives on SMF's efforts to expand and influence their higher education choices and opportunities. This chapter reinforces the long-standing importance of SMF's programming, particularly how it can give rise to dynamic processes that contribute to student achievement at the high school level, postsecondary level, and beyond. Despite challenges across the entire education continuum, SMF students persist.

Chapter 5. "Reforms" provides a practical framework of recommendations that address college access challenges in the three key areas. It recognizes that college access organizations do not operate in a vacuum and that student possibilities are circumscribed by existing regulatory and institutional environments. Reforms must target systemic and individual barriers to opportunity.

Chapter 6. "Parting Thoughts" highlights the important role SMF and other college access organizations play in helping vulnerable students to acquire educational resources that improve their higher education trajectories. It addresses how SMF might improve its programming, and it highlights the key criteria and common challenges associated with successful college access programs. SMF and other civil society actors are only part of the solution. Their work is made necessary by policy gaps in the regulatory architecture. More robust, systemic reform efforts are needed to move beyond the unacceptable status quo, especially in the areas of college guidance and affordability. This chapter provides a menu of practical policy recommendations to assist vulnerable students in achieving higher education outcomes commensurate with their potential. The chapter concludes with parting thoughts on the future of college access in the United States.

1 · ORIGINS

To encourage young people to succeed, adults often use a number of phrases: "Reach for the stars"; "Dream big"; "Make the most out of every opportunity." This was not my experience. Instead, my high school counselor steered me toward community colleges and local state schools exclusively. If I had not been exposed to the expert guidance, experiences, and strategic counseling provided by the Simmons Memorial Foundation, I might have adopted the limitations others placed on my potential. In May 2011, I graduated with honors from the University of Pennsylvania—an Ivy League institution. Currently, I work for an investment bank, and in the fall of 2012, I will attend the University of Pennsylvania Law School.

—Milton

Barriers to higher education inevitably present a dilemma for society and the individual. In the absence of equal educational opportunity, democracy suffers, talent is lost, culture erodes, and liberty is undermined. Higher education is our nation's key instrument for ensuring social mobility and stability, our most effective weapon against threats to opportunity. To perform this vital role, it must remain accessible as well as relevant to the needs and problems of contemporary society and its diverse constituencies.

The idea that attending college, or a selective college, is an attainable and a necessary step for lifelong success is not created in a vacuum. Students often cannot express ideas, realities, and dreams they do not glimpse in their current environment. Consequently, their potential remains unfulfilled. Moreover, matching vulnerable students with the more selective colleges that can tap their potential but seem out of reach or even off their radar is crucial because students attending less selective institutions may be less successful socioeconomically and in other ways.[1] In *Creating a Class*, Mitchell Stevens contends that elite colleges, in particular, serve as a mechanism by which wealthy parents pass comfortable lives on to their children. According to Stevens, elite schools are the established path for the establishment.[2] Meanwhile, vulnerable students must often find alternative, less lucrative, and more risky paths.

The failure to tap the potential of talented but vulnerable students is a national tragedy. As the Carnegie Commission on Higher Education clearly stated, "benefits from higher education flow to all, or nearly all, persons . . . directly or indirectly."[3] Education benefits include advancement of research and teaching, rapid industrialization of the economy, building character and morals, and deepening democracy by producing better citizens. Neglecting this precious resource threatens our democratic, social, and economic vitality and requires an aggressive response.[4]

Intervention is necessary to address both real and perceived barriers: Can I afford college? Can I excel academically? How will I adjust to dorm life? Can I survive at a college five hours from home? Do other minorities attend? How will I handle living with a bunch of rich kids who are strangers? Without assurances that they can succeed in competitive and complex college learning environments, students' higher education narratives remain fixed. These students need more than mere information and strategies; they need "real world" exposure that will give them a panoramic view of opportunity. However, studies confirm that "even high-ability and well-credentialed students from lower-income backgrounds face social and cultural impediments that can hinder them in the competition for higher education admissions." Lacking "the parental prodding, nurturance, and social networking typical in more affluent households, students from more modest backgrounds may not even apply to college."[5]

SMF BEGINNINGS

In 1996, my late father and I founded the Simmons Memorial Foundation (SMF), a small, grassroots, nonprofit organization designed to "develop potential on the periphery" by promoting higher education access for vulnerable students in rural southern Delaware. SMF was established in honor of my late mother, Cynthia T. Simmons, and brother, Nathaniel P. Simmons III, who both passed away in 1995. At the time of SMF's inception, I was a 22-year-old law student at the University of Pennsylvania, not much older than the students my organization served. I grew up and attended K–12 public schools in Milford, a southern Delaware town with a population, back then, of less than six thousand. I knew what it felt like to be one of only one or two black students in an advanced curriculum classroom. Unlike some of the students in my nonprofit's programs, I was better off—middle-class, a military transplant with college-educated parents. My mother was an elementary school science teacher, and my father a naval officer stationed in the Washington, DC, metropolitan area. Both of my parents grew up in the segregated South and, despite their own experiences, raised me to have a no-limits outlook. At the same time, they openly discussed the diminished opportunities they experienced in their youth.

Initially, my efforts were driven not by theory but by concrete observations, intuition, realism, and an unshakable belief in the potential of young people to transcend their circumstances. I believed SMF could fill the void left unaddressed by schools and the community. SMF reflected John Dewey's form of pragmatism, a philosophy grounded in experience and practice, and striving to translate ideas into action. Nearly a century ago, Dewey recognized the role schools could have in "countering social stratification and promoting social advancement" and, therefore, promoting equity and access.[6]

At the time of SMF's inception, the legal and political framework seemed ill equipped to address the complex obstacles our students faced. In 1998, the educational opportunity discussion focused on K–12 school finance litigation and school vouchers.[7] In the realm of higher education, affirmative action, particularly reverse discrimination against nonminorities, dominated the discussion on equity from the late 1990s onward.[8] The 1996 *Hopwood v. Texas* decision was the first successful challenge to a university's consideration of race in admissions since it had been approved by the Supreme Court in *Regents of the University of California v. Bakke*. It contributed to a hostile environment of legal and political uncertainty around admissions practices intended to further diversity at colleges nationwide, particularly selective state flagships.[9] This uncertainty persisted until the Supreme Court's *Grutter v. Bollinger* decision in 2003, which affirmed the use of race as a criterion in university admissions.[10] Due to this extended period of legal uncertainty, however, outreach programs and college scholarships targeting minorities came under assault. Some disappeared entirely due to political pressure and legal threats.

Prior to the publication of William Bowen and Derek Bok's historic *Shape of the River* (1998), debates surrounding affirmative action were largely rhetorical, ideologically driven, and without empirical foundation. Bowen and Bok's longitudinal studies demonstrated the economic payoff from having attended a selective institution, which was likely to provide "more resources, better facilities, more generous financial aid, and more faculty members who have strong reputations in their fields" and the added value of "classmates of exceptional ability, who set high standards of intellectual excellence and offer challenging examples to emulate." Bowen and Bok provided much-needed empirical content to the debate and illustrated the impact of race-sensitive admissions policies.[11]

The vulnerable students I knew rarely applied to the selective colleges or graduate schools at issue in cases like *Grutter*, *Hopwood*, or *Bakke*. Because few vulnerable students applied to selective colleges to begin with, the risk of so-called reverse discrimination was small. Even if these students applied and were admitted pursuant to a college's diversity admissions policies, displacement of traditional applicants would be negligible—only 1 to 5 percent.[12] Nonetheless, arguments over the infinitesimal prospect of traditional student displacement at selective schools overshadowed the higher education needs of many vulnerable students. Noticeably absent was the fervor to eliminate legacy admissions and other preferences that reinforce stratification at selective higher education institutions.

Such legal and political battles to preserve and promote college opportunities for underserved students were, without question, necessary and valiant, but they were not enough. They were largely defensive efforts to preserve, in my view, an already unacceptable status quo. Even when institutional discretion to promote diversity remained intact, policy makers and advocates mistakenly took the flood of applications from underserved students for granted. None was forthcoming. Despite so-called affirmative action, African American and Hispanic students are more underrepresented at top colleges today than they were thirty-five years ago.[13]

Clearly absent were *offensive* strategies to advance the higher education interests of vulnerable students in a systematic way across the entire K–16 continuum, especially the transition between high school and college. Impatient with the wasted potential, I simply could not wait for schools to improve nor could I participate in protracted ideological debates or passively hope for a political or legal panacea that might never arrive. Instead, I embraced realism: working to give students immediate, tangible tools to navigate a world where resources are not allocated equitably. Waiting for the courts, legislators, or markets—as Geoffrey Canada describes it, "waiting for Superman"—was not an option.[14]

At the time, a limited body of research, to my knowledge, addressed the problems of college access that SMF confronted. SMF had few program templates or best practices to follow and apply in rural areas. Instead, it grew organically. To directly address student needs, we implemented an array of programs—college consulting, mentoring, college trips, SAT preparation, and scholarships. The scope expanded to meet student needs that were identified over time. In addition, SMF established key partnerships, formal and informal, with community organizations, schools, and higher education institutions, particularly undergraduate admissions offices.

As a grassroots college access program, SMF leveraged social capital to promote higher education attainment by establishing direct relationships with students and parents, generating greater trust and accountability. Although today's social networking sites are popular and ubiquitous, the live, person-to-person contact SMF provided was qualitatively different. Research supports the contention that face-to-face interactions are superior in generating trust, accountability, and other benefits, yet vulnerable students often lack these types of connections.[15] A vital element of our programming included the use of volunteers' various talents and perspectives to ignite a spark in youth. With no full-time or salaried employees, SMF assembled professionally and culturally diverse volunteers to serve as mentors and to implement programming. Some volunteers became so passionate about the organization that they eventually assumed leadership positions. The diverse backgrounds and insights of volunteers, such as Brian Bell and Kwasi Asare, were invaluable to SMF. Brian Bell, a native of southern Delaware and an alumnus of Swarthmore College, became SMF's program director during its early years. Kwasi Asare, a native of Durham, North Carolina, and a Wake Forest University alumnus, became the education director.

Brian Bell and I attended rival high schools in southern Delaware. When Brian applied to college, he admittedly took a random approach, applying only to a few schools and only one very selective school—Swarthmore College. He knew nothing about Swarthmore's reputation when he applied, but by virtue of applying from southern Delaware, he was considered for and subsequently awarded the prestigious McCabe Scholarship, established by Thomas McCabe, former president and CEO of the Scott Paper Company, who was born on the Delmarva Peninsula and had strong family ties to southern Delaware.[16] Recognizing his good fortune and the empowerment that accompanies a quality higher education, Brian volunteered with SMF to help provide the strategies and insights that would maximize students' college success.

Kwasi Asare and I met as undergraduates at Wake Forest University through a mentoring program called TARGET. I had created the program with my college roommate, DeAndrei Drummond, to cultivate an interest in college among middle school students in Winston-Salem, North Carolina. When we graduated, Kwasi, an underclassman, took over the TARGET program. A couple years later, we would collaborate again through SMF. Kwasi and his parents were born in Ghana, and he had a keen interest in human development through higher education. He brought a global and cosmopolitan perspective to SMF programming.

Most of our early volunteer mentors were from the Washington, DC, Philadelphia, and New York metropolitan areas. They were graduate students, alumni of the nation's top universities, investment bankers, lawyers, consultants, software engineers, educators, artists, activists, and budding politicians. Groups of SMF volunteers would travel on weekends throughout the year to rural southern Delaware to conduct seminars and workshops for students on a broad range of topics, including college admissions, financial aid, critical thinking, and globalization. Away from southern Delaware, they continued to contact students via phone and email. We designed our live seminars to match the degree of analytical rigor students might encounter in college. Students were expected to support their opinions on current events with a convincing rationale, and we asked them to read and respond to articles from the *New York Times* and other periodicals. Over time, we hoped they would become more comfortable communicating with adults on scholarly topics and current events; this practice would ease their transition to and through college.

SMF mentors exposed students to their own personal paths to success, countering the negative messages that students might have received in their current environment. Mentors bombarded students with a range of encouraging messages, such as the following:

Never settle for mediocrity.
"I was sitting just where you are today. I was the first person in my family to attend college, and look at the things that I have been able to do. And you can do much better. Never settle for mediocrity."

Choose a college that stretches you intellectually.
"Education made the difference for me, and it can do the same for you. Choose the college environment that stretches you the most intellectually."

Education is permanent and lifelong.
"Higher education is not just about job preparation. You may lose a job. Your education is permanent and lifelong. It will allow you to approach life's challenges with greater understanding and maturity."

Leaving your comfort zone will help you grow as a person.
"Getting outside of my comfort zone to attend a selective school like Swarthmore, Wake Forest, or Penn opened new doors and possibilities; it helped me grow as a person."

College will give you a great shot.
"College won't guarantee success—that is, a high paying job, political office, praise, happiness—but it will give you a great shot at it."

Engage and make a difference.
"It is not enough to simply go to college and sit idle. Engage. Have an impact. Make a difference."

I fondly recall chauffeuring volunteers on day-long trips from Philadelphia and Washington, DC, to our usual meeting place in southern Delaware: the Seaford Boys & Girls Club, situated literally between two cornfields. I would open the Saturday morning sessions before the group of predominantly African American students with a question: "How many of you believe that a student in this room could be the next president of the United States or the next CEO of Microsoft? And be honest." I would see students look around, perhaps giggle, and then tentatively raise their hands. After a significant pause, I would say: "Well, if you didn't raise your hand immediately, or if you don't think that's a possibility, you're not in the right place. Many of you don't know what you're capable of, but excellence in anything you desire requires this type of spontaneously positive mindset and unflappable confidence." From the outset, students knew that participation in the SMF program came with the highest expectations. Heightening student aspirations is essential for higher education achievement.

A College Access Program Addressing the Application Process
SMF officially began its full-fledged college mentoring program in 1998. Our first key local partnership was not with a school but a minority enrichment program,

MERIT (Minority Engineering Regional Incentive Training). It was supported by the DuPont chemical company to encourage minorities in grades 8 through 12 to pursue engineering careers, and it benefited from a committed and charismatic leader, John Hollis, a lifelong educator.[17] An engaged parent auxiliary group also provided support for approximately fifty talented minority students from local rural public schools. As a high school student in the early 1990s, I participated in the program, but as DuPont downsized its southern Delaware presence, the program's funding decreased sharply. Although I found MERIT quite useful, I felt that with SMF's intervention, higher education outcomes for its students could reach another level.

Despite our initial well-intentioned efforts and advice, students did not apply to a broad range of schools but attended local colleges and universities. We had made a rookie mistake by assuming that the simple transmission of information would suffice. We were wrong. The students did not buy in or feel accountable, and for seniors submitting applications that first year, we came into the picture too late. In the future, younger students would benefit more from exposure to SMF and its volunteers as well as a strong, peer-driven culture. We also made greater efforts to engage parents and legal guardians, even if briefly, providing them with information on SMF's services.

We pushed forward the following year, making regular contact with students throughout the college admissions calendar. We challenged them to raise their aspirations and the amount of work they dedicated to college preparation. We provided lists of colleges, offered consistent encouragement, and made reasonable demands. Students may have found phone calls from volunteers irritating at times, but without the benefit of family or even school counselors who could shepherd them through the complex admissions process, they needed informed coaching and guidance to maximize their college selection decision, perhaps the most important adult decision in their lives thus far.

Heightening Student Aspirations through College Trips

In our second year, students applied more broadly. They were admitted to a wider range of schools, among them very selective, out-of-state private colleges, including Dartmouth, Swarthmore, Wesleyan, Wake Forest, and the University of Richmond. The same year, Jacques Steinberg of the *New York Times* wrote a series of articles about his experiences as an observer in the admissions department at one of the most selective liberal arts colleges in the country— Wesleyan University in Middletown, Connecticut.[18] He would eventually turn these articles into the best-selling book *The Gatekeepers* (2002).[19] We shared some of his insights with our students and challenged them to apply to Wesleyan and other selective colleges. Three of eight high school seniors in our program applied and were admitted to Wesleyan that year, due in part to Steinberg's writings.

Even after they were admitted, these three students, whom I call the Wesleyan Crew, did not fully realize the magnitude of their achievements. Some viewed college more as a commodity than a "differentiated" experience, resulting in individual benefits, including productivity, earnings, health, and political participation, as well as public benefits, including economic growth, scientific progress, and social equality.[20] Unlike more privileged high school juniors and seniors who visit colleges with their families, neither the Wesleyan Crew, their parents, nor many of their high school counselors had ever set foot on these elite campuses. The Wesleyan Crew, in fact, had no intention of visiting Wesleyan for an admitted students day. None of them had spent much time outside of Delaware and had no one to take them to Connecticut. Among the best and brightest, but without the opportunity to visit the campuses, our students would never be able to visualize the academic, social, and aesthetic dimensions of the elite college experience. Without this vision, walking away from such a rare opportunity would be too easy.

Therefore, I chaperoned all three on a long train ride from Wilmington, Delaware, to Middletown, Connecticut, to attend Wesleyan's admitted students programming. They stayed overnight with current Wesleyan students and participated in activities with other admitted students throughout the weekend. Like a proud parent, I attended a few events with them, including then-president Douglass Bennett's welcoming remarks, outlining Wesleyan's approach to education, and a leisurely campus tour that yielded a pristine view of the Connecticut River. It was my first visit to Wesleyan as well. We even had a private meeting with Freddye Hill, dean of students, who generously gave us her time and attention. She had grown up in the same Tampa, Florida, neighborhood as my mother. This important personal meeting with an administrator communicated to my students the various support structures and resources the university had in place.

To say that three African American students from rural southern Delaware public schools stood out would be an understatement. Most students of color, even those from low-socioeconomic-status families, appeared to come from highly regarded private and public feeder schools, usually in the Northeast. Visiting the college campus and traveling the Northeast corridor was an eye-opening experience for my students and more so for me. I will always remember the four of us on that train adventure. What stands out was the students' curiosity as we passed town after town, city after city, state after state.

Despite the trip, none of these students attended Wesleyan. They enrolled at the University of Delaware, Temple University, and Wake Forest University, my alma mater. None of them chose the most selective school among their options. Their decisions were not based on finances, because they qualified for significant need and merit-based financial aid grants. In fact, one of the three received a full-tuition grant from Dartmouth College. This experience revealed the complexity of the college decision for vulnerable students: family, peers, teachers, counselors, and other relationships matter. In many cases, they and their families did not differentiate among colleges or recognize the benefits of attending the most selective. Acceptance was only part of the issue; getting students to attend was equally, if not more, challenging.

At first, it was difficult to view these results as an overall success. Looking back, that year marked a turning point for SMF. The Wesleyan Crew, with their impressive list of college acceptances, set a high bar and had a large impact on future group expectations. Although the Wesleyan trip did not lead to enrollment at that school, it led to an annual college trip to different regions of the country. In less than three years, we would return to Wesleyan with twenty-five potential students. This time, a current Wesleyan student welcomed us to campus—he had been one of our own SMF participants.

One of SMF's most memorable and ambitious college trips took place in November 2002. Thirty students traveled to the Northeast to visit a number of colleges, including the University of Pennsylvania, Swarthmore College, Wesleyan University, Columbia University, and Yale University. For many students, the New York City leg of the trip was the highlight. A guided bus tour of Manhattan allowed them to see Harlem, Times Square, the upper West Side, and the former site of the World Trade Center—Ground Zero.

Our students had traveled several hundred miles, and a scheduling mix-up brought us to the Columbia University campus on a day when the admissions office was closed. Luckily, Peter Johnson, the senior associate director of admissions, happened to walk by on what he thought would be a quick visit to his office and noticed us. I spoke to him privately about the situation and our students. Without hesitation, he sprang into action and coordinated guided campus tours. In the meantime, he prepared a room for a private information session and ordered pizza for the entire group of students and volunteers. When the students returned from their tours, they were escorted into a meeting room (rather than the standard admissions room), where they were seated in large leather chairs around a square table. Mr. Johnson told them that they were sitting where Columbia University's Board of Trustees, some of the most powerful people in the country, regularly meet. We stayed in that room for two hours, while Mr. Johnson and his assistant gave insightful admissions advice, both general and specific to Columbia. What started out as a potential disaster turned into an amazing display of professionalism, generosity, and kindness. I have never had the opportunity to adequately thank Mr. Johnson. He could have done the bare minimum, but he clearly believed in our organization's mission and our students, Columbia-bound or not. Our students never learned of the averted disaster; all they remember is being treated with the utmost respect and hospitality.

In subsequent years, the SMF trip exposed students to various college environments—public, private, liberal arts, and historically black—early in the selection process. Over time, we made several trips, becoming familiar with selective colleges from New Haven, Connecticut, to Atlanta, Georgia. These opportunities gave students a better frame of reference in the college-planning and decision-making processes. They experienced much more than standard tours and information sessions. During the day, they visited a diverse array of cultural sites, such as Ground Zero, Monticello, the U.S. Capitol, and Ben's Chili Bowl, a popular Washington, DC, hamburger joint. In the evenings, we hosted banquets with guest speakers, including distinguished local professionals, college alumni, professors, and administrators. Many of them joined us for intimate dinners and stimulating discussions. Through these chance meetings, lasting mentoring relationships and connections formed, which enriched students' lives.

SMF trips always enlisted parents as chaperones; some had not attended college. In our view, parents must see what their children are experiencing to remain engaged in the process. By word of mouth, the trips' popularity spread throughout the community, and every year the demand increased. SMF college trips provided exposure to new people, perspectives, and places and generated excitement about college for students and their parents. The opportunity to navigate college campuses, towns, and cities mitigated intimidation and increased the likelihood that students would apply to and attend selective out-of-state colleges.

Enrollment

From SMF's third year onward (2000–2001), a cultural or mental shift occurred. Driven by peer expectations, students applied broadly. We contracted with the Princeton Review Foundation, which had a successful history of providing SAT preparation for underserved populations, although its former president, Jay Rosner, was and remains a staunch critic of the SAT's fairness.[21] The program initially increased our students' standardized test scores significantly, making them more competitive in the admissions process. In our fifth year, thirteen seniors averaged 4.5 acceptances each, for a total of 57. Most of them also made the leap to attend more out-of-state and selective universities. In about five years, students from some of the most underrepresented demographics were admitted to, attending, and succeeding at, some of the most selective colleges in the nation. SMF's admission statistics looked like private or prep school results, not the achievements of a small group of underrepresented students.

In the summer of 2006, I accepted a faculty position at Wake Forest University Law School in Winston-Salem, North Carolina. As a consequence, SMF's operations relocated, but full-blown programming did not resume until several years later because SMF needed time to study the community's needs, demographics, high schools, colleges, and valuable local partners. With the benefit of experience and a substantial body of research on college access, North Carolina presented an opportunity to reach another level of effectiveness. In summer 2009, SMF launched a revamped version of its college-mentoring program in North Carolina. Today, our primary meeting place is no longer the Seaford Delaware Boys & Girls Club but a classroom on the campus of Wake Forest University, which has generously opened its doors to SMF's talented students from the surrounding community.

Shifting Narratives

After only four years of programming in North Carolina, SMF's results are quite impressive. Nearly 100 percent of our students enroll in college, and the overwhelming majority will graduate within four to six years. The most impressive result is the significant number of students attending selective public flagships as well as private institutions within and outside of the southeastern United States. Underresourced high schools that rarely saw their students attend such highly selective universities as Princeton and Harvard are witnessing a narrative shift.

Despite the change in setting and its years of operation, SMF remains a small, intimate program. I began providing college access programming when I was about 22, closer to the age of the students SMF assisted. Today, at 44, I am their parents' age. Since SMF's inception, I envisioned that enlisting recent college graduates and current students would be necessary since my impact as a near-peer mentor would diminish as I grew older. I always hoped that SMF alumni who had benefited from our programming would return to assume an active role in the organization. In 2010, SMF came closer to that goal when alumna Kathryn Riley, a recent Swarthmore College graduate, enrolled at Wake Forest University as a graduate student in chemistry and became our program director. Her efforts contributed significantly to our success. Today, Kathryn Riley, PhD, is a chemistry professor at Swarthmore College. During the same period, we engaged Allyson Diljohn as our chief college counseling consultant. She is a seasoned professional with valuable experience as an admissions counselor at a top-25 national university, and she held senior college counseling posts at an elite boarding school and a private school. Her insights, born of expertise, ensure that SMF students, no matter their station, receive first-class guidance. Allyson is a personal counselor who is available—via phone, email, text, and Skype—to assist students and their families.

SMF now boasts a distinguished group of alumni, many of whom remain a part of our network, working with our students both as volunteers and as interns. Among former SMF participants are current students at, and graduates of, some of the most prestigious higher education institutions in the country: Cornell University, the College of William and Mary, Davidson College, Duke University, Harvard University, Howard University, Morehouse College, Oberlin College, Ohio State University, Pomona College, Princeton University, Spelman College, Swarthmore College, University of North Carolina at Chapel Hill, University of Pennsylvania, University of Virginia, Wake Forest University, Wesleyan University, Yale University, and many others. They are business executives, educators, scientists, lawyers, graduate students, clergy, bankers, activists, and leaders in their chosen communities. Notably, a significant number of SMF alumni have pursued careers in education and/or serving vulnerable populations. The SMF alumni network continues to grow stronger.

Admissions statistics alone do not adequately capture SMF's enduring impact on some students' lives. The following letter from an alumna and former foster child illustrates SMF's deep impact on student trajectories:

> Good Afternoon,
>
> I happened to come across something on the Internet with the announcement regarding me winning the [SMF] Scholarship. I was Susan Johnson at that time. This is completely random, but just in case I never did thank the organization, I wanted to do so now. I was given a great opportunity to become someone despite what my circumstances dictated. Thank you all for believing in me and helping me to believe in myself. Your organization gave me a foundation on which I built. I was able to go to Spelman College in Atlanta, GA, and then went on to get my master's degree from Georgia State University. I am in the process of publishing my first book under the author pen name of Constance Russell. Thank you all for my push and I pray that your organization is blessed simply because you blessed my life.
>
> Sincerely
> Susan Franklin

Accompanying such a brave group of students on part of their educational journey is an honor, an inspiration, and the highlight of my professional career. Today, SMF and thousands of other civil society organizations work to transform the higher education trajectories of vulnerable students in the face of an inadequate K–16 bridge: the lack of effective government and institutional policies that provide meaningful college counseling for the nation's high school students. At its core, SMF's success over two decades reflects the transformative impact of minor college counseling interventions on the college choices of vulnerable students. The steps taken to advance higher education access for vulnerable students will have profound consequences for our nation's future prosperity.

SYSTEMIC IMPLICATIONS: THE HIGHER EDUCATION SORTING PATTERN

A larger proportion of the U.S. population has access to higher education than in most developed countries,[22] but the system itself is imperfect and characterized by structural obstacles.[23] It reflects a troublesome sorting pattern that leads vulnerable students to cluster at less selective institutions while their privileged counterparts cluster at selective four-year colleges. Although vulnerable students have the same *desire* to attain a bachelor's degree as the privileged, they remain much more likely to end up attending a two-year college, for-profit college, vocational school, or no college at all, with differential socioeconomic consequences.[24] Less selective higher education options are important to access for vulnerable groups, but they are oversubscribed.[25] The absence of quality college guidance contributes to this problem.

Attaining higher education has two separate but related dimensions: a quantitative dimension related to increasing the absolute number of vulnerable students who attend college; and a qualitative dimension related to the type of higher education setting they enter.[26] At first glance, the absolute expansion of higher education opportunities would be expected to close rather than widen socioeconomic disparities, but left unaddressed, the institutional sorting pattern perpetuates inequality and reifies existing class, racial, and social hierarchies.[27] Applying to college, particularly a selective one, is not analogous to a consumer purchase of a commodity.[28] It requires an informed strategy and often technical expertise to navigate a complex process. Vulnerable students have the most to gain by employing expert strategies often used by more privileged students. All too often, they receive inadequate guidance without outside intervention.[29] SMF, like other college access organizations, intervenes to counter these troubling trends.

Divergent College Application Patterns

Selective college admissions practices support an uneven competition between high-achieving privileged and high-achieving underprivileged students, who often approach the process differently. Interventions can alter and refine college selection strategies and shift individual student trajectories.[30] For illustrative purposes only, considering the application and selection process as an investment decision involving a portfolio of college options may be helpful.

A study by Caroline Hoxby and Christopher Avery maps the application patterns of high-achieving affluent students and their lower-income counterparts. It finds that the affluent students are likely to apply to a mixture of institutions: several selective "match" schools where the student is likely to be admitted, a couple of "safety" schools, a state flagship university, and several selective "reach" schools.[31] Professional advisers often encourage their clients to apply to several institutions as a diversification strategy, particularly in the reach category, to achieve better outcomes. Affluent high-achieving students generally dislike nonselective schools and strongly favor reach schools.[32] They favor four-year colleges with higher sticker prices, which are often associated with higher per-student spending and resources, and they may also apply to highly selective arts schools and music conservatories.[33]

This path differs significantly from the one followed by high-achieving low-socioeconomic-status students.[34] They tend to favor nonselective colleges and those with lower sticker prices.[35] Many apply only to nonselective colleges or a nonselective college and a minimally selective one.[36] Specifically, they apply to community colleges or local four-year institutions that generally invest less in their education on a per-student basis. They rarely apply to specialty art schools and music conservatories, and while they favor in-state schools, they do not exhibit a preference for public flagship universities.[37] Only 8 percent apply to a mixture of match, reach, and safety schools.[38] The remaining 39 percent employ such ad hoc strategies as applying to one less-selective state school rather than a state flagship or applying to one selective, private, out-of-state college that has fewer resources than other private match schools. Hoxby and Avery acknowledge, "it is almost never sensible for a low-income student to apply to a single private, selective college: such a student can use competing aid offers to improve the aid package at his or her most preferred college."[39] This study is not the first to identify the disparate application patterns of wealthier and poorer students, but it is the largest, with a national scope.

To the informed college admissions professionals and researchers, vulnerable student application approaches often seem ad hoc, idiosyncratic, and illogical, and they often yield poorer returns, but their difference from those of other socioeconomic groups is not coincidental.[40] College admissions counseling has become a lucrative industry in this country. Affluent families will pay thousands of dollars to expert college counselors because they want their child to secure that coveted spot at a highly selective university. These services can start well in advance of a student's senior year. For example, an eighth grader can receive guidance on the types of courses and activities that will appeal to college admissions officers. Most often, proprietary college counseling services include helping families generate a list or portfolio of colleges; reading and editing college essays; and sometimes providing mock interviews to assist student applicants. SMF provides similar services free of charge. Even when privileged students do not hire college advisers they can still rely on college-educated parents and social networks for information, guidance, and encouragement.

For students who can afford it, standardized test preparation is another advantage. An entire industry depends on the notion that SAT performance can be enhanced by coaching, yet many students either do not receive or cannot afford it.[41] Scholars, such as Joseph Soares, who have identified the shortcomings of the SAT as a predictive instrument, acknowledge that the prevailing status quo in college admissions and the ubiquitous *U.S. News & World Report* Best Colleges ranking system strongly rely on the SAT. According to Harvard law professor Lani Guinier, the status quo in college admissions sanctions a narrow vision of merit—a "testocracy."[42] The ability to assemble a winning application to a selective university or college often correlates with socioeconomic status and other vulnerability factors.

The Importance of "Matching"

Even when vulnerable students do apply to college, they often "undermatch" or "mismatch."[43] In this context, *matching* means that students enroll in the type of college whose criteria match their high school qualifications.[44] Steering vulnerable students toward more selective colleges and universities that match their potential maximizes their prospects for success.[45] For example, students of all racial backgrounds attending a selective institution are more likely to obtain a degree on time than similarly qualified students who attend less selective institutions. Research indicates that college match has a particularly significant effect on minority, low-income, and first-generation students. According to Alon and Tienda, "Minority students' likelihood of graduation increases as the selectivity of the institution attended rises."[46]

Attending a more selective school may yield an array of other important benefits: economic premiums in the labor market, access to exceptional alumni and peers who elevate career ambitions, access to top-tier graduate and professional school programs, and increased civic engagement and social capital.[47] Graduates of elite private colleges earn almost 40 percent more per year than graduates of less selective public colleges, and attending an elite college significantly increases the probability of pursuing graduate study at a similarly prestigious research institution.[48] These benefits are often heightened for vulnerable students. Economic returns for minorities at selective universities may be several times greater than those for white students, leading Bowen and Bok to conclude that "providing opportunities for minority students at high-quality institutions has been a good investment."[49] Studies also suggest that increasing the number of vulnerable students at selective institutions "may raise national income, as these students appear to benefit most from attending a more elite college."[50] Discrepancies in higher education outcomes are thus not a product of simply attending college but rather a product of the type of higher education environment. Neither the qualitative nor the quantitative dimension can be overlooked.

These discrepancies also hold for vulnerable students who participate in Advanced Placement (AP), International Baccalaureate (IB), and honors curricular programs. The AP program is administered by the College Board and offers college-level courses in the high school setting in a variety of subject areas. The IB program is described as "a rigorous international program of study that originated in Switzerland and has spread to more than 100 nations." High school students in either program can earn college credit by scoring at a proficient level on a final examination.[51] Generally, these top-tier curricular programs enhance the likelihood that students are prepared for, and apply to, a selective college or university, and they signal to colleges that a student is college material. Vulnerable students are generally underrepresented in these advanced programs.[52] Moreover, those who are taking them often do not reap the potential benefits because they do not understand the complex college selection process.[53] Strong qualifications do "not alter the reality that these students often come from families and neighborhoods that are less able to provide concrete support and knowledge about the college admissions process."[54] Although, in theory, they are "in a position to conduct wider college searches that include more selective colleges, many do not understand the broad range of colleges to which their qualifications afford them access."[55]

These outcomes are troubling because they represent both underperforming students unable to take advantage of college opportunities and highly qualified students slipping through the cracks.[56] A wealth of research indicates that undermatching among high-achieving vulnerable students is a problem of national significance.[57] Studies in Boston, Chicago, and North Carolina reveal how highly qualified vulnerable students suffer "in the absence of structured support or guidance from adults at their schools or from other role models who could shepherd them through the postsecondary process"; consequently, they "struggle to complete . . . basic step[s] toward four-year college enrollment."[58] Specifically, the North Carolina Public School study identified differences in college graduation rates for students attending the more selective state universities. Students who undermatched were 15 percent less likely to graduate in six years.[59] Most important, the undermatch problem *concentrated at the application stage*, where only 36 percent of students who undermatched even applied to University of North Carolina at Chapel Hill or North Carolina State, and 28 percent chose to attend a less selective school after having been accepted at University of North Carolina at Chapel Hill or North Carolina State University.[60] Like other studies, the North Carolina Public School study cites the lack of information, planning, and encouragement as potential factors in undermatching.[61] The incidence of student mismatching reveals a disturbing nationwide trend. My experiences with SMF confirm its prevalence in North Carolina.

Match is simply one aspect of college choice, and there are certainly legitimate reasons to consider a "safer" and "more comfortable" less selective or less costly institution.[62] Some scholars promote high-quality vocational training as an alternative higher education pathway in addition to four-year colleges.[63] However, the college decisions of vulnerable students, in the absence of adequate guidance, tend to be ad hoc and haphazard.

Nationwide efforts are needed to improve the process by which students are sorted into higher educational settings that often fail to encourage them to realize their full potential. Reforming high school college counseling is crucial to repair the bridges to college access and completion for all qualified and interested students.[64] Simply put, each student "should be made aware of the full range of higher educational opportunities available to someone with his or her credentials and then encouraged to reach for the most challenging opportunity that is a realistic option."[65]

SMF and the students it serves operate within both micro and macro contexts. As the following chapters argue, higher education narratives for vulnerable students must and can change; we cannot afford to waste talent on the periphery.

2 · THE SMF COLLEGE ACCESS PROGRAM

> Talking to the mentors, who were in various stages of their professional careers, I realized something key to personal success—the fact that my life was in my hands. With attained information and guidance from the Simmons Memorial Foundation, my limitations were shed and horizons broadened, opening my life to endless possibilities.
>
> —Kevin

This chapter provides a detailed description of SMF's program features as well as the geopolitical environment in which it operates. Our study methodology and student interviewee demographics are briefly described. This information will provide context and a better frame of reference for the analysis of student interview responses in the subsequent chapters.

SMF'S COLLEGE ACCESS PROGRAM

SMF's experience is not unique to Delaware or North Carolina and reflects the work of many college access organizations (CAOs) nationwide. CAOs like SMF fall squarely under the civil society umbrella as nongovernmental organizations that receive limited or no government funding. They play an important role in propelling students forward in the absence of adequate college counseling in our nation's public schools.

The number of these organizations has grown considerably over the past two decades. Approximately 2,500 programs form the consortium National College Access Network (NCAN),[1] but many informal organizations, programs, and individuals providing college access services are unlikely to be affiliated with NCAN and the National Association for College Admission Counseling.

Although CAOs can work nationally, most choose to work regionally. According to NCAN, states average about 44 programs. States with the fewest include Arkansas (2), Nevada (4), and various U.S. territories (the Virgin Islands, Guam, Puerto Rico). States with the most programs include California (249), Kentucky

TABLE 2.1   College Access Organizations (CAOs) by State*

State	Number of CAOs in State	State	Number of CAOs in State
Alabama	54	Montana	18
Alaska	10	Nebraska	15
Arizona	27	Nevada	4
Arkansas	2	New Hampshire	10
California	249	New Jersey	29
Colorado	98	New Mexico	38
Connecticut	23	New York	113
Delaware	13	North Carolina	104
Florida	61	North Dakota	7
Georgia	45	Ohio	92
Hawaii	54	Oklahoma	54
Idaho	7	Oregon	40
Illinois	86	Pennsylvania	65
Indiana	49	Rhode Island	9
Iowa	31	South Carolina	42
Kansas	34	South Dakota	7
Kentucky	154	Tennessee	55
Louisiana	33	Texas	143
Maine	11	Utah	23
Maryland	39	Vermont	11
Massachusetts	84	Virginia	55
Michigan	75	Washington	70
Minnesota	81	West Virginia	18
Mississippi	20	Wisconsin	51
Missouri	39	Wyoming	27

Average of 44 CAOs per state, approximately 2,500 in the United States.

* See Access Program Directory, College Access, http://www.collegeaccess.org/accessprogramdirectory/reports.aspx.

(154), Texas (143), New York (113), and North Carolina (104), and. Table 2.1 lists CAOs state-by-state.

Types of Services

Individual programs perform a variety of services for various demographic groups, but most provide college admissions advising, career exploration/counseling, advice on securing financial aid, and college fairs featuring college admissions personnel. Like SMF, many programs perform various services for their target populations. A few focus more on financial services, defined by NCAN as "loan provision," "administering scholarship programs," and "fee payments for tests, housing and admission applications."

Target Populations

CAOs generally make their services available to specific populations. The most commonly targeted are low-income, first-generation prospective college students. Fewer programs work with undocumented students, foster children aging out of the system, or English-as-a-second-language students. Most work with high school students, but a fair number work with elementary and middle school students. A smaller number work with adults.[2]

Time and Location of College Access Programming

As reported to NCAN, programs take place at various times: during school hours, after school, during the summer, and at specific events. Most programs take place either at a school site or on a college campus. According to NCAN, a surprisingly low number of programs take place at a remote college center or library.[3]

SMF'S POTENTIAL ON THE PERIPHERY PIPELINE INITIATIVE (3PI)

SMF's college access program—The Potential on the Periphery Pipeline Initiative (3PI)—is a collaborative outreach program that draws on nonprofit, public, private, and university resources to bridge the gap between vulnerable students and selective colleges and universities nationwide. It has four basic goals:

1. Facilitating access and achievement for vulnerable students at selective colleges and universities nationwide
2. Developing and identifying a pipeline of academic talent among vulnerable student populations
3. Providing the highest quality college consulting to vulnerable students at no cost
4. Operating as a *de facto* feeder system for selective universities whose missions include educating talented students from diverse backgrounds[4]

In addition to the above goals, SMF's college access program has several key elements, captured in Figure 2.1.

SMF is primarily a regional CAO that helps vulnerable students navigate the standard college admissions process. It provides a range of services, including seminars on such topics as college admissions, career exploration, financial aid, and college survival skills; expert personalized college counseling; mentoring; college trips; standardized test preparation; and scholarships. It does not provide academic remediation but encourages critical thinking on a range of questions and helps students to identify academic enrichment resources. SMF's college selection

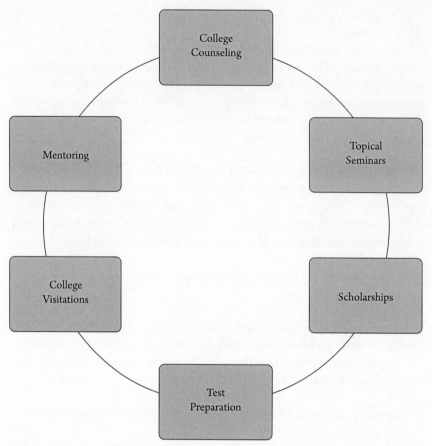

FIGURE 2.1. Simmons Memorial Foundation's Potential on the Periphery Pipeline Initiative (3PI) college access program elements

focus results from recognizing organizational strengths in specialized expertise and employing resources in an efficient manner.

SMF Program Strengths

With over two decades of SMF program experience, certain strengths have emerged. A brief synopsis follows.

Personal Connection. Despite the advent of the Internet and social media, SMF strives to maintain a personal connection with students and to cultivate a shared sense of accountability. Even in an age of information overload, some students get lost, and their doubts about their ability to meet the expectations of the college application process can lead to poor educational choices.

SMF is small enough to provide a tailored, boutique experience for its students. We take the position that no two students are alike. Close relationships are the catalyst that differentiates SMF from other programs that adopt a more corporate interface with students and their families. SMF serves pizza and beverages at most of its seminars, not to address hunger but to cultivate a greater sense of community and shared experience. We give free affinity items, such as polo shirts, portfolios, water bottles, and other items that include the SMF logo. SMF has, on occasion, sent care packages to students during their first year of college as a demonstration of support. We often furnish college admissions information, presentations, and handouts through a portal on our website and distribute them in hard copy along with college guidebooks, SAT-preparation sample tests, and other handouts at sessions. This approach may seem outdated and superfluous given the easy availability of the Internet, but we believe that students and their families get a stronger sense of belonging from receiving tangible, in-kind benefits from our program.

Our annual college trip, involving overnight visits to a range of colleges, is based on the same philosophy of shared group experience. For students, the college trip reinforces the importance of relationships and service to others through a range of elements: witnessing campus life, interacting with outside speakers, observing parents and SMF alumni serving as chaperones, and sharing group meals. In sessions and on trips, we call ourselves a family. Together, these practices contribute to a more personalized experience.

Environmental Setting. Today, SMF's seminars are usually held on the campus of Wake Forest University in Winston-Salem, North Carolina, where the executive director is on the faculty. However, on occasion, they are held in high schools or at program partner sites. A college access program's setting, in my opinion, can influence students' higher education aspirations. There is no better place to espouse the benefits of a college education than a vibrant college campus that students observe firsthand. They are outside of their "comfort zone"—that is, their high school classroom—and must adapt to the new setting. This exposure enhances their enthusiasm, builds confidence, and minimizes intimidation.

Our topical seminars occur periodically throughout the year, often coinciding with benchmarks in the college admissions calendar. In our experience, programs with their own institutional base of operations have more opportunities to establish an independent culture among program participants.

Flexibility. SMF's small size adds to its flexibility, allowing it to deliver extensive programming and large results by maintaining a personal touch. As a small, regional organization without hierarchy and bureaucracy, SMF can make quick adjustments to its programming. While organizations must be able to adapt and evolve, they must also embrace a sustainable mission and not stray from their core commitments.

Low Cost. SMF has developed a cost-effective way to deliver high-quality admissions advice to students at no cost to them. The spirit of volunteerism and mentoring is part of the SMF brand. Since its inception in 1996, it has had no full-time employees but instead leverages volunteers and pays consultants and contractors as a cost-reduction strategy. SMF's executive director has volunteered his time for over two decades. Students and parents know that SMF personnel, volunteers, and advisers are driven not by financial gain but by a keen interest in helping students. Donors and grantors also realize that their contributions to SMF do not pay employee salaries or significant overhead but directly support the delivery of student services and outcomes. SMF's primary sources of financial support are individual donations, donations from large as well as small businesses, and grants.

Partnering. Partnerships with high schools and other educational organizations are an important part of SMF's strategy and success. No matter how well designed, intentions and plans will fail without the commitment and shared investment of partners. Key partnerships with area high schools, especially underresourced schools, are critical to our mission. An effective complementary relationship between SMF and high schools is important because student exposure to SMF programming is intermittent, while their high school contact is continuous. We also establish relationships with education-focused organizations, such as YMCAs and Boys & Girls Clubs, and even share our expertise with other college access programs that serve similar student populations. Our goal is not to compete but to advance student educational trajectories and complement other forms of college guidance.

Establishing formal and informal partnerships with selective college admissions departments and marketing our college access program has a value beyond recruiting or building a student pipeline. Keeping abreast of admissions trends and the perspectives of college admissions officers is invaluable. By understanding these so-called demand-side considerations, we can identify opportunities for students and institutions. As advocates, we leverage these relationships to benefit our student participants.

Student Selection Criteria. SMF is a selective enrichment program for high-achieving students, which distinguishes it from other programs and signals value to students, families, and colleges. Our selective orientation and limited scope and scale are pragmatic organizational choices. With limited resources, SMF cannot solve every barrier to college access, especially academic remediation, so we specialize in providing the highest quality college counseling and support services to academically talented students from vulnerable populations. With approximately seventy students in our pipeline, we can deliver individualized attention. Many programs tackle too many problems with limited resources and expertise. SMF is designed to deliver win-win results to its stakeholders: students receive the highest quality college consulting at no cost, and selective colleges gain access, free of charge, to a talented group of underrepresented public school students who are better prepared to navigate, contribute, and succeed in college environments.

Because program participation is not open ended, students generally meet the following criteria:

- Enrolled in grades 9 through 12 in a public high school
- In the top 10 to 15 percent of their high school class
- Engaged in a rigorous high school curriculum, taking Advanced Placement International Baccalaureate, or honors classes

They must also be members of vulnerable groups; that is, facing one or more factors that might limit their chance for success. These risk factors include, but are not limited to, lower socioeconomic status, living in a rural or inner-city environment, underrepresented minority or ethnicity status, undocumented immigration status, membership in a historically disenfranchised group, and limited parental educational attainment. SMF owes this vulnerability concept, in part, to a classification created by the W.K. Kellogg Foundation.[5] Its freshness, breadth, and avoidance of politically charged stigma compared to other concepts appealed to us. Although the overwhelming majority of SMF students are self-identified underrepresented minorities, our program serves other vulnerable populations as well.

Recruiting. Students can become SMF program participants through several grassroots channels. Outreach targets local high school administrators, counselors, and teachers as well as community organizations. Partner high schools and community organizations, such as the local YMCA, recommend students who meet SMF criteria. Students can also apply directly. SMF often attracts students by word of mouth; satisfied participants and their families are an excellent recruiting resource. These direct mechanisms ensure greater access to SMF's programming and acknowledge that intermediaries may not always adequately communicate information about SMF and its value.

Geopolitical Environment: Delaware and North Carolina as Microcosms of the Nation

Delaware. The challenges SMF faced in Delaware are not isolated; they resonate nationwide. Although a tiny state, Delaware is a perfect microcosm of the national experience with regard to class, race, and other concerns. It has both northern and southern sensibilities. The city of Wilmington in the north is less than 30 miles south of Philadelphia and resembles other Rust Belt cities both aesthetically and culturally. It is the professional and industrial center for the entire state: a hub for chemical companies, banks, and corporate lawyers. By contrast, southern Delaware's local economy is dominated by agriculture and tourism near the coast. It is small-town America, and, at the time of SMF's inception, each town generally had one high school that everyone—wealthy, poor, white, Hispanic, Asian, black—attended. It has the look and feel of the rural American South.

Southern Delaware is part of the Delmarva Peninsula, a region encompassing parts of Delaware, Maryland, and Virginia and bordered by the Chesapeake Bay to the west and the Atlantic Ocean to the east. In a sense, the towns, counties, and people of the peninsula have more in common with one another than with their respective states. James Michener's novel *Chesapeake* romanticizes this region, which was largely disconnected from the mainland until construction of the Chesapeake Bay Bridge in 1952.[6] Its picturesque beaches, wetlands, farms, small towns with Victorian homes, and unique cultures make it a popular tourist destination. However, the local agricultural economy significantly restricts career options. Delaware's two southern counties, Kent and Sussex, have the highest poverty levels in the state—often higher than the national average. Geographic isolation amplifies information deficiencies among vulnerable families, and professionally and culturally diverse mentors are rare. Today, while the national average for students pursuing some form of higher education is 68 percent and Delaware's state average is 60 percent, only 56.4 percent of graduating high school seniors in Delaware's southernmost county pursue higher education.[7]

Although Delaware was a part of the Union during the Civil War, it remained a slave state during the war. Following the Supreme Court's decision in *Plessy v. Ferguson*, it amended its constitution in 1897 to require separate schools for white and black children.[8] It did not have a genuine public school system until 1921, when a newly passed education law required an "equivalent," albeit segregated, education for white and black students.[9] The success of this effort was due in large part to the financial, philanthropic, and political efforts of Pierre S. du Pont, Delaware's premiere industrialist. He contributed a total of $10 million to improve education throughout the state, and to silence public objections, he funded $2.6 million for the construction of segregated schools for black students, donated at no taxpayer expense.[10]

Nevertheless, Delaware's segregated public schools were never equal. As late as 1950, there were no public high schools for African Americans south of Wilmington. Pivotal 1950s court cases illustrate the persistent inequities. Two of the five cases consolidated into the landmark *Brown v. Board of Education* decision—*Bulah v. Gebhart* and *Belton v. Gebhart*—concerned Delaware public schools.[11] In both, Chancellor Collins Seitz, although upholding *Plessy*, ordered the immediate desegregation of two public schools in 1952, and the Delaware Supreme Court affirmed this ruling.[12] These were the only *Brown* cases in which the NAACP prevailed at the trial level. Seitz's order was eventually affirmed by the U.S. Supreme Court in *Brown*.

Louis L. Redding, a prominent Delaware civil rights attorney, represented the plaintiffs in these cases. He was a product of Delaware's segregated public school system, graduating in 1919 from Howard High School, Delaware's only college preparatory high school for African Americans at that time. He subsequently attended and graduated from Brown University with honors in 1923 and attended Harvard Law School, where he was the only African American in the 1928 graduating class. In the same year, he became the first African American admitted to the Delaware Bar and remained its only African American member until 1956.[13]

Higher education among blacks and whites in Delaware reflected a similar pattern of sobering inequity. In 1891, following the passage of the Morrill Act, federal legislation to create land-grant colleges, Delaware chartered the State College for Colored Students, which eventually became Delaware State University.[14] Notably, the college did not offer a four-year degree until 1932. Underfunding by the state was a continuing problem, despite contributions from Pierre S. du Pont for new campus buildings.[15] The state's flagship, the University of Delaware, did not admit blacks until after the 1950 decision by Vice-Chancellor Collins Seitz in *Parker v. University of Delaware*.[16] This decision from the Court of Chancery, the state's equity court, enjoined the University of Delaware from excluding black applicants under the separate-but-equal doctrine because Delaware State College and the University of Delaware failed to meet *Plessy v. Ferguson*'s equivalency requirements.

While Delaware was an important battleground in the effort to advance educational opportunity nationwide, SMF, nearly two decades ago, confronted the vestiges of its historical disenfranchisement of African Americans.

North Carolina. Like Delaware, North Carolina reflects the country's divisions along the lines of politics, class, race, and place (rural versus urban). North Carolina is the ninth-most-populous state, boasting three major metropolitan areas: the Research Triangle, including Raleigh, Durham, Cary, and Chapel Hill; the Piedmont Triad, including Winston-Salem, Greensboro, and High Point; and the Charlotte metropolitan area. The areas outside these cities are largely rural. North Carolina boasts a diverse landscape that includes beaches in the east and mountains in the west.

Winston-Salem (estimated population 225,000), SMF's current home, was once known as the Camel City for its close connection to the R.J. Reynolds Tobacco Company. It is located in the Piedmont Triad region, approximately 25 miles from Greensboro, site of the 1960 sit-ins so pivotal in the civil rights movement. Four courageous North Carolina A&T University students directly challenged the injustice of segregation at a Woolworth's lunch counter. Within two months, the actions of the "Greensboro Four"—Ezell Blair Jr., David Richmond, Franklin McCain, and Joseph McNeil–were repeated in 55 cities in 13 states. Dining facilities began to be integrated in the summer of 1960.[17]

From an educational perspective, Winston-Salem reflects a tale of two cities, where the socioeconomic imprint and other vestiges of racial segregation are manifest in the college aspirations of today's students. Here, SMF encounters college access problems for vulnerable students similar to those in Delaware a decade earlier against a backdrop of economic, racial, and residential segregation. The small rural towns of southern Delaware generally had one high school that students of all backgrounds attended. Winston-Salem's high schools reflect a twofold stratification: different schools have different socioeconomic and racial demographics, and within schools, low-income, minority, and other vulnerable students are tracked into less rigorous coursework that does not adequately prepare them for college. Despite the implementation of school-choice mechanisms to promote greater socioeconomic and racial diversity, high schools in eastern Winston-Salem, such as Parkland and Carver, remain low income and predominantly minority, while high schools in the western part, such as Mt. Tabor and Reynolds, are predominantly nonminority and more affluent. Top students from Mt. Tabor and Reynolds commonly attend selective colleges like Emory, Davidson, Duke, University of North Carolina at Chapel Hill, and others, but top students attending high schools in eastern Winston-Salem rarely do.

Although North Carolina has one of the best public higher education systems in the country and offers more higher education options than Delaware, many vulnerable students who should be admitted to nationally ranked private and state flagship universities do not apply and are not enrolled. Instead, they mismatch in their college choices; that is, based on their high school qualifications, they enroll in a college with a lower selectivity level than the category of college that would have accepted them.[18] William Bowen's Crossing the Finish Line documents this troubling mismatching pattern among North Carolina students.[19] However, as SMF's experience reveals, student trajectories can be altered with programmatic intervention.

North Carolina is also emblematic of the political dysfunction and gridlock gripping many state legislatures across the country. Parochial and short-term interests have resulted in the reversal of decades of improvement to a once-heralded K–12 and higher education environment that expanded access across demographic categories.[20] Regressive legislation, such as the infamous House Bill (HB) 2, the "Bathroom Bill," voter suppression attempts along racial and political lines, and draconian educational proposals, have tarnished North Carolina's reputation as an example of southern progress.[21]

METHODOLOGY

This book uses qualitative research methods and draws upon insights from multiple disciplines. Given its focus on a single organization and a single group of students, our findings may not be generalizable, but they are quite suggestive of the influence college access interventions have on students' higher education trajectories. The results reveal novel insights and new avenues of inquiry.

Data Sources

Primary data sources for this study include former SMF student interviews collected over a twelve-month period, internal SMF organizational documents, and eyewitness accounts. Our analysis of interview data applied a methodology similar to Strauss and Corbin's Grounded Theory to categorize and extrapolate concepts and theories.[22] Analysis is drawn from reports, statistics, laws, regulations, policies, and secondary source materials. The book engages and references academic research related to college access to provide greater context for the SMF interviews.

SMF Student Interviews

To perform this study, our research team secured institutional review board (IRB) approval from Wake Forest University to conduct interviews involving human subjects. All recruited participants received private communications via email, social media (e.g., Facebook and LinkedIn), or phone calls describing the study. In recruiting study participants, our research team relied on internal SMF program contact information, primarily emails. Recruiting emails, including consent forms, were sent to 136 former SMF participants. Ninety-one (66 percent) opened them; 31 (approximately one-third of the recipients) responded and agreed to participate in the study.

Consent forms alerted participants to the slight risk that third parties might identify them indirectly by linking information from other publicly available sources. To minimize this risk, our study makes use of pseudonyms to protect the identity of study participants from third parties. Participants were also given the opportunity to withdraw from the study and/or to choose not to answer questions that might involve private or sensitive information (e.g., professional status and family background) at any time in the interview process.

Between October 2013 and October 2014, I conducted thirty-one semistructured interviews with former SMF student participants. All interviews were conducted and audio-recorded with the participants' consent through private teleconferencing to reduce privacy risks. The recordings were later transcribed manually and then coded. Each interviewee was assigned an anonymous number for purposes of coding the data and a pseudonym to provide anonymity in publications. Each interview lasted approximately 1 to 1.5 hours.

All interviewees were asked the same general set of questions, developed from concerns raised in the college access literature. The interviews were semistructured; that is, participants could elaborate on a question, and the interviewer could ask follow-up questions to clarify and further develop the response. This format encouraged more open-ended responses and flexibility. Student participants were not provided with the interview questions in advance; all their answers were spontaneous. Whenever possible, the book attempts to preserve their authentic voices.

A specific strength of the semistructured interview is its ability to capture unfiltered attitudes—positive, negative, and indifferent—toward SMF's assistance, college access, relationships, the application process, financial aid, and the challenges vulnerable students experience during college. These perspectives reflect student participation across two states and approximately fourteen years. Rather than working with aggregated data, our research team identified and analyzed individual student responses. Although we had no control group, we can compare and contrast the responses of our two distinct student populations, one from rural southern Delaware on the Delmarva peninsula, the other from the more urban Piedmont Triad of North Carolina.

Strengths

Flexibility is a major benefit associated with qualitative methodologies. Most quantitative studies on precollege outreach programs measure only whether they contribute to higher college admission rates. What happens inside these programs to explain how and why they do or do not succeed remains opaque. Quantitative approaches alone do not adequately tell us how students perceive or respond to program interventions.

Instead of simply providing aggregated data that boil college access down to binary paradigms, such as college versus no college, this book attempts to answer the following types of questions from a student vantage point: Which tactics work? Why are some organizations unsuccessful? What do students really think about these programs? Can organizational success be attributed to the integration of various elements or an individual element? Does the program's size or scope matter? How do students, with the benefit of advice, arrive at their decisions? How important are extrafamilial relationships (e.g., social capital) to student college choices? Do college access programs influence personal development and perspectives? What is the long-term impact of college access programming? Aggregated quantitative data cannot adequately capture the complex interactions between individual and organizational features, tactics, and contexts that may influence student outcomes.

Qualitative interview analysis is well suited to identifying the multiplicity of college access themes addressed in student responses. Compared to typical multiple-choice survey formats, qualitative interviews prompt many responses that the interviewer did not anticipate and were not addressed by the survey, and more nuanced responses, including "if A, then X, but if B, then Y." Such responses make explicit connections to other questions in the interview protocol.

Generally, interview responses can help to assess knowledge, competence, exposure, and skill acquisition, answering questions such as, "What did you learn about the college admissions process and financial aid?" Additionally, qualitative methodologies and rubrics have expanded to capture information beyond these typical assessments of learning and achievement. Instead, researchers are assessing, for example, how students' participation in a college access program might transform their world perspective, perceptions and understandings of their abilities, motivations, and growth, as well as influence their educational, even their life, trajectory.[23] Admittedly, all learning brings about change, but qualitative methodologies have the potential to differentiate between transformative and more incremental changes and experiences. A significant number of our study participants were years removed from their SMF and college experiences and, with the benefit of hindsight, able to offer more reflective responses on transformative impact.

Employing qualitative methodologies to assess the affective impact of an engaged learning experience, such as participation in a college access program or internship, is a valuable exercise with potentially broad implications. In a volatile fiscal and political climate, program funding and investment decisions are based upon impact assessments. They must not focus simply on knowledge acquisition and competency but discern the more holistic impact of college access programming on students. Ignoring a student's perceived change in such dimensions as confidence, pride, identity, positive outlook, social capital acquisition, and educational trajectory may significantly undervalue the impact of many worthwhile programs and overstate the relative impact of others.

Limitations

Selection Bias and Confirmation Bias. A wealth of research shows that interviewees, like other human beings, are subject to certain biases,[24] and our study had the potential for selection bias.[25] Students who did not have a favorable college experience or were unwilling to share a negative SMF program experience were probably less likely to participate in the study. Another type of bias commonly associated with interviews that may have limited our study is confirmation bias, when people select facts to support their preexisting beliefs.[26]

Familiarity. The interviews were conducted by the author, executive director of the SMF program, who is well known to most, if not all, study participants. Consequently, they may have been less willing to share negative critiques of the SMF organization and been more positive than if the interviewer had been an independent investigator. To ameliorate this effect, the study asked a question designed to capture critiques indirectly. For example, it requested feedback and solicited recommendations to improve the organization's future programming.

Paradoxically, familiarity is also a significant strength of the study. The trust I have established with student participants makes them more likely to share personal details concerning their family, socioeconomic, and educational histories. It may also make them more forthcoming with personal information and more comfortable overall in the interview sessions. At times, I drew on my knowledge and familiarity with participants in asking follow-up questions.

Lack of a Control Group. SMF program activities, like those of most CAOs, were never carried out in anticipation of experimental research. Our overall aim is to provide vulnerable students with high-quality college access programming, not to withhold such services. As a consequence, formulating control groups to balance the present study was impossible, suggesting potential limitations in two areas: comparing outcomes for students who received SMF programming versus similarly situated students who did not; and isolating the relative effectiveness of various programing elements, such as mentoring, by comparing participants who were mentored versus others who were not. The lack of a control group of students who did not receive programmatic interventions is a limitation that may lead to artificially inflated estimates of program impact or the erroneous conclusion that a program is ineffective.

In evaluating college access programs, positive changes in cognitive, identity, and social-emotional development that are simply a by-product of normal maturation rather than specific program interventions must be considered. However, a number of recent studies, using randomized testing to evaluate the impact of college guidance and youth mentoring interventions, provide additional evidence to which we can compare our results.[27] Similarly with regard to evaluating the relative effectiveness of various program components, randomized trials described in the literature have assessed the specific impact of various types of college access interventions.

SMF Student Interviewee Demographics

This book's analysis draws heavily upon interviews of thirty-one former SMF program participants. Their ages ranged from 18 to 31. Our sample was divided almost evenly between the first seven years of the SMF College Mentoring program in southern Delaware (1998–2006) and the most recent seven years in Winston-Salem, North Carolina (2007–2014): 55 percent from southern Delaware and 45 percent from the Piedmont Triad. In addition, our sample was divided roughly equally between men (48 percent) and women (52 percent). All study participants self-identified as minority, twenty-eight as black/African American and three as Hispanic. One participant was an undocumented immigrant.

All study participants attended public high schools and were enrolled in honors, AP, or IB coursework. A majority, 52 percent (16 out of 31), were first-generation college students. At the time of the study, 68 percent (21 out of 31) had received their undergraduate degrees, while 32 percent (10 out of 31) were still enrolled at their undergraduate institutions and working toward their degrees. At

TABLE 2.2   General Demographic Information of Study Participants

	Number of Participants	Percentage of Participants
Gender		
Female	16	52
Male	15	48
Race/Ethnicity		
Black/African American	28	90
Hispanic	3	10
First-Generation Students	16	52
Financial Issues Important	24	77
State of Residency		
Delaware	17	55
North Carolina	14	45

TABLE 2.3   College Information on Study Participants

	Number of Participants	Percentage of Participants
Tier of Institution		
Top 25	10	32
Top 50	18	58
Outside of Top 50	13	42
Type of Institution		
Public	12	39
Private	19	61
HBCUs*	5	16
Ivy League	6	19

* HBCUs are higher education institutions established prior to the Civil Rights Act of 1964 with the primary intention of serving African American students.

the time of the study, participants were either attending or had attended the following categories of higher education institutions: top 25 (32 percent; 10 out of 31); top 50 (58 percent; 18 out of 31); outside top 50 (42 percent; 13 out of 31); public colleges and universities (39 percent; 12 out of 31); private colleges and universities (61 percent; 19 out of 31); historically black colleges and universities (16 percent; 5 out of 31); and Ivy League (19 percent; 6 out of 31).[28] An overwhelming majority attended selective universities, defined as institutions that reject more applicants than they admit. Table 2.2 summarizes study participants' demographic information, including gender, race/ethnicity, first-generation status, financial sensitivity, and state of residency.

TABLE 2.4   Undergraduate Institutions of Study Participants

Undergraduate Institution	Number Who Attended or Are Currently Attending
Baylor University/Swarthmore College*	1
College of William & Mary	1
Cornell University	1
Davidson College	1
Delaware State University	1
Duke University	1
Harvard University	1
Howard University	1
Morehouse College	1
North Carolina State University	1
Princeton University	1
Spelman College	2
Swarthmore College	1
Temple University	1
University of Delaware	3
University of North Carolina–Chapel Hill	3
University of North Carolina–Charlotte	1
University of Pennsylvania	2
University of Virginia	1
Wake Forest University	5
Yale	1

* The school listed first is the institution from which the student ultimately graduated. The second is the institution the student initially attended, then transferred.

TABLE 2.5   Graduate/Professional Schools of Study Participants

Graduate/Professional Institution	Number of Participants Attended or Currently Attending
Emory University School of Law	2
Fulbright Scholarship	1
Georgia State University Master of Social Work	1
Neumann University Master of Science in Strategic Leadership	1
Southwestern Baptist Theological Seminary Master of Arts in Marriage & Family Therapy/Counseling	1
University of Delaware Master of Arts	1
University of Delaware Master of Science	1
University of Pennsylvania School of Education	1
University of Pennsylvania School of Law	1
Wake Forest University Master in Science of Accounting	1
Wake Forest University Doctoral Program in Chemistry	1
Washington & Lee University School of Law	1

TABLE 2.6   Postgraduate Employment of Study Participants

Employment	Number of Study Participants
Consulting	1
Entrepreneur (Bakery)	1
Human Resources	1
Investment Banking	1
K–12 Education	2
Large Corporation	1
Nongovernmental Organization (NGO) (Environmental)	1
Nursing	1
Postdoctoral Fellowship (Government Laboratory)	1
NGO (Education)	1

Table 2.3 summarizes the tier and type of higher education institution that study participants attended or were attending.

Table 2.4 shows the undergraduate institutions the thirty-one study participants attended or were attending.

Among students eligible for graduate and professional schools, 67 percent (14 out of 21) had attended or were attending. One study participant was awarded a Fulbright Fellowship to pursue postgraduate studies. Table 2.5 lists the graduate or professional schools that study participants attended or were attending.

Table 2.6 captures the general employment areas of study participants who completed their undergraduate, graduate, or professional degrees and were not currently pursuing graduate or professional education.

The foregoing discussion provides context for the analysis of student interview responses in the following chapters. The next chapter captures the diverse college access challenges vulnerable students face regarding high school, affordability, and postsecondary education.

3 · CHALLENGES IN COLLEGE ACCESS

I think that the mixture of the marvelous and terrible is a basic condition of human life, and that the persistence of human ideals represents the marvelous pulling itself up out of the chaos of the universe.... Here, the terrible represents all that hinders, all that opposes human aspiration, and the marvelous reflects the triumph of the human spirit over chaos.

—Ralph Ellison[1]

This chapter describes the obstacles that conspire to thwart vulnerable students' higher education achievement through the lens of student interview findings and academic insights. Specifically, this chapter analyzes the diverse challenges students face in three key areas: at the high school level, college affordability, and at the college level and beyond. These challenges are multilayered, systemic, and individual. They demand an aggressive, well-executed response.

HIGH SCHOOL CHALLENGES

To be honest, I didn't even know my counselor until my senior year in high school.

—Harold

Submitting a college application is perhaps the most important act a high school student can take because it sets in motion numerous life-shaping events. Still, many talented, vulnerable students do not receive the assistance that would enable them to convert their high school achievement into an educational outcome commensurate with their potential. This broken K–16 bridge, characterized by disparities in guidance along with other obstacles, contributes to an ominous sorting pattern with systemic national implications. Our findings and the results of other academic research involving randomized trials with control groups reveal that targeted guidance makes a significant difference in whether and where underrepresented students attend college.[2]

This section captures SMF students' high school experiences as they pertain to college guidance. Students vividly expressed the challenges they faced across many areas: weak college-going cultures, limited structural support for preparing college applications, limited support from teachers and counselors in the college selection process and their lack of encouragement to attend selective colleges, low expectations and bias, familial influence, extrafamilial relationships, and limited opportunities to acquire social capital. These concerns are outlined in the students' own words.

The High School College-Going Culture

A college-going culture in high school is important because it "cultivates aspirations and behaviors conducive to preparing for, applying to and enrolling in college. A strong college culture is tangible, pervasive and beneficial to students. It may be developed in a specialized section of a school, such as within a magnet program or small learning community. However, the ideal college culture should be inclusive and accessible to all students."[3]

In interview responses, SMF participants told us whether their high school experiences included an enriching college-going culture. Students who indicated that their high schools had strong college-going cultures provided some qualifications and a more nuanced picture upon closer review.

Student Insights Regarding College-Going Culture

Norman and Steven noted that many of their classmates attended local community colleges and in-state public institutions. Norman, a male African American from North Carolina, stated:

> I would definitely think of it as college-driven in the sense that students go to all different types of colleges, whether that's a few years [of] technical college or just a local community college up to, of course, the university.

Steven, a male, African American, first-generation student from rural Delaware, added:

> The majority of the students who graduated from my high school went to the local community college, Delaware Technical Community College, or one of the state universities, University of Delaware, and some students attended [an] HBCU—Delaware State University.

Robert told us that at his school, some benefited from a college-going culture and some did not. Robert, a male African American from rural Delaware, said:

> I would suppose that [my high school] had a strong college-going culture about it, particularly if you were maybe of a certain socioeconomic status.

Kathleen indicated that her International Baccalaureate (IB) magnet program had a strong college culture, and counselors and teachers pushed her to apply to colleges. However, she acknowledged that her experience was not necessarily indicative of the entire student body outside of the IB magnet program. An African American woman from North Carolina, Kathleen shared the following:

> It was a lot stronger, as far as more competitive and prestigious schools, with the IB program. I was surrounded by a lot of students who planned on going to college and a lot of teachers who encouraged students and helped students out in the college process.

In contrast, students who indicated that their high school did not have a strong college-going culture offered qualifications that reflect intraschool differences among student subgroups. James noted that certain classmates who were enrolled in an advanced curriculum, such as Advanced Placement (AP) courses, were more likely to attend selective private and out-of-state universities. James, a male African American from rural Delaware, remarked:

> We did not have what I would call a strong college-going culture but . . . there was a large section of students that were graduating but would then go on to take blue-collar jobs or technical jobs outside of the school. For those of us who did go to college, the primary locations for college were sort of based upon what class level you were in and when I say class level, [I mean] if you were [in] the honors program or college prep or the level below that.

Damien also noticed that his high school did not focus on preparing him or his classmates for the four-year university experience. A male, African American, first-generation student from rural Delaware, Damien answered as follows when asked whether his high school had a college-going culture:

> I would say no, and the reason I would say that is because I looked at the statistics a while ago [and] about 44 percent [of students], if I'm not mistaken, actually went on to some sort of higher education. And then of that 44 percent, a certain portion of them went to traditional four-year colleges, a substantial portion goes into vocational or some sort of other program. There's not a strong emphasis on traditional four-year degree enrollment.

These student responses underscore the lack of a college-going culture at their high schools and show the context in which many make college-related decisions. Specifically, many interviewees felt that their high schools did not have strong college-going cultures or that the college-going culture was largely contingent upon socioeconomic status, participation in a magnet program, or placement in an honors program. Research shows that the lack of a college-going culture contributes to lower student aspirations and reinforces poor educational decision making. Based on my SMF experience, this negative environmental factor can significantly impair vulnerable student college selection and higher education attainment.

Limited Structured Support for College Applications

Of the students who identified a strong college-going culture within their respective high schools, few actually said their high school offered structured college application support to students. Structured support is important because it routinizes the guidance students receive—making it available to all students—rather than more ad hoc and haphazard approaches that may ignore too many vulnerable students. Structured support does not necessarily guarantee individually tailored application support or even high-quality support. It does, however, ensure that all students, at a minimum, receive some base level of application support.

Student Insights about College Application Support

Louis indicated that his school provided such support only if students initiated the process. A male, African American, first-generation student from rural Delaware, Louis commented:

> I don't remember there being any college assistance, any structured college assistance beyond—I do remember announcements for any high school seniors who are interested in learning more about college, please see your counselor. But beyond that, we didn't have any structured meetings or organized sessions.

Che and Barbara felt that their high schools and counselors should have done more to help students with the college application process. Che, an African American man from rural Delaware, stated:

> I thought that if there was a sort of system in which you could have more individual meetings to find out where the student's head was in terms of what they might have wanted out of their situation that there would have been a more nuanced approach to college [applications]. I know for myself my ambitions were larger than to stay within Delaware, and [if] I had that conversation or had a platform to have that conversation with my guidance counselor, we could have come to some sort of agreement in which we would have not wasted each other's time. I guess [that] is the best way that I could put it. But I think that certainly having more individualized approaches and then perhaps having something in which there were partnerships between colleges and the guidance counselors to bring in and show students and have them meet maybe admissions persons or what have you, if that's even possible, I thought that would have been really helpful for me.

Barbara, an African American woman from rural Delaware, added:

> To my knowledge, I absolutely feel that they could have done more. I feel certain students, mostly white students who had parents who were either well connected or business owners, they received a lot more [help] . . . [and] enthusiastic counselors than people who were not white.

These student responses highlight a major perceived weakness in public high schools: the absence of structured application support for large numbers of students. Even where students receive support, many must "opt-in," or proactively seek college guidance and support, which constitutes yet another obstacle for vulnerable students. The lack of standard or individualized college application assistance from high school counselors may have only a nominal impact on students whose parents or family friends can help them with their college applications or who can afford a private college adviser or tutor to assist with SAT preparation and college applications. For vulnerable students who do not have access to outside resources and relationships, the lack of information and assistance at the high school level can have a detrimental impact on their future educational choices and opportunities.

Limited Involvement of High School Counselors and Teachers in the College Search and Application Process

A subject related to the lack of structured application support is the amount of support students actually receive from their counselors and teachers. Relationships with teachers and counselors are key resources that impact the college selection process for vulnerable students. Teachers and counselors, who have more consistent contact or access to vulnerable students, are critical touchpoints for students. Our interviews capture divergent student experiences.

Student Insights about High School Counselor and Teacher Involvement

Scott and Betty stated that their counselors and teachers were actively involved, providing them with helpful information and advice. Scott, a male African American from North Carolina, said:

> I felt as though [they were] very involved. . . . And definitely the lead counselor, she was definitely very friendly. I would frequently stop by the office to discuss scholarship information. . . . I had a history teacher, who [was] also my golf coach, who would frequently ask me where I was in my college search, how I was doing on my application. . . . definitely I thought it was a great—a good environment.

Betty, a female, Hispanic, first-generation student from North Carolina, added:

My college-application process or searching for college didn't really start for me until senior year. And I was helped so much by my guidance counselors and a lot of my close teachers. [I] had really good relationships with them, and they really helped me a lot, and they gave me advice and helped me get in touch with other people. . . . They were very instrumental in helping me get to where I am today.

Leo reflected that while his guidance counselors were not involved in the college search, they were helpful in going over his essay. An African American man from North Carolina, Leo commented:

[From] an actual search aspect, I wouldn't say my counselors were very involved. . . . That was mainly through external things, [college-access programs] like SMF and Crosby Scholars. But, on the application side, they were very helpful. They proofread my essays . . . and that was very helpful for the process.

Alisha and Tawnya appreciated their counselors staying on top of the process and helping them to stay on track with their applications. Alisha, a female, African American, first-generation student from rural Delaware, shared the following thoughts:

Well, I had a [good] relationship with all my teachers and my counselors, so they were very involved. I just had to tell them what I was interested in, and they helped in terms of recommendations or preparing me for tests like the SAT. And my counselor was really good about staying on top of me to get my applications in and finding money to apply for the SATs and applications for colleges.

Tawnya, a female, African American, first-generation student from North Carolina, added:

They were very involved. I think the guidance counselor that I had—and I cannot remember her name, but, I mean, she was great. She would stay on top of me while making sure I was involved in the things that I wanted to be, not just the things that would make me stand out, but the things that I actually wanted to do. And that would also help me stand out on college applications, and she helped me apply—I was able to check out one of those books that you can use for different colleges, different scholarships, and opportunities. She was on top of me about getting waivers for applications and [attending] college tours. She was amazing.

Roxwell praised his teacher, who acted as a counselor and helped by keeping him on top of applications and the SATs. An African American man from North Carolina, Roxwell remarked:

I look at him more as a counselor. He was definitely proactive. He made sure that we were on top of our applications and with SATs. [If] there was a recommendation [he wrote], he always wanted to get your status as far as getting accepted. I definitely give him a lot of credit just for keeping me on track and making sure I had everything.

Danny emphasized the difference in the college application approach for students involved in the IB program. An African American man from North Carolina, he stated:

I found that they were very involved. They were very helpful, especially in the IB program because it did have the strong college-oriented approach. A lot of teachers are willing to help us with stuff like reading over our [college] essays. They were always encouraging us—basically, college was very important in the program. There was always emphasis on preparing us for higher education, especially with the global approach of the IB program. They were extremely helpful, I would say. I didn't really go to my guidance counselor as probably most of us should have, but I had a decent relationship with the guidance counselor.

SMF participants who cited a lack of counselor and teacher involvement made important observations. Marvin, a Hispanic man from North Carolina, found that family and outside academic advisers were a more helpful source of information:

Well, my high school is the biggest high school in Winston-Salem with 2,000 [students], so my counselors were unfortunately not very involved, and at times I even thought they were very unhelpful in the college-application process. So it was me and my family and an academic adviser that I had that helped me apply for college and scholarships, but my high school counselor was not very involved.

Rocney, Virgil, and Jennifer, all from rural Delaware, were disappointed overall with the interactions they had with their counselors. Rocney, an African American man, said:

But in terms of the schools that I ended up applying to, I applied to none of the schools that were [actually] recommended to me [by counselors and teachers], and I was still pretty successful in my college process. But I don't attribute any of that success to my guidance counselors.

Virgil, a male, African American, first-generation student, added:

On a scale of one to ten, as far as my experience [with counselor and teacher involvement], I would say about a one.

Jennifer, an African American woman, asserted:

I think they could have been more supportive. I think they could have offered more programming for students who were interested in attending college. If they did not want to be the resource, then bringing in resources that could assist students, but especially students who were coming from families where they were the first-generation students and hadn't had the experience before, [and] didn't have any relatives or anyone in their family [to] provide them that coaching.

Finley and Jaya, also from rural Delaware, noted that their guidance counselors provided them more with general tools than specific advice. A female, African American, first-generation student, Finley commented:

The guidance department did not do a great [amount] of emphasis on college preparation for those students whom they saw to be self-sufficient. They would give us the general tools that were needed as far as how to apply for financial aid, how to search for colleges, how to generally fill out a college application, but then I guess the assumption became you are on this educational level, you should be able to handle this on your own. But the door [was] open. If we asked— the guidance department—they were there, but they never really pursued the students.

Another African American woman, Jaya, added:

Our counselors and our teachers were supportive [in that] they were willing to help us with admissions essays and, of course, letters of recommendation. But in terms of helping us to decide where to apply, there really wasn't much guidance in the school setting.

Our findings regarding the dearth of structured application assistance, limited counselor and teacher engagement, and the lack of encouragement make clear that too many students do not receive adequate guidance from their high schools. After nearly two decades of assisting students, a consistent theme among SMF students has been the lack of high school counselor involvement in the college application process. These findings are consistent with nationwide statistics illustrating the dearth of college counseling at public schools. The national average is 1 counselor for every 470 students.[4] Under these circumstances, the explanation for why high-achieving vulnerable students do not apply to college or do apply but to less-selective schools is all too obvious: no one is encouraging them or guiding their choices.

A confluence of factors contributes to the lack of effective college guidance. Research illustrates that counselors are undoubtedly constrained by time, resources, and expertise. However, SMF student interview responses reveal that the problem is not so simple; counselors and other secondary school actors also show misaligned incentives, low expectations, and bias.

Misaligned Incentives

Teachers, counselors, and administrators function within a social and professional context. They are part of an organization and a broader community. When faced with competing demands, they must inevitably prioritize their time and effort. In some environments, they may prioritize to maximize their career and social advancement. For example, a counselor may have to decide whether to assist an affluent student whose parents are actively engaged with the school and "well-connected" in the broader community, or to help a low-income minority student whose parent's work schedule limits school engagement. The counselor may often choose the former in the absence of incentives to do otherwise. Thus existing incentive structures may deflect college advising priority away from vulnerable students, especially where the risk of social and occupational backlash is minimal.

The daily decisions and nondecisions of school actors have a strong impact on student outcomes. Recognizing this reality, we must consider how best to align their interests to promote greater accountability to *all* students, irrespective of social markers. No matter how well written a law, statute, regulation, or policy targeting student college counseling needs, implementation and execution by human actors will determine tangible success.

Low Expectations and Bias

Many studies of college access ignore messy factors like bias and lower expectations for vulnerable students. This exercise is dangerous and self-blinding. A number of SMF respondents perceived a lack of concern about their individual college selection process and low expectations for their higher education potential and prospects among their counselors and other school actors. I have heard SMF students express these views anecdotally for nearly two decades.

Life-changing decisions about whether and where to attend college are not made in a vacuum. Even for highly resourced families, the admissions process is chaotic, but for underresourced families with limited histories of higher education attainment, it is almost a locked door. Whether the indifference or depreciation vulnerable students experience is a function of cultural, racial, and class bias, low expectations, or misaligned incentive structures, the results are the same: their college aspirations are diminished, and society may lose the benefit of their contributions.

All human beings, even those with the best intentions, are prone to explicit and implicit bias. Academic research reveals that beyond explicit bias, nonminorities and minorities alike harbor implicit negative biases about minority groups.[5] Implicit bias theories stand in "contrast with the 'naïve' psychological conception of social behavior, which views human actors as being guided solely by their explicit beliefs and the conscious intentions to act." Instead, people "do not always have conscious, intentional control over the processes of social perception, impression formation, and judgment that motivate their actions."[6] These unconscious along with conscious mental processes inevitably influence how counselors and teachers view and interact with vulnerable students in the college selection process.

A study by Anthony Greenwald and Linda Krieger shows the pervasiveness of implicit bias against vulnerable groups. Respondents evidenced a 69 percent bias in favor of whites over African Americans and a 94 percent bias for rich over poor people. The study also suggested that "*any* non–African American subgroups of the United States population will reveal high proportions of persons showing statistically noticeable implicit race bias in favor of EA [European/white Americans] relative to AA [African Americans]." Sadly, the education level of respondents did little to change the degree of implicit bias favoring whites over African Americans. Respondents with some graduate-level education, a subcategory where high school counselors likely fall, favored whites over African Americans by approximately 63 percent.[7] Given these findings, we can surmise that the same unconscious mental processes influence how counselors and teachers might view, evaluate, and interact with vulnerable students in a high school setting.

Bias, whether actual or perceived, implicit or explicit, is a problem for students. Our attention to bias is warranted because students exhibit an acute awareness of how others view their potential, often negatively, due to their minority status or class. School personnel may frame their higher education opportunities narrowly and discourage their effort and persistence in pursuing and selecting a college education. Some participant responses mention slights, or what academics label *microaggressions*, from classmates, counselors, and teachers.[8] These findings are particularly troubling because vulnerable students, according to studies, are more dependent on their school counselors and teachers for college guidance. Our student interviews capture student perceptions of others' low expectations and bias. These responses powerfully illustrate how bias from secondary school actors, such as teachers, counselors, and administrators, can negatively affect vulnerable students' higher education achievement and persistence.

Student Insights on Low Expectations and Bias

Florence told us that her guidance counselor instructed her to look at schools that were not as high caliber as Duke or Yale. Florence, a female, African American, first-generation student from North Carolina, stated:

> My guidance counselor . . . was kind of active. She gave me papers to fill out for scholarship opportunities, but I don't think she really helped me with my college search because I remember the whole time . . . I only talked about Duke, I was like

Duke is where I want to go . . . she told me to look at schools that were underneath that, but I knew I wanted to go to a Duke-caliber school or something above that. But it was awkward because she wasn't really encouraging me to reach out [to] the Duke[s] and Yale[s] and everything.

Jennifer, an African American woman from rural Delaware, told us how her counselor discouraged her aspirations, leading her to question whether to trust the counselor's judgment:

I didn't feel like she had my best interest at heart. Like I said, she didn't even want to help me graduate early from high school. I don't think that she believed that I could do the work and I could be successful in college. And any time you have a school administrator who doesn't even believe in your ability, that's difficult. I didn't trust her judgment on anything from that point forward.

Raine and Aja said they felt that other students were more of a priority to their guidance counselors. Raine, an African American woman from rural Delaware, commented:

I'm not saying race was a factor, but it was a predominantly white high school, and so it seems like a lot of the local scholarships and grants or whatever were given to predominantly white kids. I was involved, very involved, in track and field, and I ran cross-country. I was the president of the Cello Club. I was the vice-president of the Key Club. . . . But it just seemed like I didn't get too much of any help when it came from the counselors at my high school.

Aja, another African American woman from rural Delaware, added:

Education opportunities, even special programs like the Academic Challenge program, it's only available to a select few. I happened to hear about it by chance, but the information about the program was never given to me directly by the school due to my race.

Early in SMF's history, student sentiments like these prompted staff to make direct contact with their high school counselors to tell them the students were participating in SMF programming and to explain our general organizational purposes. Beyond raising their awareness of SMF and the possibility that they might recommend potential program participants, these calls communicated the active interest of an outside party and partner in a particular student's college selection process and outcomes. The goal, in part, was to make the counselors more accountable to the SMF student whose parents might not wield significant influence or occupy high standing in the broader community. SMF places primary emphasis on student accountability, but its seminars often provide students and parents with strategies for holding school actors accountable for contributing to their college application and selection process. Although, today, SMF representatives are less likely to phone high school counselors to discuss specific students, our concerns about indifference and bias persist.

In addition to the respondents' own doubts concerning college, they exhibited an awareness of how others might negatively perceive them and their potential. Although quantifying the impact of negative third-party perceptions and biases on student achievement is difficult, they are neither insignificant nor innocuous. Sometimes they provide additional motivation for students "to prove them wrong." At the same time, they add an unfair burden to already encumbered vulnerable students. While some students feel pressure to match or to live up to their family's history of lofty higher education standards, vulnerable students may feel added pressure to assert and to justify their simple presence in certain college environments.

In many ways, SMF students are no different than other students making the transition to college. Despite their overall confidence, they harbor some doubts and uneasiness: they want to know whether they can compete academically; whether they will be homesick so far from family and friends; and whether they will fit in with other college kids from different social, economic, and cultural backgrounds. Naturally, some of these concerns are more acute for vulnerable students than their more advantaged counterparts, and they must be dispelled. Students without the benefit of a wider safety net or a firm foundation must be assured that they will be fine in dynamic, competitive college learning environments. Programmatic interventions can provide a corrective and stabilizing force against a backdrop of structural and environmental obstacles.

Limited Opportunities for Social Capital Acquisition

Relationships matter in the college selection process. Social capital acquisition is a crucial factor in changing the higher education narrative of vulnerable students. College access is not simply a matter of what students know but who they know. The popularity and value of social networking sites, such as Facebook, Instagram, LinkedIn, and Twitter, reflect the power of social capital, but it is not a recent phenomenon. Alexis de Tocqueville acknowledged its role in the United States long before it emerged in the social science literature:

> Americans of all ages, all conditions, and all minds are constantly joining together in groups. In addition to commercial and industrial associations in which everyone takes part, there are associations of a thousand other kinds: some religious, some moral, some grave, some trivial, some quite general and others quite particular, some huge and others tiny. . . . Nothing, in my view, is more worthy of our attention than America's intellectual and moral associations.[9]

Definitions of social capital vary, but all agree that it accumulates from the relationships we build with others.[10] Robert D. Putnam notes that "a considerable
body of research dating back at least fifty years has demonstrated that trust, networks, and norms of reciprocity within a child's family, school, peer group, and
larger community have wide-ranging effects on the child's opportunities and
choices and, hence, on his [or her] behavior and development."[11] Bourdieu
observed that "social capital is the aggregate of the actual or potential resources
which are linked to possession of a durable network of more or less institutional-
ized relationships of mutual acquaintance and recognition—or in other words,
to membership in a group—which provides each of its members with the back-
ing of the collectivity-owned capital, a 'credential' which entitles them to credit,
in the various senses of the word."[12] The emerging consensus is that social capital
centers on the resources people secure "by virtue of membership in social networks or other social structures." It has "three basic functions ... applicable in a
variety of contexts: (a) as a source of social control; (b) as a source of family support; (c) as a source of benefits through extra-familial networks."[13] The concept
is particularly useful in explaining the acquisition of higher education benefits
accruing to individuals by virtue of their participation in social networks.[14]

For our purposes, social capital is derived from a range of sources, including
connections to family and community members as well as extrafamilial ties with

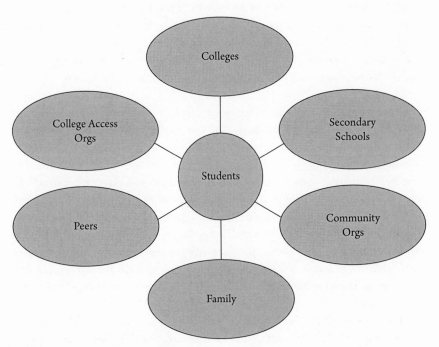

FIGURE 3.1. Sources of social capital

individuals, members of organizations, and groups.[15] Figure 3.1 illustrates the varied sources of social capital for a high school student that are acquired through relationships to individuals or individuals embedded within organizations and institutions.

The Importance of Relationships Rich in Educational Knowledge and Resources

The lack of key family relationships through which students can gather knowledge about higher education options places vulnerable youth at greater risk of securing less favorable higher education outcomes. For example, youth from single-parent, low-income households, in general, tend to have fewer opportunities for social capital acquisition due to the absence of a second at-home parent. Frequent changes of residence and the daily struggle to make ends meet can curtail ties to adults in the surrounding community.[16]

In relation to higher education, young people may compensate for the lack of immediate family or community relationships that are rich in higher education resources with more remote extrafamilial relationships that are.[17] It is important to note that everyone has social capital, but it is not always relevant to higher education.[18] Consider the following example: Student A has limited higher education emphasis or knowledge in the home and/or limited access to college information via immediate family relationships. Alternatively, Student B has the same familial lack of access to college information as Student A, but she has extrafamilial ties with school counselors, teachers, college access programs, other students, and mentors, who emphasize higher education attainment and provide a mechanism through which she can acquire valuable college information. Here, Student B's extrafamilial networks can offset the lack of college information within her immediate family.

Social science research demonstrates the influence of extrafamilial relationships on higher education outcomes, the job market, and beyond.[19] However, youth from poor urban or isolated rural communities often lack social connections beyond their immediate family and community that would enable them to acquire information about valuable higher education and career prospects.[20] In the urban context, the flight of middle-class families significantly limited the opportunities for social capital acquisition for inner-city populations, and modern patterns of gentrification have pushed poor families further to the periphery. Wacquant and Wilson observe that "not only do residents of extreme-poverty areas have fewer social ties but also . . . they tend to have ties of lesser social worth, as measured by the social position of their partners, parents, siblings, and best friends."[21]

In New York's Chinatown, Miami's Little Havana, and Los Angeles's Koreatown, contacts may provide resources, such as "start-up capital . . . tips about business opportunities, access to markets, and a pliant and disciplined labor force." Still, even where ethnic and cultural enclaves might serve as vital resources for community members seeking to establish a business, these ties are often limited geographically and in scope and may not extend to higher education goals.[22]

Rural isolation significantly limits opportunities for social capital acquisition.[23] Scholars, policy makers, and institutions have paid much less attention to the college guidance needs of rural compared to urban populations. This rural blind spot contributes to greater geographic determinism. According to Durham and Smith, the "educational attainment of adults living in rural areas has consistently lagged behind their urban counterparts."[24]

All these circumstances inevitably contribute to less desirable higher education outcomes among vulnerable students. In theory, reforms targeting social capital acquisition could serve as a valuable proxy for family and other resource-rich connections through which vulnerable students can acquire information and resources related to higher education. Public schools have the potential to function as social network hubs where students and parents could access valuable information enabling them to convert student academic preparation into favorable college admissions and other higher education outcomes. However, most public schools, along with local, state, and federal policy frameworks, do not adequately address the impact of social capital acquisition on higher education access.[25]

Social Capital Acquisition and Inequality

Unequal access to various types of capital—human, financial, social—across demographic groups and among group members causes social inequality. Unequal social capital acquisition has two dimensions. The first reflects (1) prevailing institutional practices, rules, cultural norms, and social structures that deprive a group or group member of opportunities; and (2) differential investments by a group or group member that result in a shortage of social capital.[26] The second dimension occurs when the same quantity or quality of social capital generates a "differential return or outcome for different members of social groups." Such differential returns may come from (1) a person's reluctance to mobilize social capital or a cognitive deficiency that prevents effective mobilization, (2) differential efforts by intermediary agents in the network chain, and (3) differential institutional and organizational responses to an individual's social capital.[27] This return differential, among other things, captures the impact of institutional bias where, for example, whites with the same quantity or quality of social capital as African Americans generate greater rewards in the labor market, such as position, titles, prestige, and earnings.

Social interactions often take place among people with similar socioeconomic characteristics and lifestyles.[28] Establishing connections with others generally takes more effort from vulnerable students, which may contribute to inequities in social capital and status attainment. Such disparities have ramifications for educational and career advancement.[29] For example, low-income minority students may have to engage in strategic behaviors to access resources beyond their immediate social circles and neighborhoods, working harder to find professional mentors and establish ties with institutional agents like counselors, teachers, and administrators.[30] In discussing social capital acquisition, we must understand that a group's or student's investment in social relations to generate educational returns does not operate in isolation. Structural and institutional barriers play a significant role in limiting social capital acquisition, which, in turn, limits higher education attainment.

Social Capital's Far-Reaching Impact through Direct and Indirect Relationships

Direct and indirect relationships reveal the potential power of social capital. Social capital acquisition often involves a chain of actors. To secure a resource, such as information about a particular college, Student A may encounter Individual B, who does not have the information but knows Individuals C and D, who do. Here, Individual B's social networks can become resources for Student A. Social capital is generated through Student A's direct connection to Individual B and indirect connections to Individuals C and D. Student A's social capital and networks extend as far as their direct and indirect ties.[31] Figure 3.2 reflects the direct and indirect ties that contribute to a person's social capital.

Relationship to Other Forms of Capital

Most modern social science accepts "capital deficiency" theories, which hold that poor academic performance is caused by "lack [of] resources needed for academic

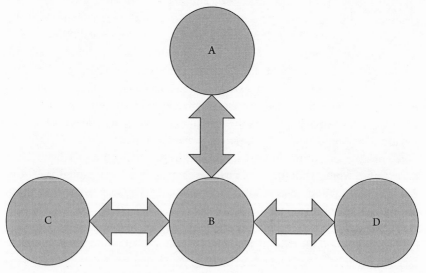

FIGURE 3.2. Direct and indirect relationship ties

success."[32] Social capital is a catalyst for securing other valued forms of capital, such as human capital, financial capital, and cultural capital, which are more tangible but not more important. Figure 3.3 captures this relationship.

Social scientists describe the important catalytic function of social capital as follows:

> People gain access to social capital through membership in networks and institutions and then convert it into other forms of capital (such as education) to improve or maintain their position in society. When children are connected through ties of kinship or friendship to people who can help them prepare for college—socially, psychologically, culturally, and academically—then those ties constitute a source of social capital.[33]

Human capital (e.g., skills and education) and social capital both contribute to societal advancement and are mutually reinforcing. Better-educated individuals with significant human capital tend to operate in social circles that are rich in social capital related to higher education. In the context of education, "well connected parents and social ties can indeed enhance the opportunities for individuals to obtain better education, training, and skill and knowledge credentials."[34] For

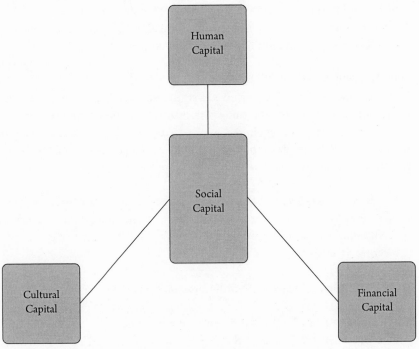

FIGURE 3.3. Social capital's relationship to other forms of capital

vulnerable students with limited familial higher education attainment, social capital networks are particularly important for gaining access to colleges that will meet their potential and needs. They provide information and resources that enable students to capture other forms of capital helpful for higher education success and beyond.[35]

Peers, community groups, nonprofits, family members, teachers, counselors, administrators, and acquaintances all contribute to student success in the college application process. The confluence of these relationships and their contributions to social capital acquisition are reflected in our interview responses. SMF respondents' experiences reinforce the need for more effective interventions to promote social capital acquisition.

Family Influence

Family influence strongly impacts students' higher education choices. Not all parents or families have the same degree of knowledge or experience with higher education to transmit to their children. The absence of higher education knowledge and experience among immediate familial members does not mean that such family members are unsupportive or unhelpful. In fact, a significant number of student responses reveal the opposite. For example, a parent or grandparent can promote and reinforce the importance of higher education in the home without having attained a degree. Notwithstanding, good intentions alone are insufficient. If the goal is informed decision making and successful participation in a highly competitive selection process, inadequate information and ineffective strategies, in my experience, can undermine the best of intentions.

Student Insights on Family Influence

Family members were actively involved in the college application and selection process for just over half of the study participants. Interview responses capture the ways in which family members assisted students. Tammy and Armando revealed how their families supported them by giving general encouragement. Tammy, an African American woman from North Carolina, stated:

> My mom was very involved. She went on every college tour that was sponsored by SMF, and she also took me to college events . . . so my mom was very involved and learning with me because of course she hadn't gone through that experience before as a teenager.

Armando, a Hispanic man from North Carolina, added:

> My dad helped me a lot. He was pushing me, reminding me . . . and I'm so grateful because they [my parents] helped. They were very involved and they made it so much easier.

Cathy and Ronalda shared that they had family members with some college application experience, which was a plus in their application process. Cathy, an African American woman from North Carolina, remarked:

> My mom was very involved, and mostly because she has three other kids before me—who went to college and did the college application process—she knew a lot of stuff about it.

Ronalda, an African American woman from rural Delaware, added:

> I think my parents were involved as much as they could be. I mean, my mom had attended college, but the process had changed significantly since she had applied . . . so I feel like they were supportive and helping me to meet deadlines and filling out all the paperwork that was required of them.

Marie, Russell, and Chad found siblings and other extended family members important in providing encouragement and support for their higher education aspirations. Marie, a female, African American, first-generation student from rural Delaware, commented:

> Because I was an only child, and at that time, I was the only individual who would be going to college, my family placed a great emphasis on their desire for our success. Anywhere that I needed the help or where they saw that I was lacking, there were aunts and cousins and my mom and my grandmother, who were there to jump right in and help me with it.

Russell, a male, African American, first-generation student from rural Delaware, added:

> I would say that my sister was very involved. My mother was as involved as she could be, but given that she didn't go to college herself and did not have a lot of insight around getting into college, there wasn't a whole lot that she could provide. But in terms of going over information with me and [discussing] why I made the choices I made in terms of which colleges I was applying to, she was definitely very involved. In terms of helping me figure out where I wanted to go to school and certain schools to look at, I would say my older sister definitely was very involved in helping me with those decisions.

Chad, an African American man from North Carolina, had a similar experience.

> In [the] college search, they [my parents] were not very involved at all. I remember the biggest involvement was [from] my brothers. They really pushed

me . . . to apply. They knew that I was smart. And not only smart, but [I] actually worked hard because that was a difference between me and them. They were smart, [but] they were [less disciplined], and so they were [saying] you can get into these Ivy League schools or MIT or something like that. They really pushed me to give my best in [the] application [process]. . . . [For] writing the essays and everything, my mom helped me out heavily with that because she already had two sons that already went through the process.

Lauren and Allena shared the importance of communicating expectations with parents. Lauren, a female, African American, first-generation student from rural Delaware, said:

Out of everyone, I would say probably my mom helped me the most. We were [on the same page] as far as finances because she knew she wasn't able to help me [financially] and also as far as location because if she needed to come and get me, she wanted it to be within driving distance. Even the University of Delaware looks like maybe two-and-a-half hours away. She would say that would be the longest distance that she could afford to travel at that time. So I think we were probably on the same page as far as finances and as far as location.

Allena, an African American woman from rural Delaware, added:

My dad convinced me to go to Delaware State. He was looking at the cost factor because they could not afford for me to go to school. And they were not sure of what the economy would do. And they knew that I was a really good student. They just didn't want to see me graduate and [not] be able to have a job to pay off the student debt. So they were really looking beyond just here and now.

SMF participants whose families were not actively involved in the college application process explained how it affected their college aspirations. Earl and Alexa shared that their parents and family members steered them away from applying to selective schools due to distance or cost. Earl, a male, African American, first-generation student from rural Delaware, remarked:

On a scale of one to ten, one. The discussions that I had with my parents about school selection, school applications, boiled down to a few conversations, and that was when my mother . . . didn't want me to go to school too far away from home. That was really the only involvement that my parents had in my entire application process.

Alexa, an African American woman from rural Delaware, added:

They didn't at all, actually. I had made up my mind that I would attend the school that granted me the most money. . . . I came from a low-income family, and I knew they wouldn't be able to fully support me financially.

Thomas and Jeanne stated that they drove their own college selection process with limited intervention from family members. An African American man from North Carolina, Thomas said:

[My family was] not that involved because growing up, I was pretty independent, and my mom always had a lot of confidence in me and knows that I know how to take care of things and get things done on my own. And my parents or mostly my family, they weren't really that involved in my whole application process. A lot of it, I pretty much did on my own by researching schools, finding the applications online and doing the essays.

Jeanne, a female, African American, first-generation student from North Carolina, added:

Not very [much]. I always did these kinds of things on my own, so I've always done the research; I've always done the paperwork, the applications, all that just by myself. And my mom was there to support me, but she wasn't very involved.

Angeline and Makeba told us that their objective was to get as far away from home as possible. Angeline, an African American woman from rural Delaware, commented:

When I thought [about] applying to college, I was in foster care, [and] my goal was to get as far away as possible. So that was really most influential [in those] days as far as the relationships in my life at that time.

Makeba, a female, African American, first-generation student from rural Delaware, stated:

It [family] didn't [influence me]. Many people asked why I chose Spelman. I wanted to just get as far away from Delaware as I could at that time. Out of all the schools I was [admitted to], I literally just chose the school that was the farthest place away from home.

Irvina, another female, African American, first-generation student from rural Delaware, shared that SMF helped to correct her parents' misconceptions about college so that she could attend school out of state.

Yes, my family was really concerned about me leaving the state or going away because that is not something that normally occurred in my community, and within the direct community, I would have been the first, and my parents were just really nervous about the dangers, what would happen if I had homesickness and things like that. They could not just readily come get me if I was far away . . . I do not think that was a big factor because ultimately [I ended up] going away [for college], but this is probably where the Simmons Foundation stepped in as well. Having that feedback as far as it is okay for [you to go] away for [college] and having that information where I can relate it back to my family and [say], "Mom and Dad, it is okay." If you need to talk to someone, there is someone there that can fill in that information and let them know that this was a better opportunity for me instead of being directly at home.

Research overwhelmingly confirms that familial relationships play a very important role in the college application process and higher education attainment, yet parental and familial involvement varies across demographic subgroups, especially among vulnerable students. With limited familial involvement or a dearth of familial college knowledge, SMF respondents display a significant degree of independence and personal discipline, which makes high school guidance and extrafamilial relationships with SMF volunteers all the more crucial to the college selection process.

Extrafamilial Relationships

A large proportion of SMF participants stated that relationships outside the family were important in the college application and selection processes. These relationships, at times, compensated for the lack of higher education knowledge and related resources among immediate family members.

Student Insights on Extrafamilial Relationships

Kevin and Vera cited college access programs, such as SMF, as helpful in their college selection process. Kevin, a male, African American, first-generation student from rural Delaware, said:

I think, outside of my family, I had my peers or other students who I was in class with and even in the MERIT program [a Delaware-based college-access program] and SMF, we pushed each other a lot, and I remember there was like a very healthy competition among us where we always were asking well, what school did you apply to, and what is your list? We always looked at each other's list and just to see [did] I get the same school? [We'd ask] who got into which school, and once you got in, we're celebrating together, and I remembered having conversations about who is going to go the farthest away from home, and are you okay with that? We had ongoing conversations about what our prospects even were and a healthy competition about which school did you get into, how many did you get into, where do you think you're going to go? So it felt like we had a community of learners that continue to push each other . . . throughout our senior year.

Vera, a female, African American, first-generation student from rural Delaware, shared:

I think ultimately the people outside my family really coached me to go [for] the better school and opportunity. My counselor, Mr. Howard, the MERIT Program, and the Simmons Foundation really were impactful on my decision of going away for school. I had a lot of people in my church community who were [not] exactly my family who had not attended college themselves but maybe their children had, and they let me know how great an opportunity [it] would be for me to go away and get the outside perspective over my managing of things.

Stacee, a female, African American, first-generation student from North Carolina, found out-of-school programs and summer camps helpful.

I think I did a lot outside of school as far as programs and summer camps and just the people that I met in different programs that I was in—just made the process a lot easier because I learned so much about how to apply and what to expect in college and doing college tours and trips and all that stuff really helps a lot. . . . I saw that NC State was the best option, and what sealed the deal for me was I pretty much forced [my best friend] to also apply to NC State because she was one of the students who didn't think that she would go to college. She didn't think that she would ever get into a good school, and she didn't want to go to a school that wasn't reputable, academically. So she was just throwing her hands up already, and I told her, "I will work through [the application with you] if you actually put extra effort into it." And so we did it, and she got in, and so we both ended up at NC State.

The confluence of higher education resource-rich relationships and their contributions to social capital acquisition are reflected in our interview responses. Through such relationships, SMF students are able to access higher education knowledge and strategies that propel them to better outcomes. To understand the full impact of social capital acquisition, we must emphasize that group or student investment in social relations to generate educational returns does not operate in isolation. As mentioned, social capital acquisition is often constrained in two important ways, which result in inequality of opportunity and outcomes: (1) the lack of quality or quantity of resource-rich relationships, and (2) differential returns on the same quality or quantity of resource-rich relationships for any number of reasons, including institutional bias.

COLLEGE AFFORDABILITY CHALLENGES

> I definitely think one of the biggest obstacles to higher education is the cost. I think in a lot of cases, the cost is getting prohibitively high. And that's definitely the problem because we don't want to be a society where only the elites can afford to send their kids to college, because that just perpetuates inequality.
>
> —Zoey

This section captures a ubiquitous challenge through an analysis of interview findings related to SMF students' perspectives on college affordability. Cost concerns are the most salient factor for vulnerable students pursuing higher education. Accordingly, they require special treatment in this book. College selection is a two-part process that includes the general application for admissions and the determination of financial aid. The latter is especially important for vulnerable students, who rarely discern their ability to afford college until the admissions process is completed. In my experience, many families, without accurate information and support, make decisions driven, in part, by misinformation and sometimes fear. Here, the structural problem of college affordability significantly impacts higher education outcomes. Addressing financial literacy and providing accurate financial aid information is vital. However, these steps alone are not enough to address the deeply entrenched structural problem of college affordability.

Disturbing National Demographic Trends Reveal Financial Inequities

Despite the historical expansion of higher education opportunities to broader segments of the populace, the current regulatory architecture has not caught up, inadequately addressing the needs of low-socioeconomic-status (SES) students and sometimes forfeiting the benefits of wider participation. A wealth of research highlights the strong correlation between low SES, an important measure encompassing family income, education, and occupation, and limited higher education attainment. As Professor Howard Gardner of Harvard's Graduate School of Education notes, "tell me the zip code of a child and I will predict her chances of college completion and probable income; add the elements of family support (parental, grandparental, ethnic and religious values) and few degrees of freedom remain, at least in our country."[36] Research consistently shows that finances are the primary deterrent to college enrollment for academically qualified students.[37] In 2008, the postsecondary enrollment rate of recent high school graduates for the lowest quintile of American families was 55 percent, compared with 80 percent in the top quintile, but this measure understates the gap because it includes only those who have graduated from high school.[38] Low-SES individuals constitute a significant proportion of the nation's populace, spanning many demographics, including gender, race, ethnicity, and geography. Most low-SES students in the

United States are white, but low SES is more concentrated among minority populations, particularly Hispanics and African Americans.[39] Figure 3.4 illustrates low-SES student concentrations across the United States.

Nationwide, approximately 51 percent of the students enrolled in public K–12 schools come from low-income families, and that number is growing.[40] In certain regions, such as the South, the percentage of low-income students rises above 60 (see Table 3.1). Of the 18,010,223 students enrolled in "Southern" public schools in 2013, 57 percent were considered "low income." Here, the South encompasses Alabama, Arkansas, Florida, Georgia, Kentucky, Louisiana, Maryland, Mississippi, North Carolina, Oklahoma, South Carolina, Tennessee, Texas, Virginia, and West Virginia.[41]

In 2006, the Advisory Committee on Student Financial Assistance estimated that between 2000 and 2010, 1.4 to 2.4 million students from low- and middle-income families would be academically qualified for college but would not complete a bachelor's degree due to financial obstacles.[42] This population of academically prepared students presents an opportunity to raise the nation's college-degree production and further the public good. A wealth of recent research illustrates that too many capable low-SES students are derailed in their pursuit of a college degree. Low-SES constrains not only a student's choice about whether to attend college but also where, and income gaps alone may actually understate the degree of imbalance.

Discrepancies in household wealth reflect an even dimmer outlook. The Great Recession exacerbated decreases in household wealth as well as intra- and inter-group wealth gaps. Between 2005 and 2009, U.S. household wealth fell 28 percent. Compared to a 16 percent decrease for white households, Hispanic household wealth fell 66 percent, and black household wealth 53 percent. Median household wealth for whites is roughly 18 times greater than that of Hispanic households and 20 times more than that of black households. These wealth gaps are the largest since the government began recording the statistics over two decades ago.[43]

SMF respondent perspectives and academic research confirm that financial barriers, real and perceived, often block higher education access for vulnerable students. Financial impediments are especially important for vulnerable students, who rarely discern their ability to afford college until the admissions process is completed. They face an array of challenges, questions, and anxieties: How much money should I borrow for college? Is a selective private college worth the price premium? Is early decision for me if I don't know whether my family can afford the school? What are the repayment terms on these loans, and who is ultimately responsible—my parents, me, or both? What return can we expect on this educational investment?

Affordability is crucial for college choices in a time of state budget cuts, soaring tuition costs, economic stagnation, shifts away from need-based aid, and rising numbers of low-income applicants. Variations in family financial literacy also

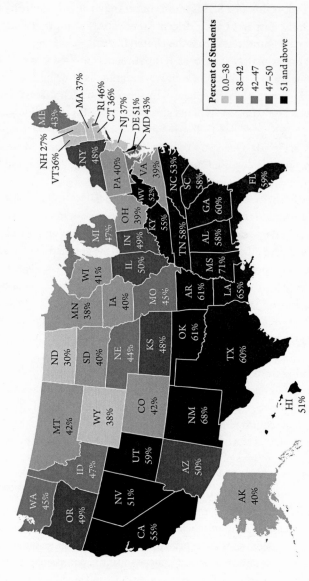

FIGURE 3.4. Percent of low income students in U.S. public schools, 2013. National average: 51 percent. Southern Education Foundation/SouthernEducationFoundation.org. *Source:* U.S. Department of Education, National Center for Education Statistics, Common Core of Data.

TABLE 3.1   States with a Majority of Low
Income Students in Public Schools:
2013—Southern Education
Foundation

State	Rate (Percent)
Mississippi	71
New Mexico	68
Louisiana	65
Oklahoma	61
Arkansas	61
Georgia	60
Texas	60
Florida	59
Utah	59
Tennessee	58
South Carolina	58
Alabama	58
Kentucky	55
California	55
North Carolina	53
West Virginia	52
Hawaii	51
Nevada	51

influence student choices. Organizations like SMF can assist by offering sound financial advice and making students aware of financial aid resources and future career prospects, but alone, they cannot overcome the structural obstacles low-income and working-class students face.

The Shift to a Market Paradigm

The direction of the debate on college access at the outset of the twenty-first century reflects a paradigm shift in which higher education is less a state responsibility and more a market-driven private good to be purchased and financed by the individual. Lani Guinier notes that prior to the Reagan administration, higher education was perceived to be "a public good to be funded by the government." Reagan's 1988 budget proposal, according to Michael Hout, stated, "students are the principal beneficiaries of their investment in higher education. It is therefore reasonable to expect them—not the taxpayers—to shoulder most of the costs of that investment."[44] This trend is a reversal of state-centered expansion, public subsidies, and nonprofit organization and has led to greater emphasis on concepts, such as privatization, competition, strategy, performance metrics, and efficiency.[45]

Historically, government intervention has been more pronounced in the K–12 context. U.S. students and their families are expected to pay for some portion of their higher education, but in some other developed countries, governments assume a much greater role. As the market-based perspective has gained traction domestically, higher education is increasingly viewed as an industry, and students as customers. Such a perspective has significant implications for how institutions serve, attract, and cater to students. Moreover, we must keep in mind an assortment of well-documented market failures that often work to the detriment of vulnerable students.

The reform discussion often misconstrues the higher education market, student choices, and various types of market failure. The federal government's demand-side subsidization and portable financial aid programs bring benefits to millions, but without adequate guidance and support, ill-informed, vulnerable students may be duped into selecting inferior educational options. Such market failures contribute to and reinforce stratification patterns among demographic groups. The market's invisible hand may run counter to the interests of vulnerable students and broader community and societal goals. Intervention can move that hand to support vulnerable students.

During interviews, student respondents discussed the many factors that influenced their college decisions: academic reputation, geographic location, programs of study, diversity, and cost. One factor, affordability, stands out. The obstacles to financing college are both real and perceived, but in practice, the difference is moot because both real and perceived obstacles influence behavior; false perceptions about a student's ability to afford college, left unaddressed, may have long-term negative consequences on his or her higher education and economic outcomes. Among student respondents, a supermajority cited financial considerations as important to their family when they were applying to college. Their candid responses reflect the cloud that financial concerns cast over life-altering educational decisions.

Student Insights Regarding College Affordability

Irrespective of their own financial circumstances, when asked about obstacles to higher education facing vulnerable students, Vicky and Shirley indicated that they felt pressure to attend a less expensive school rather than a more reputable selective college. Vicky, a female, African American, first-generation student from North Carolina, commented:

When it comes to higher education, I think oftentimes, minority students or students coming from the lower socioeconomic backgrounds are funneled into community colleges and/or state schools simply because they feel that will be the best choice financially.

Shirley, an African American woman from rural Delaware, said:

> One of the biggest [obstacles] are just finances. A lot of students don't know what is out there for them, scholarships as well as the financial [aid] process; some people just figure because I'm poor and my parents don't know any better, I can't do it because they don't have the money. They don't realize that there are loans, there are scholarships and things of that nature.

Julius and Princess admitted that sticker price swayed their decisions. Julius, an African American man from North Carolina, asserted:

> I feel that—probably the most significant [obstacle] is—a lot of people are intimidated by the price tag. . . . it's just that they don't know the information on scholarships; they don't know information on financial aid to be able to seek out the help they need to go to school. And I feel like that's very sad.

Princess, a female, African American, first-generation student from North Carolina, simply stated, "I was very quick to limit . . . school [options] based on the sticker price."

Rita, an African American woman from rural Delaware, and other students observed that high costs penalize the poor and offer a way for the elite to send their children to college, perpetuating inequality between the poor and the rich. Rita said:

> I would really focus on [not] making it so much of [a] penalty to be poorer . . . because when you don't have as much money, you end up taking out these loans, and you have to pay it back, and I think that kind of renews the cycle.

Corrine, a female, African American, first-generation student from rural Delaware gave a detailed account of her family's struggle after the 2008 financial crisis. She knew that in her family's precarious circumstances, finances were going to be a primary concern in the college discussion.

> Everybody knows that during 2008, we had that financial recession, and because of it, my father—he does masonry work and brickwork—so he was out of a job. He had his own business, but because of the economy, he ended up losing his business, and he was out of a job for about eleven months to almost a year. And that was really hard for my family because we were only using my mom's income, and my mom, she made only about $32,000 for—I think there were about five or six people living in our house—and that was difficult not only financially, but also emotionally, especially for my dad, who was very used to being the provider for

his family. And having to watch him sit at home—it was really sad, actually. I sympathized with him.

Because of that situation, my family got really behind in bills, so when it became two years later, and my dad finally did get a job ... I remember coming home from church service one day, and my dad's car was actually being repossessed, which was really an interesting experience to have ... when you are a senior, [and] you are thinking about going to college. We were behind on bills, our job position was a little [more] stable, and we [were] thinking about attending [a] university. And I think that is where I was, and my mind said, "Money was a huge factor in attending college."

Seth and Serge also knew that finances and scholarships would most likely define what college they attended. Seth, an African American man from rural Delaware, noted:

Well, at first [finances] were very important. My brother had gotten into a normal [four-year college] and didn't go because my parents didn't think that he could afford it.

Serge, a Hispanic man from North Carolina, remarked:

[Finances were] very important for my parents since I'm not a citizen of the United States. I couldn't apply for financial aid from the government, so any kind of scholarship, it would have to be some private organization, and so scholarships like the SMF scholarships were very important to me. There was a point where my parents told me that if we didn't [get] enough money ... I can't get to school, and at that point, it was really a stressful time, [and] I'm glad that it worked out.

Rhona and Kendall acknowledged that their concerns were partially self-created and reflected a desire not to burden their families with additional financial hardship. Rhona, an African American woman from rural Delaware, remarked:

I think at the point of application where I didn't know anything about potential financial aid or scholarships, I was probably more concerned about [finances] than my parents were. I would say that they were hopeful for scholarship money because they knew that they couldn't cover the whole cost, but ... they weren't deterring me from [applying to] any schools, and they never even said after I applied, "if you don't get any scholarship money to that school, then we might not be able to afford it." So they never really put that idea into my head. But I think maybe [it was] just a concern of [mine] putting that burden on my parents.

Kendall, an African American man from North Carolina, noted:

My greatest worries were paying for college because I come from a single-parent household. My mom is a teacher, so she doesn't have a lot of extra income. And I guess that was probably my greatest worry. I wasn't too worried about getting in because I knew I'd get in somewhere, at least one of the schools I applied to. I guess it just came down to I hope I get scholarship money, so that meant whether I'd go to school and not have to worry about the financial burden.

Caroline and Gillian were concerned about accumulating student debt and knew that was something they did not want to deal with after college. Caroline, a female, African American, first-generation student from North Carolina, asserted:

I don't think I applied to Duke, but another thing for me was just the cost. So I just figured I wouldn't want to spend $40,000 a year on my college education, so I chose the best schools for a good price—where I could get a great education for a good price, and I could stay relatively close to home because my mom would not have liked it if I moved halfway across the country. . . . So [my mother] wanted me to go to Duke and to Wake Forest, and I was like, no, I'm not going to do that. She [says], you can get scholarships. I'm [saying] there is no [way]. Elon was a good example because I applied there. Their tuition isn't that bad, and they gave me a scholarship, but . . . I [didn't] want to be in debt by the time I graduated . . . I just didn't want to do it.

Gillian, a female, African American, first-generation student from North Carolina, added, "I was really concerned about student debt. I knew I did not want to take out loans. I knew I didn't want to be in debt forever. So that was a huge concern for me."

Sometimes students and their families harbor relatively equal degrees of concern; sometimes students harbor more or less concern than other family members. This mismatch can be an added source of stress for students and families, but it can also generate frank conversation on financing college.

Student financial concerns persist during and after college. Sterling and Vacha reported that their family financial situation changed. Sterling, an African American man from rural Delaware, noted:

I think it was kind of volatile. My freshman year of college, when they were helping me, both of my parents worked. Then my sophomore year, only one of my parents worked. In my junior year, they both worked, and senior year, both were out on disability. And so, needless to say, there were wild income variations given those things.

Vacha, a female, African American, first-generation student from rural Delaware, remarked:

But in going to Temple, I wasn't able to go my second year. I actually stayed home the second year just because the finances were so high my freshman year. When I did go back what I considered to be my junior year, I doubled up [on courses] so that I still got out on time. I ended up doing the four years in three because I had to sit out a year to catch up on the financial piece.

Some respondents experienced greater financial volatility during than before college. For some, the primary breadwinner in their household experienced unemployment or disability prior to or during their college enrollment. Families with several college, high school, or college-age siblings were more likely to have acute financial concerns.

College affordability is a serious obstacle for middle, modest, and especially low-income families, and it will continue to grow for vulnerable students for the foreseeable future. The choice of where students attend college and how they pay for college impacts much more than the initial college decision. Many vulnerable students continue to experience financial volatility during and after college. Financing higher education has lifelong ramifications for future standards of living and wealth generation. Poor college selection and financing choices on a grand scale could deepen existing wealth disparities among demographic groups rather than close them. College advising along with financial guidance takes on added importance in this context. College selection and finance are in essence quality-of-life decisions for vulnerable students.

COLLEGE-LEVEL CHALLENGES AND BEYOND

I got exposure to the Wharton School of Business, which made me curious. I didn't know any business people; I didn't know anybody who owns businesses, who actually even owned their home, living in southern Delaware. I had no concept of investing; I had no concept of money. So being exposed to the Wharton School of Business got me curious, and I thought, well, hey, they're not smarter than I am, and I can learn it if they can. And that's what got me interested in financial services and advising specifically. I think it definitely altered my trajectory, definitely exposed me to people who had a lot of great ideas and just a lot of great qualities.

—Jorge

This section analyzes interview findings related to SMF students' challenges and experiences at college. Specifically, this section examines student perspectives on (1) their academic preparation for their respective college environments, (2) their social and cultural preparation, (3) the college's diversity and fitting in with other students, (4) cultivating relationships with professors, and (5) persisting through college obstacles. The student perspectives suggest how college access organizations must look beyond the admissions decision and pay attention to factors that enable students to persist at the college level and beyond.

Academic Preparation

College transition places many demands—academic and nonacademic—on students.

> In order for students to move from high school to college-level work, they must have basic skills (mathematics and reading) and content knowledge in core academic subjects. Equally important is having core academic skills such as thinking, problem-solving, writing, and research skills that can be used across subject areas that will allow students to engage in college-level work. Finally, meeting the developmental demands of college requires students to have a set of behavioral and problem-solving skills, sometimes termed noncognitive skills, that allows them to successfully manage new environments and new academic and social demands.[46]

The demands vulnerable students face are magnified and more complex.

Student Insights on Academic Preparation

While a slim majority of SMF respondents indicated that their high school adequately prepared them academically for the transition to college, their specific responses indicate that in some areas, preparation was lacking. Fela and Brooke stated that the IB program generally helped in their transition to college. Fela, an African American man from North Carolina who attended Wake Forest University, stated:

> I think that the international baccalaureate program at [my high school] definitely prepared me for undergraduate [work at] Wake Forest University, especially more so than a lot of the students who didn't come from that type of background, since they did maybe AP or honors in their high school. Just because the International Baccalaureate program has an emphasis on writing, I've been writing pretty high quality since high school, and I think it was definitely an easier transition when I got to college, and a lot of my peers were complaining about papers and having to write, I was already used to having to write papers, having to write fairly lengthy papers that were up to a certain standard. And it was definitely a lot easier to transition because I already had that under my belt.

Brooke, a female, Hispanic, first-generation student from North Carolina who attended Duke University, added:

> It's a tough question to answer because I did IB, and tons of students here [Duke] also took IB, and they agree with me that it was harder and more stressful than

college, but it's really different. The academic coverage is the key difference of [college] academics [as] was the studying and learning how to learn the material—that was the biggest transition difficulty.... It's really different because I think in college, you have to be able to synthesize the information more and be able to remember things more. I think high school did prepare me for college but in a different way, and I think I have learned along the way how to teach myself more.

Todd and Wanda felt that the IB and AP programs were helpful, but their other high school classes were not necessarily at the level needed to assist in their transition. Todd, a Hispanic man from North Carolina who attended Princeton University, remarked:

I think, on the whole, the IB program did provide good training in terms of the rigor in some of the assignments, but it was definitely a mixed bag. The science and math program at my high school was not up to par to what I came across in Princeton. And that I feel actually decided some of my later college major decisions.

Wanda, a female, African American, first-generation student from Delaware who attended Wake Forest University, said:

Some of my AP classes prepared me for academic rigor, but the rest of my classes did not. I remember taking statistics in college [at Wake Forest] versus taking statistics in high school, and there were things that ... we had no idea about because I was not taught it. There [was] definitely a gap there.

Other students agreed that their high schools did not adequately prepare them for college from an academic perspective. George and Judith spoke about specific deficits in research, writing, and studying skills they felt they brought from high school. George, a male, African American, first-generation student from rural Delaware who attended Wake Forest University, commented:

I remember being on campus. I didn't understand what it meant to research ... [or] write academically. Those were challenges for me in my first year.

Judith, an African American woman from Delaware who attended Swarthmore College, added:

I think I had the fundamentals that I needed to start college, but I didn't have the studying skill sets. So I guess I wasn't challenged enough in high school to the point where I really had to study for anything, and I was quite unprepared for the challenge of reading on my own and learning some of the material on my own and preparing myself for exams.

Raul and Ayden indicated that their overall college course load was significantly more challenging and felt their high schools had not prepared them for that level of work. Raul, an African American man from rural Delaware who attended the University of Pennsylvania, said:

I don't [think I was adequately prepared academically], and I think that was indicative of my first semester at Penn where I got the lowest GPA in my total experience at Penn. . . . I just felt as if the work was next level than what I had in [high school] even though I was at the top of my class.

Ayden, an African American man from North Carolina who attended the University of North Carolina at Chapel Hill, agreed:

Well, it did what it could for a high school, but the thing is, with college, there is so much more downtime, and the professors expect so much more. While high school did prepare [me] for night[ly] homework and studying . . . it wasn't quite helpful for getting ready for the extent [of] how much you need to do.

Some interesting themes emerge from these responses. North Carolina IB students generally gave a more favorable assessment than non-IB students. Rural Delaware study participants had a much less favorable assessment of their academic preparation than North Carolina participants. Research illustrates that access to a rigorous curriculum is a serious concern for vulnerable students. It correlates with college attendance as well as selective college attendance. A recent investigation by the *Raleigh News & Observer* and the *Charlotte Observer* found that higher income North Carolina public school students in Forsyth and Guilford counties, where SMF operates, are twice as likely to be recommended for advanced coursework compared to less affluent students with the same academic credentials.[47]

Cultural and Social Preparation

Affluent students can more easily maneuver the campus social environments. This advantage may translate into greater ease interacting with professors and academic competition. Meanwhile, vulnerable students can experience "social anxieties and create social silos as a result of cultural differences learned in family structures." The social distance students experience "can result in academic underperformance or even cause students to drop out of college."[48] Only a small number of participants believed their high school provided adequate cultural or social preparation for college.

Student Insights on Cultural and Social Preparation

Liz, Maris, and Erin pointed to their active involvement in high school programs, which prepared them both culturally and socially for college. Liz, an African American woman from rural Delaware who attended Swarthmore, remarked:

> My high school was more conservative than Swarthmore but because I interacted with different people in high school through sports or through band or the people who were in my AP classes or in some of the general classes I took, I think that equipped [me] to deal with . . . people from different backgrounds and with different personalities. So I felt pretty well adjusted, socially.

Maris, an African American woman from rural Delaware who attended Howard University, said:

> Socially, yes, because I was very active in high school. So when I got to college I was very active. . . . So I would say from that aspect, yes, but . . . I felt like it was kind-of me. I took the opportunities in high school and took the transition right through college.

Erin, an African American woman from North Carolina who attended the University of North Carolina at Chapel Hill, added:

> Because I've been used to diversity, it's something that is easy for me . . . and then I feel like I was very involved in high school. So I do feel like, socially, I was prepared as well.

Glenn, Francine, and Chandra, all from rural Delaware, spoke on how interacting with students from diverse communities was a difficult change. Glenn, a male, African American, first-generation student who attended Wake Forest University, commented:

> I think when I got [to] college, [it] was a change for me to be around a lot of different people from different places and to socially interact with them.

Francine, an African American woman who attended the University of Pennsylvania, agreed:

> I was so sheltered. I don't think there's anything they [my high school] could have done because, I mean, I'm from [rural] Delaware, and I went to school in Philadelphia. So that is that; I don't know that there is too much that they could have done.

Chandra, a female, African American, first-generation student who attended Temple University, added:

> Cultural preparation—like I said, it was me and four other individuals [in high school] who pretty much [stuck] together. I didn't draw much from the school culturally. . . . Sussex County being a small town area and what I consider to be a [racially backward] area, they didn't have an interest in educating us on African American history . . . which is what drove me to choose African American studies as my major. But socially, being that Temple was in the city . . . [there] was a whole lot of adjusting that I had to do along the way.

Tyrell and Milan stated that they were not prepared for the socioeconomic differences between them and their classmates. Tyrell, an African American man from rural Delaware who attended the University of Pennsylvania, stated:

> I think that from a social and cultural standpoint, I was also not prepared. It just so happened that I went to a [college] with the majority of kids that went to private schools or went to boarding schools, and I was probably by far the least wealthy of my immediate peers until I sought out and found people of similar socioeconomic status over time.

Milan, a Hispanic man from North Carolina who attended Princeton University, added:

> Even though I came from a pretty [well-]educated and, I would say, [upper] class family, it was not to the level of some of the students here at Princeton. And that was something [that took] some getting used to.

Payton, a female, African American, first-generation student from North Carolina who attended Harvard University, found that interacting with students who had limited access to students of different races was an adjustment.

> I don't know, I feel like I had to offer the black perspective to the white people and black people here [at Harvard], so that's been interesting simply because being used to being around black people all my life is not always the story for every other black person here. That was definitely interesting.

Ann, an African American woman from rural Delaware who attended Delaware State University, felt that her church rather than her school helped in her social and cultural preparation.

> I think my involvement in church prepared me to be more well-rounded socially. I'm very involved in church so . . . I knew how to communicate. I wasn't very

antisocial, was very involved. I had great skills of networking with people. High school did not prepare me socially or culturally.

Lawrence, an African American man from North Carolina who attended Cornell University, had difficulty adjusting to his school's social scene and felt he was unprepared for the change.

> The social life . . . was Fridays, Saturday, Thursday, Wednesday, people like to go out and drink then get drunk and party and all that stuff. . . . I thought that stuff was . . . a myth. Then I found [out] it was not a myth, and so I wasn't quite prepared for that.

For most of the student respondents, college involved some social transition. Fewer first-generation students indicated that high school adequately prepared them socially as compared to students whose parent or parents attended college.

Fitting In at College

Although many respondents indicated that high school did not adequately prepare them culturally and socially for the transition to college, a clear majority indicated that they did fit in. In addition to generally positive assessments of fit, most participants indicated that they cultivated friendships across class, racial, ethnic, and religious boundaries. A recent national study documented that students who experienced "greater satisfaction with racial harmony on campus" showed stronger gains in critical-thinking skills. In addition, students who enrolled in a school that they perceived to be more accepting of diversity realized greater benefits.[49]

Student Insights on Fitting In at College

Thompson, an African American woman from rural Delaware who attended Howard University, found that she fit in by finding a community of students to whom she could relate on an intellectual level.

> I felt at home at Howard, and I felt that I finally had come to [a] community in which people could look like me and not feel . . . like I was an exception . . . because of my level of intelligence and my academic [interests].

Mirlaine and Greta fit in and found friends through their involvement in sports. Mirlaine, an African American woman from rural Delaware who attended Swarthmore College, said:

> I think, initially, I relied on being part of a sports team to make friends, but beyond that, especially when I chose a major, and I had some minors, I began to interact with people outside of my team and who were from different backgrounds. And

so for the most part, I felt like I was able to make friends and fit into [the] land-scape at Swarthmore.

Greta, a female, African American, first-generation student from North Carolina who attended Yale University, added:

> I am on the track team here, so I met a lot of different people through track, and of course you bond automatically because you're a team, but also at Yale we have resi-dential colleges, and so it's like a microcosm of the college—of the university itself. And living in a college, you're here for four years and just meeting everyone from everywhere, from Pakistan, Korea, Japan, everywhere. It's amazing just being able to say things about my own culture and listening to them [about] their experiences at their home. And . . . this summer I was with a lot of different people, and I actually made friends with a guy from China, and now we're really close friends. So it's just a great experience for me meeting all these different people and people [of different] religions and talking to them about what we believe in, but in an intelligent way and not judging based on what they believe in, but just to understand them more.

Telly and Meredith pointed to student organizations or sorority involvement that helped them make friends and fit into the college scene. Telly, an African American man from North Carolina who attended Wake Forest University, stated:

> Yes, I would definitely say I fit in, and that's one of the things that I think is valu-able about Wake Forest is . . . the size, it's small. . . . I'm not going to say it's very easy, but it's not hard to find a niche and get in where you fit in because when you have a small campus like this, I feel there's an opportunity for everybody to excel in some area. Everybody can [become] somebody. That's kind of clichéd, but I really believe that. And I definitely have made friends across different racial and ethnic lines, just based on different common interests, such as I was on the pep team my freshman year, the Screaming Demons, and also at Wake Forest, we have random room assignments as freshmen.

Meredith, an African American woman from rural Delaware who attended Dela-ware State University, added:

> I did fit in. I became a member of Alpha Kappa Alpha [sorority], but before I was AKA, I still was very involved and exposed to different people. I'm an agriculture major, so my major was predominantly white at a historically black college and uni-versity. There were kids from farms that were studying to be chemists where we were taking the same classes. Culturally, I was exposed to quite different people, and I was very open to making friends with anybody. My study-mates were from different countries and different religions.

Belinda and Charleston felt that they fit in, especially with students from their own racial communities. Belinda, an African American woman from North Carolina who attended the University of North Carolina at Chapel Hill, commented:

I do feel like I fit in very well here, and I found my niche . . . most of my closer friends are African Americans, but I do have a lot of friends who aren't. But I think one population I haven't really [interacted with are Asian students]. I don't really find myself surrounded by [Asian students], as far as the clubs I'm involved in. So I don't really have any close Asian friends, but I'm working on it. I do have a lot of African friends who are international students, and . . . I've realized African and African American are two different things. So now, [I am] part of the African Student Organization and the African dance group, so I've really found a place with international African students.

Charleston, an African American man from rural Delaware who attended the University of Pennsylvania, said:

I at first did not feel as if I fit in, but I was an athlete in college, and so I was able to develop a friend group based upon being involved in athletics. Afterwards, I made friends almost exclusively in the black community. Although Penn is a predominantly white school, the black community there is sizeable, enough such that you don't really need to go outside of it to have friends, and for whatever reason, those are the people that were most similar to me. However, within the black community, I did in fact make friends across class levels. In fact, I would say probably 75 percent of my friends were top 1 percent income families.

Tasha and Heller not only made friends but also spoke to the diversity of their peer group at their respective universities. Tasha, a female, African American, first-generation student from North Carolina who attended Harvard, stated:

I have one white roommate, one Korean roommate, and we're still close; my white roommate, she's actually still my roommate going into our third year, and we're different on so many levels. I think even though my main friend group comprises predominantly black people, I definitely have friends and acquaintances across almost every social boundary or social category that there is.

Heller, a Hispanic man from North Carolina who attended Princeton University, added:

Actually, I did feel like I would have some trouble fitting in just because the caliber of some of the students here is just impressive. I mean, it's incredible. Geniuses, there's no other word for it. And I thought I was a genius. I mean, I thought I was pretty, well, [smart], but when I came here, it's like, wow, I'm pretty dumb compared to these kids. I've actually been surprisingly successful. And I think part of it was just my background of having lived in different countries, having lived among different ethnic and socioeconomic groups. I made a good amount of friends across cultures, across socioeconomic groups, across . . . race and ethnicity. Yeah, it's pretty diverse.

Mirande and Stefano shared with us their experiences of making friends with students from different countries. Mirande, a female, African American, first-generation student from rural Delaware who attended Wake Forest University, stated:

There had been times when I felt that I did not fit in, but this is my senior year, and looking back, I think that I did a pretty good job in finding diversity here. My roommate, she is from Hong Kong; one of my roommates, she is from Persia; we had two friends who are from upper-class communities. . . . I think as far as connecting with more diverse people, we were able to do that pretty well, and I think my school had those [people].

Stefano, a male, African American, first-generation student from rural Delaware who attended the College of William and Mary, added:

Whether we're talking about food, whether we're talking about the types of things people eat, I was . . . exposed to people who grew up in different hemispheres, so I had friends from . . . South Korea; I had friends from China; I had friends from India, Pakistan, and Iraq, from South Africa or Ghana. My social network became international instantly when I stepped on [the] college campus.

The very small number of respondents who provided more negative assessments of fit and making friends across boundaries mentioned certain factors, such as race and class, as impediments. A few cited partying cultures, emphasizing heavy drinking, to which they were not accustomed. Some noted feeling as if they did not fit in initially but acknowledged progress over time. Generally, respondents noted racial diversity in their respective student bodies. Past and present student athletes indicated that they had a ready-made support group that may have eased their early college transition.

In theory, the college experience should enhance vulnerable students' social capital by forming new relationships outside their previous social circle. However, social capital acquisition is not that simple: it reflects both the number of social connections and the returns on them. Research indicates that vulnerable students may have to exert greater effort to acquire resource-rich relationships because of the general human tendency to associate with people who share similar demographic characteristics and markers.[50] For example, low-SES students may have to exert special effort to establish relationships with the majority of wealthier students at an elite university. The converse is also likely true—wealthy students have to exert greater effort to establish relationships with low-SES students—but the two groups are not similarly situated. Given the small number of low-SES students attending the typical elite university, wealthy students enjoy many more opportunities to establish resource-rich relationships with little effort. Even in the college environment, accessing resource-rich relationships and generating returns from them pose greater challenges for vulnerable students.

Ultimately, a supermajority of student respondents indicated that they chose the right college. Even after acknowledging difficulties early in or throughout their college careers, they came to the conclusion that they had made the right choice. Students who were most unsure of their decisions cited a lack of academic guidance and an unsatisfactory racial, social, or cultural climate. The favorable responses were roughly similar for current college students and graduates.

The Importance of Diversity

Student responses regarding diversity, when coupled with college fit, provide greater insight into their thought process and college experience. Our findings confirm the general assumption that underrepresented students overwhelmingly emphasize student body diversity, broadly defined, when selecting among college environments. Slightly less than a supermajority of our respondents cited the importance of diversity in their decision, but their responses indicated a more nuanced, fluid, cosmopolitan, and pragmatic understanding of diversity than many academic and mainstream depictions.

Student Insights on the Importance of Diversity

Leon, an African American man from rural Delaware who attended the University of Pennsylvania, shared that he was most interested in intellectual diversity:

> I do not believe, ex ante, diversity from an identity standpoint was an important factor to me when I chose Penn. I had always assumed that all elite schools would be predominantly white institutions with scattered minority populations, so I did not really think about diversity in the traditional sense. I will say, however, that intellectual diversity was something that I considered. I wanted to be in a place that was well-regarded in as many disciplines as possible. It was important to me to attend a school that would give me as many pathways to excellence as possible.

Carla and Etan wanted the opportunity to interact with students of different nationalities. Carla, an African American woman from rural Delaware who attended Swarthmore, stated:

I think it was important to me to be able to interact with people from not just different states but different countries, which is something that Swarthmore gave me, but I don't know that I gave it a ton of weight, and I think that's just because I grew up in a high school that wasn't necessarily extremely racially diverse, and I really hadn't had any kind of issues with regard to race during my upbringing. So it didn't really make me feel uncomfortable to be at a school that might be predominantly white, but I am really thankful for the opportunity to have gone to a more diverse school.

Etan, a Hispanic man from North Carolina who attended Princeton University, added:

I think that it [was] a factor, but for me—the most important student diversity was more in terms of country-wise than anything else. I did want a school that had a large international contingent.

Gerri, an African American woman from rural Delaware who attended Spelman College, wanted to attend a school with students from differing socioeconomic backgrounds.

When I thought of diversity [it was not] so much as far as . . . race and ethnicity . . . but more so background, so different socioeconomic backgrounds.

In contrast, Kimberly, an African American woman from rural Delaware who attended Swarthmore College, found that the lack of racial diversity ultimately affected her college experience:

[When I applied to college I did not give] as much [attention to diversity] as I should have. And it ultimately led me to transfer after my freshman year.

Bessie, a female, Hispanic, first-generation student from North Carolina who attended Duke University, was disappointed when she visited what she thought was her dream school:

I realized, where's the diversity? I felt out of place. I didn't like that feeling and that moment, I felt really disconnected . . . because I knew Wake Forest had always been my dream school, but then that was also a wake-up call for me that maybe it was . . . like an empty dream or maybe it wasn't exactly what I'm looking for.

Eva and Barthe said that racial diversity was important to them in picking the colleges they would attend. Eva, a female, African American, first-generation student from rural Delaware who attended Temple University, noted:

But I have to say that after I did do my visit to Temple, which is where I ended up going, and I saw the larger number of African American individuals mixed with [whites] that was what I think sealed the deal for me because it wasn't necessarily [an] HBCU, but it had a higher [number] of African American people that I could pull from and still pull from other cultures too.

Barthe, a female, African American, first-generation student from North Carolina who attended Harvard, added:

I also looked at diversity. I really looked at diversity—were there any black people going to the school? And then when I went to visit, I looked at what the dynamic was racially on campus because that was just important to me.

A significant number of respondents indicated that diversity was not a major concern in their decision-making process. Oliver, an African American man from North Carolina who attended Wake Forest University, attended a predominantly black high school and wanted a college experience that would enhance his exposure to different types of students.

Actually, I didn't think about it that much because—now I'm thinking about it—like all of those schools that I applied to were predominantly white institutions. And so I didn't give diversity too much thought. I knew I probably didn't want to go to a historically black college or university just because most of the people in my family had gone to those, and so I had kind of grown up around that culture, especially people in my family. . . . And I had also attended majority-minority schools for most of my life. I went to a black elementary school. My middle school and high schools were both majority black, and so I know I wanted a different experience than that. And so, when it came down to college applications, I didn't apply to HBCUs, and I didn't really think too much about [racial] diversity.

Wendell, another African American man from North Carolina who attended Wake Forest University, did not think about the importance of diversity when applying but realized it upon attending:

I'm not sure I just didn't really think about that. In my high school but specifically in the IB program, there was definitely a diverse group of people. . . . We definitely had diverse groups, so I didn't really think too much about diversity. I felt like [diversity is] just simple to get at Wake [and] that I would be adding diversity to it. Obviously from the outside looking in, some of the programs that I attended at Wake, the overnight programs, I was with more multicultural students of color than the white students. I had no problem with going to a predominantly white institution, but I guess at that point in time, I wasn't really weighing [heavily] on diversity at that time. I guess I see the importance now though for sure.

Clarion, on the other hand, an African American man from rural Delaware who attended Davidson College, had experienced being one of very few minorities enrolled in advanced coursework in high school.

Actually, I didn't give much weight to student diversity because at that point, I already [had] the experience of being one of two black people in the class for an entire . . . [school] year. So, at that point, student diversity wasn't really the most important thing in the world to me. It wasn't really important at all to me, to tell you the truth.

Statements that diversity was not an important factor in the application process do not indicate students' general views on the importance of diversity. For vulnerable students, attending a majority selective institution might allow them to experience greater diversity. Similarly, attending a majority-minority institution, such as an HBCU, might allow them to experience greater intragroup diversity.

Ironically, the dialogue on college diversity often focuses on minority students (e.g., race, ethnicity, class), particularly their need to adapt socially and culturally to the new college environment. Meanwhile, the adaptation narrative for majority students is often weak. High-achieving, affluent, nonminority students are less likely than vulnerable students to encounter people of different class and racial backgrounds throughout their educational and professional experiences. Placing the adaptation burden overwhelmingly on vulnerable students is unfair; this overemphasis sidesteps and even undermines an important aspect of progressive education—facilitating cultural understanding, competence, and empathy. The continuing number of campus incidents reflecting student and administration missteps, insensitivity, ignorance, indifference, and hostility related to class and racial differences is a harsh reminder of how existing institutional efforts to promote cultural competence are insufficient.

Discussions of diversity and group differences often ignore the obvious importance of similarities among different groups, which may provide crucial insights into formulating solutions. According to Hoxby and Avery, once they apply to a specific college, high- and low-income students exhibit similar patterns in terms of their probability of enrolling and, most important, progressing toward a degree. Notably, this pattern holds for selective colleges. The data do not support the notion that low-income students have poor outcomes or are "overmatched" or cannot make "cultural" adjustments when they apply to, and enroll at, selective colleges.[51]

Relationships with Professors

Professor–pupil relationships and interactions are an important pillar of higher education enterprise promoting knowledge exchange. Through relationships with professors, students may access additional instruction and enrichment, mentoring, research opportunities, recommendations and references for graduate school and the job market, as well as many other benefits. Notably, a supermajority of SMF student respondents indicated that they cultivated relationships with professors despite occasional challenges.

Student Insights on Relationships with Professors

Carl, an African American man from rural Delaware who attended the University of Pennsylvania, spoke of the difficulty he had in cultivating relationships with professors at a large university:

> It was a little bit harder for me. At Penn, it's a larger school, and it really depends on your major whether or not you have access to professors, and I was in a major that was pretty large. It's philosophy, politics, and economics, and the professors there are less inclined to speak with you. I didn't develop any relationships with professors that I took on a day-to-day basis, but I did develop relationships with professors that were [advisers to] student groups that I was involved with while I was in leadership positions.

By contrast, Lilliana, a female, African American, first-generation student from rural Delaware who attended Wake Forest University, felt that the small size of her university made it easier to connect with her professors.

> Yes, that's another value of going to a small school like Wake Forest, is because class sizes are so small. Professors have, I guess, a lot more time to spend with individual students, and so I've definitely been able to cultivate good relationships with my professors, especially as I've gotten older, and I've realized . . . the value of that because I think by coming as a freshman, you don't really realize just how valuable it is to develop that type of good relationship with the professor and how unique that is among a lot of institutions. Whereas my friends at Chapel Hill don't have as much access to the professors as I do at Wake Forest, where I can just pop [in] at their office or go out to lunch with them at the Magnolia Room or I can just meet them for coffee at Starbucks.

Phillip and Melissa noted specific professors who helped them throughout their college experience. Phillip, an African American man from rural Delaware who attended Davidson College, asserted:

I was feeling down on my ability, and then I ended up [taking] a class my first semester as a sophomore that the teacher really took an interest in me, and he actually brought up thinking about law school, which is where I ended up . . . he was a Political Theory teacher . . . and I ended up taking a bunch of classes [from him], and we ended up forming a great relationship.

Melissa, an African American woman from rural Delaware who attended Delaware State University, added:

The dean of the College of Agriculture, which was my major—ag business—I made sure that we had that relationship where we would stay in touch on scholarships [and] if there were any current events. I was definitely at the front of my class for every class I took and made sure I asked ample questions, [and] always had access to my professors. If I had questions, I'm going to email them. I made sure that I was front and center, that the professor knew me, and that I was able to understand any class before I was taking the full unit and did homework.

Based on these responses, relationships with professors qualitatively enhance the college experience for students. Some respondents acknowledged difficulties establishing more meaningful relationships with professors. They cited class size and personal discomfort in proactively seeking those relationships. Certain participants cited greater difficulties earlier in their college career than later. All participants acknowledged the importance of forging relationships with professors, and several expressed regret over not doing so. SMF's high school programming provides guidance on how students can capitalize on their college experiences by engaging with professors early and often.

These findings on forging relationships with professors rebut some common assumptions, myths, and doubts about vulnerable students' ability to adapt to college, particularly smaller selective college environments. The respondents' experiences should also erase some doubts vulnerable students themselves may harbor about whether they will fit in at selective institutions. Respondents exhibit a high-level of adaptability, tolerance, and appreciation for different environments and people.

Persisting through College Obstacles

The Roman poet Horace wrote, "adversity has the effect of eliciting talents which in prosperous circumstances would have lain dormant."[52] This quote captures a common theme that pervades the SMF respondents' experiences: the influence of perseverance. Professor Tammy Duckworth and others examined a noncognitive trait, "grit," which they define as "working strenuously toward challenges, maintaining effort and interest over years despite failure, adversity, and plateaus in progress."[53] Specifically, their study examined educational attainment among adults, the retention of cadets at the U.S. Military Academy at West Point, grade-point averages among Ivy League undergraduates, and the ranking of participants in the National Spelling Bee. Study findings indicate that grit, under certain cir-cumstances, may have a greater impact on success than standard measures of intel-ligence. According to the authors, "the gritty individual approaches achievement as a marathon; his or her advantage is stamina."[54] Although the grit hypothesis has its academic critics, perseverance and persistence are key attributes of SMF students.[55] The words from the following respondents vividly capture the attri-butes of perseverance and persistence.

Student Insights on Persisting through College Obstacles

Citing Horace as an inspiration, Matthew, an African American man from rural Delaware, recounts how perseverance and persistence helped him throughout his experience at University of Pennsylvania and how he strengthened those virtues at Penn.

There's an old Roman poet who has a phrase that I often recite to myself that per-severance is the secret of all triumph. And I say that that really speaks to the way in which I try to live my life and the way that I think about what I had to do.

When I first came to Penn, I came out of my first semester with a 2.9 GPA, which is something that I had never seen before or thought of. But I was able to raise my GPA to the 3.4 to 3.5 range and get into a top-ten law school because I didn't give up in that moment, and I didn't sort of expect from myself that I would do less well than the other students, and that was just simply because of perseverance. And I think that having that is probably a key component. Whether you're rich or whether you're poor, the ability to struggle through something, I think, is prob-ably the single most important life skill that you can have.

From an integrity standpoint, I think that integrity means being honest and truthful, but it also means having an expectation of yourself that will allow you to propel yourself to greater heights and deeper depths. And what I mean by that is just what are the things that motivated me while I was at Penn, when I saw other people succeeding and doing things, and I would have conversations with guys in the dorm, and, I thought, these people are no smarter than I am; they're no more qualified than I am. Why can't I do what they are doing? And just having that per-sonal integrity within myself to say, "Hey, I'm just as good as everybody else," was a life skill that I developed and strengthened at Penn, which allowed me to sort-of grow my expectations and expect more of myself in an increased rate at which I picked things up and was able to overcome the deficit that I came with from high school.

And I think just being flexible, that would just mean to me being able to get along with and understand people from different places, social classes, and avenues, and being able to rock with whatever sorts of things being in those social groups required. As I mentioned before, a large portion of my friends are from upper-income families, and I did not know how to sort-of liaise with those people until I got to Penn and learned how to be flexible, learn from your experiences, but then also learn from other people's experiences, and when you can draw from other people's experiences, when you're faced with a challenge, you're able to problem solve and troubleshoot in the way that you wouldn't necessarily be able to if you were only sticking to your own path and that was it.

Gabrielle and Sally had encouraging words for the next generation of students. Gabrielle, an African American woman from rural Delaware who attended Spelman College, commented:

Go for it! I think that any obstacle can be overcome, so don't focus so much on what's negative and what doesn't look good, well, go for what you believe you can do, and everything will work itself out.

Sally, a female, Hispanic, first-generation student from North Carolina who attended Duke University, added:

Continue fighting for your college [education] and don't give up. I know sometimes it can be difficult for minorities, but don't compare yourself to other people who have had more opportunities in the past that probably put them at an advantage but just continue doing what you enjoy and what makes you happy, and great things will come from that.

The political discourse and academic literature tend to objectify vulnerable students, looking at them exclusively through the lenses of race, ethnicity, socioeconomic status, and other circumstances completely outside of their control. These students are reduced to numbers, anonymous statistics, products of dysfunction, and deficits. At the same time, their enduring positive attributes, such as discipline, perseverance, adaptability, and empathy, which enable them to triumph over obstacles, are too often ignored.

Now that I have described the matrix of college-access challenges vulnerable students face—at the high school level, with college affordability, and at the college level—the next chapter explores how SMF programming specifically addresses them.

4 · THE ROLE OF SMF INTERVENTION

I was smart, but I was a poor kid. I didn't really know a whole lot about what options were available. So being able to go on college trips to see colleges outside of just the Delaware region, meeting mentors and—SMF mentors that had gone to various schools, really good schools, and done well at these schools—and just being able to see people that looked like me that had done well and sort of broken that misconception that I had about whether or not I can make it definitely helped me to see how broad my opportunities were and led me to look for schools outside of that region and to go after those really good schools that maybe I didn't really know if I could get into or not.

—Gregory

This chapter illustrates how SMF intervenes to address college access challenges in three key areas: (1) high school level, (2) affordability, and (3) college level and beyond. Student interviews and academic insights reveal how participating in a college access program contributes to a dynamic process from which vulnerable students acquire valuable resources related to higher education success. The impact of SMF's intervention is not limited to information transfer but extends to attitudes, aspirations, exposure, and academic survival skills.

HIGH SCHOOL LEVEL

The Importance of Quality College Selection Assistance

The previous chapter illustrated the varied challenges that undermine student access to quality college selection guidance. This dearth of resources contributes to a local as well as a national systemic pattern where vulnerable students make ad hoc and uninformed higher education choices. In response to these challenges, SMF has developed low-cost, high-quality methods to deliver vital support services.

SMF's Approach to College Selection

SMF does not espouse a one-size-fits-all approach because every student is unique. For example, in our experience, a student's preference for one college or university can easily change between the beginning and the end of senior year. Sometimes students need encouragement to target selective schools because they are selling themselves short. In other instances, they may need an honest discussion about their academic record and should adjust their application strategy by adding some less selective but still very good schools to their list to ensure a better admissions yield. Research shows that interventions can ameliorate ad hoc student college decision-making processes. SMF's programming recognizes and targets the chaotic human side of decision making that does not follow a linear pattern, especially for teenagers. Our program's effectiveness depends on students' engagement, flexibility, and openness to advice throughout the college search and selection process, which can begin well in advance of the senior year. SMF must also persist and systemically engage students throughout the college admissions process.

SMF's college access program elements include (1) year-round seminars on such topics as college admissions, career exploration, financial aid and planning, and college survival skills; (2) expert personalized college counseling; (3) mentoring; (4) SAT preparation assistance; (5) college visits; and (6) scholarships.

In interviews, respondents were asked to reflect on whether SMF influenced their college search and application process and, if so, how. A supermajority said SMF's role was significant. A consensus supported its value, yet the individual responses provide a more textured and interesting picture. The wide range of responses captures the various ways SMF programming affected individual student experiences.

Student Insights Regarding SMF Influence on College Selection

Isaac, an African American man from Delaware, stated that SMF was influential in helping him to identify the small steps he needed to take in the college selection process. SMF mentors also bolstered his confidence in his worth and what he had to offer selective colleges.

> I think SMF was probably the most positive influential factor in my college search and acceptance. I mentioned before that the school that I ended up going to was the University of Pennsylvania, and prior to a conversation with my mentor through SMF, I had no idea that the University of Pennsylvania was a good school, let alone an Ivy League school. I thought that it was just some offshoot of Penn State. And that's sort of an experience that's indicative of a role that SMF played. It sort of helped me to, one, understand that there were things greater and things that were

outside of the perspective of my community, but it also informed me with practical steps to get there, and I think that second piece is the most important thing in that people know that Harvard is a great school, but they don't know all of the small steps that it would take to have an application seriously considered. And while working with SMF, I was able to talk about what my grades were and whether or not I needed to do better or take a different class or do something differently. I was able to share my SAT score and find out that, hey, if you want to be successful at that level, you need to get to at least this minimum threshold, and here are the resources available to you to get there. And so learning those small steps, it made things that seemed very far away more close and more into focus. And so when I applied to colleges, the reason why I applied to a bunch of really selective schools and didn't really have the concept of a safety school was because I went into my college process understanding my worth and understanding what I was going to be able to offer admissions counselors and that's 100 percent because of having access to people who had gone to selective schools, who were dedicated, and that all came from my involvement in SMF.

Sia and Leslie stated that SMF influenced their admissions process by pointing out particular institutions that could provide a quality education. Sia, an African American woman from Delaware, commented:

I received a DVD from Swarthmore about why Swarthmore, and it had testimony from students, and I had received an email from the coach. For some reason, all things seemed to point back to Swarthmore, and so I decided to take the advice of SMF and apply anyway, and I ended up receiving a scholarship there, and that's where I ended up attending. Probably the greatest influence then on my final decision was that one meeting where SMF came to the MERIT program.

Leslie, a female, African American, first-generation student from rural Delaware, added:

I had heard about SMF a little bit through the MERIT program, but my direct contact with SMF came after I had been accepted [to college], and I was trying to verify exactly what school I wanted to go to. I remember my specific phone call with Mr. Simmons, where I was caught between going to the University of Delaware or going to Wake Forest University, which is surprising now, and I tell people all the time the fact that he compared Delaware to an apple and Wake Forest to a watermelon and [asked me to consider] the fact that you can calculate you can eat a watermelon for a couple of days, but the apple you can eat for a day [as an illustration of] the size of the opportunity that will come from going to Wake Forest, and I think that conversation was really impactful in helping me decide.

Lia and Cruz agreed that SMF mentors provided helpful advice that broadened their expectations of what college had to offer and where to apply. Lia, an African American woman from rural Delaware, remarked:

> I think that SMF kind of opened my horizons because in high school, I was not really thinking about college. I was thinking, okay, get through high school and finish and figure out what's next. Well, I think SMF showed me a world outside of what I knew. So, you know, the college tours and being able to actually talk with people who have gone through that process and believe that you can do it—I believe the foundation had a really strong effect.

Cruz, an African American man from North Carolina, agreed:

> The Simmons Foundation, SMF, definitely helped to broaden my perspective on which schools I'd apply to because, originally, the only schools I was looking at were ones that were in state and so that was Chapel Hill, Duke, and Wake Forest, but then I went on the college tour, and I saw a bunch of different schools, and one of the schools that we visited was the University of Richmond. And I actually ended up applying and getting in there, and so that's one thing that SMF really did help me do was expanding my perspective and getting me to kind of look outside of my little North Carolina box and apply to a school that was outside of the state.

Angie and Hillary found that SMF could provide opportunities to talk with others who were in similar situations and to have their questions answered by mentors or volunteers. Angie, a female, African American, first-generation student from North Carolina, said:

> I think when I was in SMF, it made me just 100 percent sure that I could get to college, and I could actually succeed. We had the tours . . . and I remember we had panels from different college students, and we had discussions about what to expect in college, how to succeed, what profession you're looking for, and how to stand out, and how to proceed beyond college. I think all of that just made it a lot clearer for me because doing a lot of research and talking to my guidance counselor was very helpful, but actually being able to engage in this discussion with other students who had the same goals that I did. And I met great people there too, like other students.

Hillary, an African American woman from rural Delaware, added:

> SMF actually played a really important role because some of the first college trips. . . . My parents took me to Michigan—that was their alma mater—Delaware and some other schools. But SMF—I remember two or three [trips] where I was

able to . . . go to Penn . . . in sixth [or seventh] grade, so I knew ever since then [Penn] was my dream school.

Jessi, Burtha, and Keanu said they were most influenced by the visits to college campuses and the prep work for admission. Jessi, an African American woman from North Carolina, commented:

> One of the greatest [things] was just going to Atlanta and . . . [visiting] colleges. That was something that I probably wasn't going to be able to do without SMF, considering my mom's work schedule and money and things like that.

Burtha, an African American woman from rural Delaware, said:

> [I] didn't realize how reputable the school was. It was the number-one liberal arts college in the country at the time, very elite, very hard to get into, rigorous academics, [great] reputation. So I would say the college trip as well as talking to some of the volunteers . . . definitely helped. SMF helped me, I think I mentioned earlier, with my college essays to get admitted to school. SAT prep, ACT prep, the college visits, all of it together, I would say definitely helped.

Keanu, a male, African American, first-generation student from rural Delaware, noted:

> SMF was very helpful, and it almost taught us how to research beyond the sessions that we had. These were very informative sessions; I remember leaving with information packets on SAT prep, financial aid, college search—whereas before, [we received general information] like, okay, you're going to go to college; you're going to do this and succeed; you're going to seek out these opportunities; but SMF really helped us to figure out what those opportunities even look like and, specifically, what kind of colleges were out there, what it meant to look for a major. We were exposed to people who had graduated from college and were succeeding professionally.

Evander and Adam articulated similar positive sentiments about SMF assistance. Evander, an African American man from North Carolina, said:

> I know SMF helped me tremendously. Definitely with the information I received, going to the meetings . . . that I wasn't getting from my counselor . . . such as, for example, applying to school, you know, may be private and expensive, but . . . apply anyway because of their scholarships [and] financial aid . . . specific information, such as right or wrong things to do on an application. Definitely, all those details on my essays, I received help from Kathryn and Allyson . . . it definitely helped me tremendously.

Adam, a Hispanic man from North Carolina, agreed:

> SMF was a great resource that I used in this college application process. It was a great start because [family members] having gone to college in Colombia, none of us had any clue how the whole process worked [in the United States]. And SMF offered a lot of information on how to prepare for the SATs, on when to apply . . . and they offered a lot of information on different schools, and the things that they offered. So I used SMF a lot in this process.

Daniel, an African American man from rural Delaware, reflected on SMF's impact on his higher education expectations:

> It's really about knowledge and expectations. Many times, at least from the public school perspective in places that are not necessarily wealthy, you're not in the know in the way a kid from Exeter is in the know. Furthermore, when you're not in the know, your expectations are quite limited, so you could be just as smart as the kid at Exeter or any of these great boarding schools or private high schools, but you're just not going to reach for the same things because those things aren't even within your cognizance, and that's something that I suffered from when I was a kid, and SMF helped me to break through that. But I think that one of the main issues that we have in education today is not having the knowledge for building expectations. And when the expectations rise, then it will become the second-tier problem of distributing resources, but at the very base of it, you have to plant the desire to want more before you can even reach for more.

These responses capture SMF's multidimensional role in the college application process. Beyond merely disseminating information, it influences attitudes, aspirations, and perceptions. Moreover, extrafamilial relationships with SMF volunteers offset limited familial and school-related opportunities to acquire social capital. In this context, the volunteers act as an extended family. The interview responses reveal how SMF-based relationships provide resources they could not otherwise access.

The Importance of Mentoring

Mentoring, the act of giving advice to a less experienced person, is often mentioned and tacitly understood as an intervention promoting human development.[1] In the classic work *Meditations,* Emperor Marcus Aurelius reflects on the lessons he learned directly or indirectly from various individuals over the course of his life.[2] His inspiring acknowledgment of the relationships that advanced his development is mirrored in the narratives of today's students learning from SMF mentors how to navigate the college selection process and higher education in general.

Like social capital, mentoring is an important, relationship-based concept without a precise definition or model. Mentoring relationships can be formal and informal, professional and nonprofessional. Scholars have proposed various mentoring models, including cloning, nurturing, friendship, and apprenticeship.[3] One study offers the following useful definition of a youth mentoring program: "A program or intervention that is intended to promote positive youth outcomes via relationships between young persons (18-years-old and younger) and specific nonparent adults (or older youth) who are acting in a nonprofessional helping capacity."[4] This broad definition captures the activities of widely diverse organizations, including SMF. Although SMF's services can be described in market or business terms as high-end college consulting for high-achieving underrepresented students, this characterization is oversimplified and suggests a pecuniary and formal business transaction, an impersonal connection limited to knowledge transfer. SMF's programming is not simply knowledge transfer but a confluence of elements that form a deeper mentoring relationship, extending to college selection and beyond.

Mentoring as an Intervention Strategy

Mentoring is a popular intervention strategy in such diverse spheres of policy and practice as public health, juvenile justice, and education, yet its use has not been thoroughly evaluated, and questions about its effectiveness and the conditions required to achieve optimal outcomes for participating youth linger. The explosion of mentoring programs over the past decade stems, in part, from public and government concern for vulnerable youth. A number of federal, state, and private foundation initiatives all support youth mentoring.[5]

According to a recent study, "the argument for using mentoring as an intervention strategy is particularly strong where there is an interest in promoting outcomes across multiple areas of a young person's development," such as "behavioral, social, emotional, and academic domains."[6] Mentoring has the "capacity to serve both promotion and prevention aims."[7] In other words, "mentoring can make some things better and at the same time prevent some things from getting worse," and it "seldom leads to negative effects."[8] The outcomes for mentored and nonmentored students can be quite different. Notably, mentoring is a flexible intervention—one-on-one, group, and e-mentoring have all shown some degree of effectiveness.[9]

Mentoring's Multifaceted Impact on Youth Development

Research has established the potential positive impact of youth mentoring in three domains: cognition, identity, and social-emotional development. In practice, separating these domains is difficult because they work in concert over time. Mentoring relationships can affect cognitive development as youth refine and acquire new thinking skills. Enduring ties with mentors can also predict improvement in academic and vocational outcomes. Interaction with, and modeling by, adult mentors can be a "corrective experience," challenging negative views youth hold about themselves and demonstrating that positive relationships with adults are possible. Mentors help youth to cope and to approach even negative experiences as opportunities for learning. Mentors can help to shape youths' current and future identities, particularly enhancing their vision of "what is possible" or "what they can become." Research reveals how relationships with mentors can open doors to educational and occupational opportunities from which students construct a sense of identity and aspire toward higher education.[10]

All mentoring is not equally valuable. Certain mentoring relationships may not be as effective as others. A wide range of factors are at play, including youth demographic traits, attitudes, and social competencies; mentor background and skill sets; strategies for matching youth with mentors; and the roles mentors assume.[11] Identifying the impact of these factors is important in pursuing consistent levels of effectiveness as mentoring programs are replicated and scaled up. Certain program characteristics and design elements, such as relationship duration and mentor selection and recruitment, are associated with better youth outcomes. Long-term relationships may yield significantly better youth outcomes. Furthermore, ensuring that mentoring relationships are coterminous with the rest of the program and do not end prematurely, undermining youth expectations, is also vital. Studies find that matching the educational and career backgrounds of mentors with the program's goals increases overall effectiveness.[12]

Notably, studies suggest that mentoring may have a greater impact on youth from low-socioeconomic-status (SES) and other vulnerable backgrounds. This finding seems logical in the higher education context, where, often out of necessity, vulnerable students rely more heavily on extrafamilial networks than their more privileged peers do.[13] The idea that vulnerable students benefit significantly from third-party mentoring is also consistent with social capital theory, although competing views posit that social capital's role lies either "in communicating the norms, trust, authority, and social controls that an individual must understand and adopt in order to succeed" or as a "mechanism that the dominant class uses to maintain its dominant position."[14] The SMF experience largely reflects the former perspective, where mentoring is a tool for addressing obstacles that could limit student college and career trajectories.

SMF's Mentoring Approach

The absence of professional role models in rural and other communities as well as in families was a major influence on SMF's program design. Despite a paucity of studies specifically addressing this factor, without professional role models program effectiveness could be limited for students growing up with minimal access to adults who model educational and professional accomplishment.[15] Many SMF respondents acknowledged a lack of professionally diverse mentors in their neighborhoods or towns. They indicated that listening to the personal journeys of SMF mentors, some from similar economic and racial backgrounds, introduced them to unanticipated educational and career possibilities, which, in turn, reinforced their aspirations. Some student respondents specifically highlighted the diversity of the mentors and the importance of meeting successful mentors of color and other mentors from the same geographic area or school who had "made it."

In our experience, a student's self-determined level of initiative, positive attitude, and engagement with SMF and the college selection process all lead to better outcomes. SMF is a selective program, so many student participants perform extremely well in their respective school settings, doing the best they can with what is placed in front of them. They already exhibit positive attitudes toward higher education yet sometimes harbor doubts about being able to select and afford the right college. A part of SMF's challenge is to convert doubt and fear into confidence; its encouragement and guidance aim to reinforce positive thinking.

SMF mentoring operates on an intimate scale. It targets a specific outcome— higher education achievement—and is anchored in specific settings: a university, high school, or community partner site. Mentoring is combined with other forms of intervention, namely, seminars, college visits, college counseling, and scholarship aid. Although isolating the impact of mentoring on our students is difficult due to the lack of a control group, their interview responses overwhelmingly reveal a strong influence. Over its history, SMF has employed a range of mentoring formats, including formal, informal, group, individual, and e-mentoring via blast emails and social media. The variations have been a function of maximizing resource allocation and addressing specific student interests.

Matching and Recruiting

Studies indicate that the criteria for, and approach to, matching youth with mentors may affect program effectiveness.[16] In some instances, mentors are assigned to students based on specific interests, such as the type of college targeted or a career-related focus. In other instances, students and mentors enter into informal, self-generated arrangements through standard program interaction. Overall, SMF's flexible approach to matching youth with mentors more resembles art than science.

SMF mentors are selected from racially diverse backgrounds and usually attend or have attended selective colleges and universities. All mentors are vetted by SMF staff and receive guidance to assist them in their mentoring role. They also have access to written resources (e.g., guidebooks and training manuals). Historically, SMF mentors have been under thirty years of age to increase their ability to relate to high school students. This near-peer modeling adds credibility to the program's message. At the time of SMF's inception, I was a law student in my twenties at the University of Pennsylvania and a near-peer mentor to student participants.

This environment presented excellent opportunities to recruit mentors. Graduate and professional students are particularly experienced and adept at application processes. Recently, SMF mentors are more likely to come from the SMF alumni network.

SMF is an outlet and opportunity for volunteer mentors who want to address inequality directly and have an immediate impact. SMF's message and grassroots emphasis appeal to civic-minded, public-interest-oriented students and young professionals, who do not always get the opportunity within the school setting or corporate workplace to have a direct impact on the lives of young people. Many mentors initiate contact with SMF about the prospect of volunteering. To an extent, volunteering reinforces their professional and civic identity. Some mentors already understand the importance of SMF's work, having come to success from similarly vulnerable backgrounds, and some relish the opportunity to gain new experience with the program. The mentoring process is not one sided but an exchange benefiting both mentor and mentee.

Free services and volunteerism are part of SMF's brand. The mentors' backgrounds, experiences, and public service values connect strongly with the overall higher education goals of the program. Our mentors may dedicate an entire day to meet with students, chaperone a four-day trip, review an admissions essay, or conduct mock interviews with students on short notice via Skype. Students and parents know that SMF mentors often have busy schedules yet maintain a steadfast commitment to advancing student potential.

SMF recruits mentors who understand that their role is to impart knowledge as well as support and encouragement. Vulnerable students easily connect with mentors in a safe, nonjudgmental environment. Volunteers and program staff provide substantive instruction on college admissions and other topics. Research shows that systematic teaching and advocacy combined with mentoring improves program effectiveness.[17] The delivery of expert "how-to" information is crucial since many SMF students do not receive it from their high schools. Even when they do, topics are not addressed in sufficient depth; for example, applying to selective out-of-state institutions is often an involved process. SMF interviewees who received such assistance were able to establish individual relationships with teachers and counselors, but a supermajority of them reported the lack of structured college application assistance at their high schools.

Cross-Age Peer Mentoring

SMF relies on peer mentoring. The grade ranges for students (grades 9–12) ensure that younger students have the opportunity to witness older students successfully navigating the application process. Simply knowing that someone from the same community, school, or enrichment program has succeeded can boost student confidence and expectations. As more SMF students attend selective and out-of-state colleges, more students consider those choices. The opportunity to sit in a college classroom with like-minded students and parents focusing exclusively on ways to attain higher education is a positive, powerful experience.

Many SMF program years conclude with a seminar for the entire group in which graduating seniors describe their experiences and lessons learned through the college selection process. This capstone moment demonstrates our students' progress through the program and serves as an effective peer-mentoring tool and feedback mechanism for staff and volunteers. During these sessions, younger students often direct a laser focus on their older high school peers, who are confidently imparting wisdom from a panel at the front of the classroom. When the seniors announce the colleges to which they are headed and why, the entire group seems to rise with a sense of pride and achievement.

SMF Student Insights on Mentoring

A supermajority of our study participants found mentoring helpful in the college selection process. Note that much of the research on mentoring programs has neglected to follow students into adulthood to ascertain whether they demonstrate the long-term benefits attributed to mentoring. Such results would allow more meaningful estimations of program impact and cost-effectiveness; that is, whether researchers, policy makers, and program staff are under- or overestimating the influence of mentoring programs. More evaluations that clarify the unique contributions of mentoring in the context of a multicomponent program are also needed.

Although our interviews cannot definitively answer these questions, they do offer valuable insights on the short- and long-term impacts of mentoring from the mentee perspective. Student respondents were asked to discuss the impact of mentoring on their higher education outcomes. With the gift of hindsight, many credit mentoring and encouragement as significant, sometimes pivotal factors influencing their higher education and career trajectories.

Terry and Marian stated that their mentor was vital in helping them to choose a career path. Terry, an African American man from rural Delaware, commented:

> The only lawyer that I knew happened to also be my SMF mentor and that was extremely helpful in helping me to shape whether or not I wanted to go to law school.

Marian, an African American woman from rural Delaware, added:

> I found SMF's mentoring to be very important, as it changed the course of my life. The mentors I had the pleasure of meeting and working with through SMF provided invaluable insight and advice as I finished high school, attended college, law school, and graduate school. I still keep in touch with some of them and feel like I have friends who will be there for me if and when I need them. Without the SMF

mentors, I would not have applied, been accepted with a full academic scholarship, and attended Swarthmore College my freshman year. Furthermore, without the support of my mentor, I would not have had the courage to transfer to Baylor University after my freshman year and graduate a year early. Coupled with the transfer, I switched from pre-med to pre-law. I attribute my desire to become a lawyer to my mentor. Although he never pushed me to go to law school, I admired and respected him, so I decided to follow in his footsteps. I even studied abroad in London for a semester during law school, in part because he got an LLM [Master of Laws degree] in the United Kingdom while mentoring me.

I just realized the vital role my mentors had in shaping my career path and perspective on life. I chose public interest over corporate law partly because of my mentors' commitment to public service and giving back to their communities. I felt like I could also make a difference by becoming a public defender. All of my successes, academically and professionally, can be traced back to the loving support of my SMF mentors. I am eternally grateful that SMF existed while I was in high school. At several crossroads in my life, I was able to seek out the counsel of an SMF mentor to help me make a decision. It is very important for teenagers and young adults to be able to turn to adults who they trust to help them make life-changing decisions. SMF mentors provided that resource for me and my family.

As African American women from rural Delaware, Derrika and Stephanie found having a mentor present to answer their questions and give advice when they were not sure what to do invaluable. Derrika said:

SMF was really . . . instrumental in me making my decision then . . . we were able to filter questions through a lot of the mentors. The mentors . . . changed, and there were some things that they did the same, but it was even useful just to have different people from different backgrounds come and speak to us, to let us know—just because you're in some little town doesn't mean that you don't have the ability to make an impact.

Stephanie remarked:

If I were queen for a day, what would I do to give underrepresented minorities a leg up? One, I would give them all a personal mentor that they can email, that they can call and ask the questions that they don't really know because . . . when you're a first—[for example] I went into an area that I don't even know anybody who does what I do . . . it always helped to have a mentor where I [would say], I don't know what this is; I don't know what I'm doing, but I want to do it the best. Do you have any ideas? I think that's something that made a huge difference in my life. So, one, give them a mentor; two, I would give them some money.

Maya, a female, African American, first-generation student from rural Delaware, expressed her appreciation that her mentors were not just there to say they helped but connected with her and were willing to continue the connection even after the college selection process was over.

> I think the biggest benefit of SMF was that it was real, and it wasn't just a theoretical group of individuals that were just trying to make an impact. It was more personal, and it wasn't as if we were just a group of kids that they were trying to say that they helped, but they really engaged and helped us, and they were willing to connect and continue to be connected.

Many respondents noted the importance of having mentors who helped them succeed, which contributed to their own desire to volunteer and help other youth.

These responses paint a very promising picture of the short- and long-term effects of mentoring on educational trajectories, both tangible and intangible. Mentoring relationships are a vital part and strength of SMF's programming.

College Visits: Exposure to College Environments

Without exposure to several college environments, students might be intimidated about the prospect of attending a selective in-state or out-of-state university. These institutional labels are just an abstraction, and students have trouble visualizing themselves as part of some unknown campus environment. Exposure informs their decision making. The SMF annual college trip allows students to experience a variety of educational environments; a supermajority of respondents reported that they attended an SMF-sponsored college trip, and all of them indicated that it was influential. The following respondent reflections underscore the impact of college visits, especially for vulnerable students, many of whom would not have had the opportunity to visit many colleges and universities.

Student Insights on Exposure to College Environments

Sidney and Madison reported that their high schools did not offer the opportunity to visit the colleges they visited with SMF. Sidney, an African American man from rural Delaware, said:

> My high school didn't offer any college visitation opportunities whatsoever at that time. I don't know what they do now, but I do know that at the time . . . the concept of a college trip seemed a little bit odd to me. I didn't know that that was something that people did, but I said, hey, it's an SMF program, and it's probably something that I should attend. And so I went on my first college trip to the North Carolina region, and I was able to see . . . Wake Forest, North Carolina A&T, [Duke], North Carolina State, and UNC–Chapel Hill, and I thought that that was extremely helpful, and I applied to Duke and to Wake Forest because of that trip.

Madison, an African American man from North Carolina, agreed:

> My high school, I don't believe, had any college trips going all the way up to the Northeast . . . there's no way I would have visited any of those schools . . . had it not been for the Simmons Memorial Foundation.

Collins and Jodi found it helpful to be able to picture themselves at select college campuses as opposed to simply being told about the colleges they should apply to for admission. Collins, an African American man from North Carolina, stated:

> I would definitely say college visitations [were highly beneficial] because as a young person in general, there's really not a shortage of people who are trying to give you advice. They tend to give you a lot of different information, and a lot of times from a young person's perspective, all that stuff bleeds together. But . . . it's a lot more helpful when you actually can go somewhere and see something tangible. And so, I definitely think the college visitations were probably the most beneficial part of the program for me just because there is a chance to go and see what it's actually like on a college campus. I see what different campuses look like, see how they work, how they operate in the flesh versus just the different things that . . . people can tell you or advise you to do.

Jodi, a Hispanic man from North Carolina, added:

> Even though I didn't go to any of the schools that we visited, I learned a lot about those schools, and they helped me [know the] kind of school I wanted to go to because we went to very different schools, small schools like those in rural [areas], urban, very urban, and yes that helped me get a feel for what living in the certain schools would be like.

Like some other SMF students, Danyell was inspired by her college visits. An African American woman from rural Delaware, she had never traveled outside of her small town and remarked:

> The most helpful [SMF feature] was the college visitation. I came from a very small town in Georgetown Delaware, and I never traveled anywhere, and my parents kind of stuck to their bubble. So being able to get out and see the schools and be on campus and be able to ask questions and [get] the information about the school, scholarships or financial aid they offer . . . it definitely gave me an idea of where I wanted to apply.

The SMF annual college trip places a group of young people in a supportive "no limits" and "can do" environment centered on higher education excellence. It generates enthusiasm for the college application process and instills confidence, as students find themselves able to navigate campuses, meet students, experience new geographic regions, and get a better sense of what college entails, rather than relying on abstract anecdotes. Our destinations are selected, not randomly, but to expose our students to a cross-section of diverse institutional settings; for example, small liberal arts colleges, private universities, historically black colleges and universities (HBCUs), large public universities, urban settings, and suburban settings. Although SMF students apply nationwide, the annual college trip often targets East Coast colleges and universities largely due to geographic and time constraints.

Most recently, participants toured colleges and universities in the greater Philadelphia region: Haverford College, Temple University, University of Pennsylvania, Swarthmore College, and Duke University. It was also a cultural experience: viewing art at the Barnes Foundation, climbing the Philadelphia Museum of Art's steps made famous by the fictional hero Rocky Balboa, and dining at Jim's Steaks on South Street in Philadelphia. After years of traveling with hundreds of students, I find the experiential value of the live college visit endures. The inability of vulnerable students to visit selective colleges with their parents or high schools does not reflect a lack of interest and curiosity. Selective colleges should find ways to make their campuses more open and hospitable to vulnerable students, who may travel in large groups out of necessity. Our organizational experience indicates that if institutions open their doors, some of these students will enroll.

SAT Preparation

The historical emphasis on the SAT is unfair for a range reasons covered in the academic literature. One reason is that vulnerable students often lack access to standardized test preparation courses that would allow them to improve their college admissions chances. A supermajority of respondents indicated that they received some form of SAT preparation, while a small proportion took an extensive Princeton Review, Kaplan, or other proprietary course. In some instances, SMF provided the only SAT preparation these students received by contracting with the Princeton Review Foundation to deliver minicourses or providing free SAT preparation materials for students. Budget and logistics often prevent SMF from providing more robust preparation. In other instances, students received test preparation through their schools or other organizations. The College Board in conjunction with Khan Academy currently offers free online test preparation. SMF students are encouraged to make use of this free resource.

COLLEGE AFFORDABILITY

The Importance of Sound Financial Guidance

Approaching the college decision without ample consideration of family and personal finances is reckless. Students and parents can receive a significant amount of misinformation about their college financing options from multiple sources.

Every student's situation is unique; however, college access organizations can play a vital role in assisting students and their families. Our student respondents often acknowledged that guidance from SMF, counselors, teachers, and other third parties on the financial aid process alleviated some of the pressure they felt in selecting a college. Students and their families need factually, strategically, and economically sound guidance that is free of charge to counteract the misinformation and fear that can accompany college decisions.

SMF's Approach to Promoting Financial (Aid) Literacy

Student interview responses highlight the anxieties surrounding college costs. In this context, financial literacy and dispelling financial fears are important. Interventions targeting affordability go beyond simply providing assistance with financial aid forms. SMF financial aid presentations often compare the college investment to investment in a quality automobile, but we carefully differentiate, explaining that the value of the college investment appreciates over time, unlike a depreciating asset. The car purchase analogy allows us to explore various financial concepts, such as loans, repayment options, and interest rates. I used a Toyota Camry as my example until college costs escalated, and I began using a Lexus. This approach provokes thoughts about financial priorities and the trade-offs students and their families must consider in aiming for a quality higher education. Without hesitation, I make the case that a quality higher education is a much better long- and short-term investment than an expensive car.

Affluent families may have trouble imagining how a $100 application fee, a $75 testing fee, or a $500 deposit to secure a student's spot in the rising freshman class could determine whether the student attends an elite college rather than a local, open-access institution or, in some cases, attends college at all. Families with moderate to low economic means are much more sensitive to costs, emphasizing short-term, out-of-pocket costs over bottom-line savings. I vividly remember unsuccessfully counseling a young man to attend a highly selective private university with a total cost approaching $54,000 instead of a local, nonselective public school that cost $20,000. The student received grants and scholarships from the private institution that made his out-of-pocket costs $14,000 a year and grants and scholarships from the public school that made his total out-of-pocket costs $10,000 a year. In terms of per-student spending, reputation, and career opportunities, the institutions had nothing in common. I spoke to this young man's father, who boasted about his son's getting a scholarship from the nonselective public school; in his mind, he was saving $16,000 over the four years of his son's college education. His calculations did not consider the respective sizes of the scholarship/grant amounts: $160,000 at the private university versus $40,000 at the public school. He did not consider the loss in turning down $120,000 more in grant and scholarship money. He did not consider the quality of the education, the networks, and the impact of many other nonmonetary factors. Cost concerns often displace other meaningful concerns and may turn the college selection process into an oversimplified decision about a commodity purchase. Higher education, especially for vulnerable students, is not a commodity. It is more akin to a luxury good.[18] Research shows that where students attend college matters. The returns for vulnerable students attending selective colleges and universities are significant.[19]

For many low-SES students, their earning potential and creditworthiness jump when they enter college and may exceed their parents' earning potential by the time they graduate. The truth is that many low-SES parents will never be able to pay for their child to attend college, which is fine as long as their child can secure financial aid and limit future financial volatility by reducing the ultimate debt load to a reasonable amount. The ultimate burden for financing college often rests on the shoulders of the low-SES students themselves. These same students may provide financial support to other family members, creating additional financial burdens their affluent counterparts do not share. The irony is that these vulnerable students are often exposed to greater volatility (e.g., debt loads) in the college selection process, when their preexisting financial circumstances, even without college expenses, are much more unstable than those of their more affluent peers. The stakes for vulnerable students are extremely high: good advice may place them on track to enter the middle and upper-middle classes, while poor or no advice may reinforce a pernicious pattern of economic instability, debt, and poverty. Intervention is needed.

Student Insights on Financial Guidance

Billy, Hazel, and Aiken shared their positive experiences. Billy, a male, African American, first-generation student from rural Delaware, commented:

> I was not overly concerned about the cost of college. In hindsight, I probably should have been, but I was not when it came to actually picking schools because I had learned about need-based funding. And I learned about need-based funding through college trips with SMF. . . . My take-away from those trips was that if you are smart enough to get in, and you come from . . . a low-income family or a family where you have some sort of financial needs, the school will make a way for you to attend there. The cost did not scare me away; however, as far as my family was concerned, my parents . . . their conversation with me about cost was that you need to find a way to pay for your education because they don't have it.

Hazel, a female, Hispanic, first-generation student from North Carolina, said:

> Financial concerns were not a significant factor when I applied to college. As a first-generation college student, I did not previously know the intricacies of the American higher education system. I knew college was expensive, but I do not think

I realized back then how truly expensive it could be. I just knew that one way or another, I would be able to finance my education. Thankfully, I had several great role models and mentors in high school who encouraged me to apply to more elite colleges. One person in particular, Michael Bourke, who was my IB [International Baccalaureate] coordinator and also studied at Wake Forest, he really pushed me to look beyond the sticker prices of universities. I often shared my worries about financing my education with him, but he was always confident that through financial aid and scholarships, I would only have to pay a few thousand dollars, if any at all. He also frequently reminded me that many private, elite institutions, such as Duke, they often have more money to give in terms of financial aid, something I did not initially know about. In hindsight, people like him, other teachers, and the Simmons Memorial Foundation, they all believed in me to aim higher and provided me with insider information about the education system that I would have otherwise been clueless about. In the end, though there was a worry in my mind about how I would pay for college, financial concerns were not a significant factor when I applied to colleges. In other words, perceived college expenses did not limit me in the college application process.

Aiken, an African American man from rural Delaware, noted:

I was advised by my SMF mentor to not allow price tags to, I guess, limit where I could go, and that there were ways to finance an education, and that the opportunities that they could provide at these places would more than cover the cost in the long run. And so initially I thought that going to places like Harvard and all the Ivy League schools was going to be far too expensive even if I was "smart enough" to get in. But after . . . that conversation, [things were fine].

These responses underscore how personal advice and encouragement can influence how students perceive and approach the daunting financial aid process.

Grants and Scholarship Aid

SMF student respondents generally received significant grant and scholarship aid at their respective institutions and a lower proportion of loans. This success was a function of such factors as low expected family contributions and assistance from the higher education institutions to which students applied. As a matter of strategy, SMF mentors advised students to apply to selective, well-endowed institutions that award significant need-based grants as well as in-state flagship universities. Grants are generally larger at well-endowed selective institutions. One student found that attending the out-of-state, private Cornell University was less expensive than attending the home-state flagship University of North Carolina at Chapel Hill. Some study respondents received significant outside scholarships, such as the Gates Millennium Scholarship and the Horatio Alger Foundation

Scholarship. Notably, some individual students amassed total grant and scholarship aid, aggregated across the institutions where they were accepted, approximating a million dollars. Some students secured federal work-study and external employment during college to address costs.

Since its inception, SMF has awarded over sixty scholarships to students. These one-time awards are paid directly to the recipient's institution of choice. Currently, SMF administers three scholarships, each with its own criterion: the Cynthia Treco Simmons Memorial Scholarship, Nathaniel P. Simmons III Memorial Scholarship, and Nathaniel P. Simmons, Jr. Memorial Scholarship.[20] Internally, we call them *bridge scholarships* because these several thousand dollar awards help to bridge important funding gaps students encounter and to minimize debt loads.

Student Insights on Grants and Scholarships

Shannon and Nader indicated the importance of receiving these awards. Shannon, a Hispanic man from North Carolina, said:

> I think something that I'm very grateful for to SMF, honestly, is the scholarship that was given to me. And I really want to thank you once more for that. My parents and I—I mean, we've kind of struck a deal that I would try to fund half of my college tuition via scholarships or work or otherwise. So the scholarship search was a big part of senior year. I think $2,000 was very useful in helping achieve that goal and helping—honestly, making Princeton more of a reality than it could have otherwise been, especially given the differential in monetary financial packages that other schools were offering.

Nader, a Hispanic man from North Carolina, commented:

> Well, first of all, the [SMF] scholarship was great because my family had some trouble paying for college, and any help that we got was so valued. I was so grateful to get the scholarship last year, and that made it a little bit easier for my mom to pay for my school.

Axel, an undocumented scholarship awardee, was not eligible to receive federal or state grants at the University of North Carolina at Chapel Hill, so for him, outside scholarships were crucial.

In our experience, even small amounts—$1,000, $2,000, $3,000—can determine whether a student attends a well-endowed, selective institution or a less-endowed, nonselective institution. Resources often limit the amount and number of scholarships SMF can offer. A more robust scholarship program providing more bridge funds to more students would have substantial impact on student choices.

Student Loans and Debt

A majority of student respondents indicated that they or their families borrowed money for college. Family attitudes about borrowing for higher education varied; some expressed greater willingness than others. However, less than half of student respondents reported having significant student-loan debt. Rather than establishing an objective measure of what constitutes significant debt, our research team opted to capture respondents' subjective thoughts about their own financial situation. This approach recognizes that students' college-related decisions operate within a context and are shaped by additional subjective considerations.

Financial Aid Forms

Nearly half of student respondents indicated that they or their families experienced some difficulty filling out financial aid forms, including the Free Application for Federal Student Aid (FAFSA), the College Scholarship Service (CSS) Profile, and other institutional forms. Common problems included parents not providing tax information in a timely fashion or addressing noncustodial parent information requests. Several students indicated that they received helpful guidance from outside sources.

The Obama administration passed reforms to assist low-SES students in the college selection process by providing financial aid information earlier in the application process. The changes took effect for families seeking federal financial aid for the 2017–2018 school year. Specifically, students can submit their FAFSA in October for the school year beginning the following summer or fall. Previously, low-SES students could not discern their ability to pay for a college until after they were admitted in April. Now, they will be able to submit a FAFSA as early as October using the previous year's income data, instead of waiting until January and having to finalize their family's annual income taxes. Recognizing the need for early financial information, these practical, streamlining reforms will prevent more students from self-selecting and not applying to various colleges based on sticker price and frustration. Early information on affordability could minimize the degree of mismatching that limits low-SES students' higher education attainment. The status—permanence, enhancement, or clawing back—of these helpful reforms is a major area of concern during the Trump administration.

COLLEGE LEVEL AND BEYOND

The Importance of Postsecondary Support

Although SMF interacts with students most during high school, it intervenes in postsecondary experiences in several ways. Policy makers and practitioners must not underestimate college access organizations' downstream impact on student trajectories.

SMF's Approach to Postsecondary Support

For SMF, students' initial decision about where to attend college influences their achievement and persistence. Studies link choosing the proper higher education environment to persistence, retention rates, graduation rates, employment, and future income for vulnerable students.[21] Certainly, selective, resource-rich college environments are far from perfect and, in practice, not equally hospitable to all students, but as a professor at one, I can attest to the amount of ancillary academic and nonacademic support students have available to them: tutors; nurses, doctors, mental health and wellness experts; state-of-the-art physical facilities; nutritional choices; counseling options; study abroad and other opportunities for international exploration; internship and externship opportunities; affinity and support groups; and other relevant programming. Some have established on-campus programs specifically designed to assist first-generation college students, for example, Wake Forest University's Magnolia Scholars Program.[22]

Anecdotally, throughout my career as a nonprofit leader and professor, I have seen many vulnerable students thrive when they have access to these ancillary academic and nonacademic supports to which more affluent students have access before, during, and after college. A few examples of where these supports contributed to a student's ability to thrive include: a student making better grades when academic supports, such as free tutoring, are in place; a student receiving, for the first time, a medical diagnosis and treatment for an ailment that had gone undetected and had impaired academic performance prior to college; and a student from a small rural town gaining access to undergraduate study abroad programs and global-themed student organizations, who subsequently won a postgraduate Fulbright Fellowship.

SMF's college recommendations are not limited to a school's reputational ranking. We are concerned about the ground-level resources available and employed to support vulnerable students. For example, two Ivy League schools that both champion diversity, inclusion, and tolerance through external communications and hiring diversity professionals can manifest completely different ground-level experiences for the same vulnerable student. SMF's guidance is not based merely on a casual look, susceptible to institutional window dressing. Before recommending schools to students, SMF solicits input from many sources in addition to their own admissions professionals. We use our network to solicit unfiltered perspectives from current students, alumni, administrators, professors, and others who will provide a candid appraisal of the institutional environment. Whenever possible, we connect current SMF students with SMF alumni who attend or have attended the institutions under consideration. Students must enter college with their eyes wide open, with a broad, realistic perspective on the pros and cons.

Precollege Planning and Cultivating Student Survival Skills

College brings independence and a lot of adjustment for all students, but vulnerable students may have fewer people in their network to guide them on college matters and may be reluctant to reach out for help in an unfamiliar environment. Some form of precollege counseling is essential because, simply put, the consequences of failure are greater for vulnerable students—second chances may be in short supply.

Each year, SMF holds a session that gives students strategies for navigating the first year of college. It covers an array of topics: course selection, study habits, time management, establishing relationships with professors early and often, and finding mentors. A more detailed description is provided next.

Course Selection and Planning

Given the number of competing demands students face in the first year, SMF recommends they take a lighter course load to adjust academically and socially. They can take required coursework or heavier course loads during subsequent semesters or in the summer, but poor academic performance early in the freshman year can damage their confidence and add stress and the difficulties of rebounding. Even worse, they could fail to meet their scholarship eligibility guidelines and lose their ability to pay for college. All SMF students are given a target of a 3.0 grade point average or better with respect to their college coursework. Our goal is to instill a "can do" and "no limits" mentality and to place them in the best possible position to enhance their future choices of graduate and professional schools, internships, fellowships, and employment opportunities. The course-planning conversation sometimes requires frank appraisal of the student's preparedness for the coursework, especially when academic rigor in high school was inadequate. In some instances, we recommend precollege summer enrichment programs and coursework.

Study Habits and Time Management

SMF emphasizes diligent study habits and time management, highlighting the importance of unplugging from social media and other distractions to engage with coursework. We encourage participation in study groups and review sessions, working with tutors, and making use of libraries and private study areas on campus. Ultimately, we attempt to instill a disciplined approach to course preparation that will serve students throughout their postsecondary education.

Establishing Relationships with Professors and Other Mentors

We encourage SMF students to meet with professors early and often. We encourage them to serve as research and teaching assistants and to take seminar classes to cultivate and strengthen their relationships with professors. Beyond providing additional academic enrichment and guidance, professors will provide recommendations and references for graduate school and employment opportunities. Students are encouraged to be proactive in finding mentors and to remain receptive to mentoring. Potential mentors are not limited to professors and might include college administrators, staff, and other students.

In our live sessions, we often use current college students or recent college graduates to convey strategies for surviving and thriving during the first year of college. The authentic near-peer perspective carries credibility for the high school student. We also provide students and their families with an accessible list of dos and don'ts along with quotes from former SMF students. We make clear that we will continue to offer valuable career and academic advice as they go on to college, and we encourage them to stay in touch because former students often serve as volunteer mentors and participate in our programming. We challenge them to help others replicate their success.

Informal College, Graduate School, and Career Mentoring

Although we do not yet have a formal postsecondary and career mentoring process for SMF students at college, our informal mentoring extends well beyond high school. As executive director, I am frequently contacted by former students seeking guidance on a range of college, graduate school, and career-related questions. I either provide advice or put them in contact with others in the SMF network who can provide informed and well-reasoned guidance. I may also contact SMF college students to learn how things are going and offer advice and encouragement. During college, students may have minor or major setbacks, poor grades, financial volatility, uncertainty about their major, or an unsuccessful job search. Helping them to think through dilemmas and troubleshoot is a valuable part of SMF's programming. Below, I share our students' reflections on the impact of college and helping others because of the help they received, that is, "paying it forward."[23]

Student Insights on College's Impact on Life Trajectory

A supermajority of student respondents asserted that college had an impact on their life trajectory. For many students, college is a transformative experience, and it can catapult vulnerable students to once-in-a-generation opportunities.

Gary, an African American man from rural Delaware, stated that his college experience at the University of Pennsylvania helped him to understand different career paths and identify with people across class levels.

> I would say that Penn was probably one of the most transformative experiences of my life.... The whole college process from being a junior and talking to my SMF mentor through graduation was just a widening of perspective. I learned about things that I had no cognizance of, because no one around me knew anything about

it. I think from a transformative standpoint, just understanding what the different industries were out there, what different sort of goals were able to be obtained from a professional and academic standpoint, just learning—I guess a tangible example of that was I had no idea what investment banking was until I got to Penn, and then after I left Penn, I became an investment banker. So simple things like that were just really transformative, and really being able to identify with people across class levels was also probably the second thing, and knowing whether you're very rich or very poor, I think I can speak to your experience at least to some degree, and I think I owe that a lot to being at Penn and being in a very diverse black community.

Reina, an African American woman from rural Delaware, thought that Swarthmore provided a natural progression into graduate school.

My very first counseling session at Swarthmore . . . was [with] my academic adviser. I knew going into school . . . I maybe wanted to major in chemistry . . . although, at that time, I was unsure whether I wanted to go to medical school. And my academic adviser, in that first meeting [with me] as a 17-year-old freshman . . . [asked] have you ever thought about graduate school? . . . and I had not, but, after being at Swarthmore, it seems like the most natural kind of progression for me. And I would say, had I gone through a different school and that [was not] one of the first-time conversations I had [concerning] my academic future, I don't think that I would have continued on [the same path].

Hakim, a male, African American, first-generation student from rural Delaware who attended Wake Forest University, stated that college gave him the opportunity to learn about the person he wanted to be outside of the community he was raised in.

It opened my horizons . . . and also I got a chance to live . . . totally outside of the communities where I was raised and where everybody knew who I was and my family. So I was able to learn about the person that I wanted to be outside of my own community, which was very helpful.

Damon, an African American man from North Carolina who also attended Wake Forest, shared that his college experience allowed him to see the world differently than he had before.

Growing up, the world is . . . your family, your school, your friends, whatever activities you do. But as a college student, there's this perspective where . . . even this country that you live in is just one small part of a whole, and we're all interconnected and we're all related in some kind of way.

Richelle, an African American woman from rural Delaware who attended Baylor University, remarked that college opened job opportunities.

It opened doors for me—obviously, I wouldn't be an attorney; I wouldn't have even been able to go to law school without having gone to college. I possibly could still be in southern Delaware, where there are not a lot of employment opportunities. I could either be a nurse, a teacher, or work at a chicken [processing] plant. So yes, college definitely opened a lot of doors for me.

Robin, an African American woman from rural Delaware who attended Spelman College, found it taught her the importance of working hard toward her goals.

I really did have that experience, from child-to-woman sort of thing, where you understand what really matters and also understand that if you are going to have something, you have to be willing to work for [it].

The diversity of responses to our question regarding life trajectories illustrates the importance of exposure to dynamic college environments and the people within them. Students acquire more than basic knowledge. They acquire habits of mind, survival skills, and broader perspectives on educational, career, and life prospects. These responses reflect the nonmonetary benefits that are difficult to quantify but nonetheless extremely important for individual development.

Student Insights on Paying It Forward
SMF targets more than college admissions. It helps to prepare young people for leadership and public engagement through example. All respondents indicated that they volunteer. They were asked a number of questions about volunteering— why they do it and whether they are more likely to volunteer or to pursue public service because they participated in youth-related programs like SMF.

Harper and Tamara spoke of the importance of their own mentors and wanting to mentor others to help them succeed. Harper, an African American man from rural Delaware, stated:

I do volunteer, and I volunteer because I know that a lot of what I've done in my life sort-of [matches] in some ways that of my SMF mentor, at least slightly. And I think that the fact that this was a guy who came from the place where I came from, who then went on to do great things and go great places, but that still—stomached enough to come back to rural Delaware and find a kid in the sixth grade and say, "Hey, you can go to a good school. You just have to do these different things." If that experience had never happened to me, I don't know where I would have been, and just from that perspective and then also the perspective of my faith, I think it's important to give back to others, and so for me . . . I know that there are people out there who can succeed if they find the right mentor, and so it gives me a personal joy and a sense of satisfaction to see other people succeed from similar backgrounds as myself, and so that's why I mentor and give back.

Tamara, an African American woman from rural Delaware, added:

I think we have to bridge the gap with younger generations that are coming up. I think our kids don't really have two-parent homes and supportive parents like I had. I really want to get involved and just be that mentor to give advice and to help along with the whole college process and scholarship process. Honestly, I have older friends of mine that have children that are in college right now, and I definitely helped their kids get in college with applications and scholarships, so I think I want to do it on a larger scale.

Wilamena and Franka could see themselves creating their own outreach program. Wilamena, a Hispanic, female, first-generation student from North Carolina, asserted:

I would one day like to create my own organization like [SMF], but definitely, I think I'm much more inclined to volunteer [because of past participation]. Just volunteering in general, I think I've learned that service to others is really important to me, and I think, the society as a whole. It's something that's very important to do, and I see [it] as my duty . . . and I enjoy it.

Franka, an African American woman from rural Delaware, added:

I could even see myself starting my own type of outreach programs that [have a] science focus [and] that also would provide opportunities to discuss college and career trajectories for scientists.

Sarah and Carlina, both African American women from rural Delaware, discussed their appreciation for the mentors who helped and believed in them and their desire to do the same thing for others. Sarah noted:

I volunteer because I think just as I have been helped . . . just to see the fact that [someone is] excited about someone wanting to be there for them, and it really makes me emotional because I love that whole [idea]—someone else wanted you to succeed, and I think that's important.

Carlina added:

Well, I realized that I've been really blessed, and I realized that people poured their lives into me when they had no reason to, they were getting nothing—like SMF, you guys were, by all standards, successful young professionals; you had no reason to go to Georgetown or Seaford [Delaware] and talk to [middle and high school students] on the weekend. People poured into me when they had no reason to think or believe that there was going to be any return on that investment, so I just thought that I've entered the point in my life . . . I definitely need to be giving back and contributing to the community to help the next generation.

SMF communicates to all its participants that they will be successful educationally and professionally, yet we challenge them to aspire to more. SMF invests in student success by providing a range of free services, but in a sense, our services are not free. Our programming and modeling emphasize the importance of service to others and its inextricable link to success. We explicitly communicate to students, "If you wish to pay us back, use your talents to help others and bring others with you into your circle of personal and career success. Re-create your level of success in others." Although our focus is on the imminent college selection process, we take the long view. By contributing to vulnerable students, SMF directly and indirectly contributes to other communities, groups, and families. The respondents' perspectives on service and volunteering reveal how mentoring and program participation influence students in many contexts beyond their immediate need.

The next chapter will focus on pragmatic reforms addressing college access at the local and national levels.

5 · REFORMS

For me, education has never been simply a policy issue—it's personal.
Neither of my parents and hardly anyone in the neighborhood where I grew
up went to college. But thanks to a lot of hard work and plenty of financial
aid, I had the opportunity to attend some of the finest universities in this
country. That education opened so many doors and gave me the confidence
to pursue my ambitions and have a voice in the world. For me, education was
power.

—Former First Lady Michelle Obama[1]

This chapter provides a pragmatic framework for college access reforms with respect to high school, affordability, and the postsecondary level. College access has both systemic and individual dimensions that impede vulnerable student achievement and persistence. SMF programmatic interventions at a grassroots level function within a broader context. They complement other reform efforts and interventions. They also fill policy gaps and remediate design defects in the regulatory architecture. Ultimately, their impact depends on other interventions, practices, and policies.

HIGH SCHOOL-LEVEL REFORMS

Complementary and Supplemental College Advising

SMF and other college access organizations provide complementary college advising and information transfer, often alongside mentoring interventions, to address vulnerable students' limited opportunities for acquiring information and social capital. They would become, not obsolete, but more effective, if high schools housed a self-standing, college counseling apparatus. A multilayered approach is needed to address vulnerable student gaps in college knowledge, exposure, and other support needs. Federal and state legislators as well as private foundations should expand funding for complementary college advising programs to reinforce public school investments with another layer of support for vulnerable students.

A growing body of research illustrates how targeted college guidance can boost higher education outcomes for underrepresented students.[2] Strong, multicountry evidence also supports the effectiveness of higher education equity initiatives targeting underrepresented students. In the United States, the Meyerhoff Scholars program at the University of Maryland, Baltimore County, employs some programming elements similar to SMF's, such as mentoring, outreach to high schools, and advising, to address disparities in science, technology, engineering, and mathematics (STEM) higher education attainment among underrepresented minorities.[3] Established in 1988, the Meyerhoff program has decades of evaluation evidence documenting its success and is viewed as a national model in increasing the number of underrepresented minority students who pursue STEM PhDs. Similarly, in New Zealand, the Āwhina program has improved STEM higher education outcomes for underrepresented Maori students, employing strategies that include mentoring high school students and exposing them to various opportunities.[4] Although SMF does not specifically target the STEM fields, its programming takes similar approaches. The demonstrated impact of these equity initiatives across environments indicates that their success can be translated to other contexts.

Features of Successful College Access Programs

To assist practitioners, policy makers, and program evaluators, we identify program features associated with successful college access programs based on our interview responses and two decades of organizational experience. Although these features may be relevant to all college access organizations, they are perhaps most useful for programs with less than a hundred students.

Mixing Program Elements. College access programs should combine such programming elements as seminars, mentoring, college visitations, and scholarships, and, when practicable, sync them with the college admissions calendar. For example, seminars on the financial aid process should occur in advance of financial aid application deadlines, and seminars addressing college applications should occur in the beginning of the school year, well in advance of admissions deadlines (e.g., early decision, early action, regular decision). Seminars should occur in a safe and comfortable environment suitable for discussion and guidance and free from distractions. We recommend a strong and diversified mentoring component: one-on-one, group, near-peer, and professional. Guidance should target secondary school but continue into college and career through informal or formal mechanisms. Programs should cultivate and leverage their own alumni network to mentor and assist their current students. We also recommend exposing students to an array of institutional environments: public, private, liberal arts, technical, selective, urban, rural, and historically black colleges and universities. Ideally, students will tour such campuses, beginning as early as their freshman year of high school.

Outreach, Partnerships, and Caregiver Engagement. Successful programs employ a range of effective outreach strategies. Outreach to secondary school administrators, counselors, and teachers is important along with grassroots outreach to community partner organizations and individuals with a shared interest. College admissions office outreach and the establishment of informal and formal partnerships can enhance prospects for students and apprise program staff of key trends. Through partnerships, high school students may gain access to local college and university resources. Crucially, programs should engage with parents and caregivers, giving them the opportunity, when possible, to learn alongside their kids, especially at topical seminars. Including them can yield many rewards, including trust, good will, and better results.

Program Evaluation Capabilities and Tracking. For internal and external purposes, programs should develop evaluation capabilities. Tracking student college admissions milestones and progress—for example, applications submitted and Free Application for Federal Student Aid (FAFSA) completion—allows programs to respond to student needs in "real time" and troubleshoot problems when necessary. Effective programs can track and monitor student progress before and after college admission.

Effective Leadership. Strong leadership matters in college access programs. Certainly, program leaders should display the range of competencies normally found in nonprofit leadership. Moreover, they should have extensive higher education and professional networks to aid their students, and they should model dedication, persistence, and compassion. Leadership continuity increases the likelihood that partners will remain engaged and that the program develops a dynamic culture or ethos.

A Vital Solution: K–16 Bridge

To realize the benefits of K–12 educational investment from an individual and societal standpoint, large numbers of students must attend and complete college. High schools must not only enhance college readiness through academic instruction but *provide meaningful transitional support to ensure students actually convert academic achievement into college enrollment.* Addressing the former without the latter will lead to modest results, at best.[5] Vulnerable students are more reliant on high school counselors and teachers for college selection decisions, yet they often do not receive adequate support.[6] For students lacking family-based higher education-related social capital, extrafamilial relationships with counselors, teachers, administrators, fellow students, and other school officials become extremely important.[7] To ensure that many vulnerable students are not lost in the transition between secondary school and college, future education reforms should (1) enhance college counseling capabilities in public high schools nationwide, and (2) improve the collection and reporting of college access data.

A primary emphasis in the extensive body of literature on the K–12 system and the achievement gap pertains to the quality of teachers (e.g., experience, stability, resources).[8] However, along with test scores and teacher evaluations, college access and completion metrics reflect how well the nation's schools perform. From a societal standpoint, higher education outcomes better reflect the return on investment in K–12 education than narrow, snapshot testing metrics.[9] The dearth of meaningful college counseling for vulnerable students underscores a critical gap in education policy; namely, the failure to build an adequate bridge between public high schools and colleges. Moving beyond the status quo requires more thoughtful steps than simply leading vulnerable students into a dense forest and leaving them to fend for themselves.

Public high schools have the potential to serve as social networking stations to promote social capital acquisition and ameliorate information deficits. A wealth of social science and education research underscores how structured college counseling support for vulnerable students can have a significant impact on college access and completion outcomes for low-income, rural, urban, first-generation students, and students of color.[10] The college access puzzle is more nuanced than the standard narrative of vulnerable students having limited access to rigorous Advanced Placement, International Baccalaureate, and honors curricula. Due to impediments to effective college counseling, racial and class discrepancies in higher education outcomes persist even where high-achieving vulnerable students have access to rigorous curricula.

To better address higher education access for vulnerable students, reforms must target all phases of the K–16 continuum: K–12 academic preparation, transitional assistance between secondary school and higher education, and college-level achievement and persistence. However, the middle, transitional phase is often overlooked. Reforms in this area must be comprehensive and address emerging demographics, school quality concerns, stratification, social capital acquisition, and market failures, such as information asymmetries. Such reforms must engage all stakeholders—federal, state, and local government actors as well as higher education institutions, secondary schools, private actors, and civil society.

Impediments to Effective College Counseling

Policy makers often overlook the importance and potential of effective college counseling for promoting college access and limiting higher education stratification. This oversight is surprising, especially in light of the relative ease of improving it compared to more intractable educational problems.[11]

Resource Restraints

In most of the nation's public high schools, college counseling is severely constrained by the inadequate availability and training of counselors. Although professional groups, such as the American School Counselor Association, say that a student–counselor ratio of 250 to 1 is optimal, this state of affairs is far from typical in most public schools. In California, the ratio is closer to 1,000 students for every counselor available. In Arizona, Minnesota, Utah, and the District of Columbia, the ratio is typically more than 700 to 1. Nationwide, the average is 460 to 1.[12]

The average school counselor nationwide spends 38 minutes per year on college advising for each student.[13] The scarcity of resources requires counselors to rely on large group sessions to reach the largest number of students, yet studies reveal that students, parents, and teachers agree that more direct services are needed.[14]

Another significant finding is the degree of variation across and within school districts. Private, independent, and more affluent public schools are more likely to have organized college- counseling services.[15] Public schools—especially those in urban and rural areas and with predominantly low-income and minority students—are less likely to have adequate college- counseling resources, and their counselors tend to spend more time on psychological counseling, testing, discipline, and routine class selection, while private school counselors can focus more on college counseling.[16] The U.S. Department of Education found that high-poverty schools (those in which 76 to 100 percent of students are eligible for free or reduced-price lunch) averaged 2.8 counselors per school, while low-poverty schools (those that do not participate in free or reduced-price lunch) averaged 3.4 counselors per school.[17]

Due to school district resource restraints, counseling activities may be geared toward meeting the needs of the average or most needy students, which displaces specialized services for college-eligible students. At low-resource schools, the focus is often on ensuring that students graduate from high school rather than enroll in college. Thus, according to the U.S. Department of Education, "students who do not proactively seek contact with counselors and/or attend a high school where college enrollment is not the norm are less likely to receive sufficient college counseling."[18] The quality of college counseling is further limited by the "short-term duration of interactions between counselors and students, and barriers that limit the development of 'trusting' relationships between counselors and students, especially working-class minority students."[19] Simply put, students who have the greatest need for college counseling often "face the greatest structural barriers" to receiving it.[20] Meanwhile, high-resource schools are likely to have counseling staff who provide the hands-on, targeted approach that facilitates student access to a broader range of colleges and universities.

Competing Counselor Roles

The barriers to effective college counseling lie not only in counselor–student ratios but also in priorities and diversification.[21] High school counselors perform a variety of roles, including scheduling, school discipline, testing, college counseling, psychological development, and administrative support.[22] These diverse roles often compete for priority and inevitably limit the amount of time spent on college counseling. Conflict can arise when a principal directs a counselor to focus less on college counseling and more on discipline, proctoring tests, and other administrative duties. The emphasis may be dictated by the characteristics of the student body or the attributes of the school district.[23] Counselors often struggle to adequately provide all of these functions, and their responsibility for college counseling has sometimes been the subject of heated debate. The college advising role has variously been perceived as unseemly salesmanship, simply disseminating college planning materials, "in conflict with counselors' identities as mental health agents," or elitist in its use of "disproportionate institutional resources" for the college-bound section of the student body. The latter critique is especially suspect when considering that "almost nine out of ten students now say they plan on going to college."[24]

Counselor Professional Development and Expertise

Even assuming high school counselors have ample time to focus their attention exclusively on college counseling, most counselors remain ineffective because they have little college-related counseling expertise. Research indicates that high school counselors would benefit from professional development in advising on college access and selection.[25] O'Connor observes that public school counselors often "do not receive any meaningful training in college admission counseling," while "affluent private high schools often hire former admissions officers from well-known colleges to serve as their college admission counselors."[26] Although many states have counselor certification requirements, counselors normally do not receive intensive college counseling training, nor do they benefit from specialized academic programs targeting college access.

One study asserts that although 466 colleges offer graduate training for counselors, fewer than 45 of these programs offer a course on the college selection process, and only one required a course on college admissions counseling.[27] The constantly changing environment requires knowledge of up-to-date admissions and financial aid trends and data, but, as studies reveal, many counselors lack the requisite specialized knowledge and institutional support to secure such knowledge and related expertise. Counselors are particularly apprehensive about their financial aid expertise.[28] Degree concentrations, certificate programs, and online continuing education courses would help, and organizations, such as the National College Access Network (NCAN) and the National Association for College Admission Counseling (NACAC), already provide an array of counselor training opportunities. Perhaps well-designed and executed college/secondary school counselor partnerships would have an even greater impact.

Integrated, Self-Standing, College Counseling

Applying to and selecting a college are not like buying a commodity; a mistake can have harmful consequences. The complex process requires technical knowledge, expertise, an informed strategy, and reassurance every step of the way. Coupled with other obstacles, ineffective college counseling inevitably places vulnerable students who do not have degree-holding parents or material resources and have not been exposed to higher education settings at a distinct disadvantage; they must compete with students from privileged backgrounds, equipped with better information, better strategies, and better networks.[29] To receive a return on their educational investments, vulnerable students and their families must have "college knowledge" that elucidates the admissions and financial aid processes, and it should reach them much earlier than the twelfth grade. Some observers have suggested that college "counselors begin actively supporting students and their families in middle school."[30] Otherwise, less privileged students will be channeled toward less selective higher education options, further stratifying the higher education system. Researchers have found that "the results are sobering. . . . Students who are poorly counseled are less likely to go directly from high school into a college program—a step . . . highly correlated with dropping out of college."[31]

The availability of college counseling varies across state, district, and school lines. Variations are manifest "in the number of students per counselor, as well as in differences in the availability of a dedicated college and career coordinator and center."[32] Among private high schools, 77 percent dedicate a position to college counseling, while only 21 percent of public schools nationwide do so.[33] To prevent further stratification of the higher education system, policy makers should either mandate (approximately thirty states and the District of Columbia mandate general school counseling for students in grades 9 through 12)[34] or at least strongly encourage integrated, self-standing college counseling in the nation's public high schools, particularly in the neediest school districts.[35]

College counseling should occur alongside academic instruction in a school environment that manifests a college-going culture. The current federal and state focus on college-readiness standards has limited value if large numbers of vulnerable students either fail to enroll in college or undermatch in their choices. College counseling departments should be staffed with competent, experienced, and well-trained professionals, who focus exclusively on college-related activities.[36] These departments must have visibility, standing, continuity, and ample resources to assist students and parents effectively, and they must engage and even deputize teachers and administrators in the college-counseling process. Although teachers in most schools have a limited role in direct college counseling, some tasks could be incorporated into the classroom to build a college-going culture; for example, students could "write a college application essay in their English classes."[37] The permanence of college counseling in high school helps to create a college-going culture among teachers, administrators, and the student body as a whole, not just the proven high-achieving seniors. It could start engaging students in college access–related activities in the ninth grade; early intervention would enhance a number of admissions-related outcomes, such as standardized test outcomes, rigorous course selection, and navigating more specialized admissions processes, for example, early decision, music conservatories, and ROTC (Reserve Officers Training Corps).[38]

Today, software and technological tools, such as Naviance, can minimize the cost and time school personnel spend monitoring student progression through the college selection process and better engage parents and students. Some states and large school districts are already using these tools. Although beneficial, the role of technology in college advising should be complementary, not a substitute for meaningful human contact.[39] Streamlining the college application and financial aid processes could help to level the playing field for vulnerable students. Lawmakers and colleges should consider moving toward a paperless, consolidated college and financial aid application. A national online course on college admissions, for example, created by experts and made available to public schools nationwide, could provide a rudimentary understanding of college admissions and financial aid concepts for many more students and parents. This information could easily be disseminated through an array of social media outlets and smartphone applications. Despite criticisms, recent efforts making "college scorecard" data readily accessible to families holds promise to the extent that it contributes to informed higher education choices.[40]

Pragmatically, the implementation of college counseling reforms may require a mixture of formula-based and competitive grant programs, and budget and political hurdles may require it to occur in phases. In an initial phase, competitive grant programs could promote reforms in states, districts, and schools and among private actors. This process would identify best practices that could serve as models for broader national and systemic reforms in a later phase. During the Obama administration, the Department of Education's Race to the Top Initiative and Investing in Innovation Fund promoted state, district, and school reforms and public–private collaboration. With competitive grant programs as opposed to formula grants, the challenge is ensuring that large numbers of students in the neediest schools receive college counseling.[41] Ultimately, a meaningful college counseling reform strategy will require federal, state agency, and school district funding commitments, standards, and training.[42] Reforms must also leverage the expertise and resources of such nongovernmental organizations as NACAC, the Lumina Foundation, and NCAN and higher education institutions, particularly in training the college counselors of the future.

College Access Data Tracking and Reporting

In addition to providing funding mechanisms to enhance college counseling in the nation's high schools, Congress should create incentives for states, districts, schools, and counselors to bridge college enrollment gaps through data management and reporting requirements. States are not currently required to track the number of high school graduates enrolling in, or graduating from, postsecondary schools, but previously proposed reforms of No Child Left Behind (NCLB) legislation would have required it.[43] The Every Student Succeeds Act (ESSA) replaced NCLB in December 2015. Twenty-one states now track the percentage of high school graduates who go to college; fourteen track college grade point average (GPA), credit attainment, or other academic indicators for students from individual high schools; and nine track one-year college retention rates. The increasing number of states that track college readiness data indicates "both that states see the importance of such data in judging school quality and that they have already laid the groundwork for including such indicators in public reporting and accountability systems."[44] An enhanced federal effort to require reporting of quantitative and qualitative higher education outcomes would provide data that the federal government and states could rely on to identify problems and reward improvements (i.e., positive accountability) in schools, rather than labeling or penalizing already troubled school systems (i.e., punitive accountability).

Although the trend under ESSA is to return accountability back to the states and away from the federal government, vulnerable student populations would be better helped by incentives for structural reform everywhere than by piecemeal, state-by-state approaches (e.g., competitive grants).[45] The overall ESSA accountability framework should be expanded beyond the narrow metric of test scores to include college access data and apply to all schools receiving federal funding or operating pursuant to ESSA as well as charter and alternative schools. To ensure the credibility of its current accountability measures, such meaningful measures as college enrollment and college graduation rates among various demographic subgroups must be combined with test scores. The integration of postsecondary entry information with K–12 academic achievement data and graduation measures will provide a more accurate picture of student success. This holistic approach recognizes student needs beyond academic instruction.[46] When two high schools have similar student bodies with similar aggregate test scores, stark differences in higher education outcomes could signal limited opportunities for social capital acquisition, ineffective college counseling, and lack of a college-going culture. Higher education outcomes from admission to graduation are an important metric of high school performance and reflect the downstream return on individual and societal investment.[47] Detailed higher education outcomes can serve as important "value-added" performance benchmarks that reflect the quality of the school rather than the student body.[48]

The importance of college access data underscores the need for longitudinal systems that link K–12 data with higher education data and beyond. The Obama administration's Race to the Top program made the expansion and adaptation of statewide longitudinal data systems a priority, with the goal of making data collection efficient and relatively inexpensive. To this end, states, districts, and schools should collect college access data on qualitative markers (e.g., acceptance and matriculation at a selective four-year college, nonselective four-year college, public or private university, community college, vocational school, or for-profit institution) and quantitative markers (e.g., number of applications completed and FAFSA completion rates). These data should be disaggregated and cross-tabulated to define how various student subgroups—low-income, minority, nonminority, first-generation—fare; for example, do they attend a selective four-year college, less selective four-year college, vocational school, community college, or no college. These data should be made available to various stakeholders, such as lawmakers, school officials, parents, researchers, in a manner consistent with federal and state privacy laws.[49]

In addition to government-imposed incentives encouraging schools to develop and maintain effective college counseling and data-collection capabilities, public reporting of college access data would create incentives for schools to provide effective college counseling. Like school-district or school-level scores on such tests as the SAT and National Assessment of Educational Progress (NAEP), parents might use higher education outcome data as a proxy for school quality or, at least, a college-going culture when choosing a school for their child or deciding where to live. States and localities are not blind to factors that make schools and locales attractive to sought-after companies and their employees; for example, neighborhoods attract residents who perceive the schools as "good." Empirical data suggest a relationship between housing prices and test benchmarks; in Florida, school districts receiving an A grade for test scores witnessed an 8 percent increase in property values over school districts that received a B.[50] Test scores remain an imperfect metric for school quality, but NCLB's singular focus and the more recent ESSA emphasis on testing have narrowed the definition of a good school while crowding out other meaningful measures, such as higher education outcomes.

High School Partnerships with College Access Organizations

For high schools, and particularly counselors, teachers, and administrators, college access organizations (CAOs) operate as a complementary advising resource that provides valuable information and expertise on admissions trends and strategies for vulnerable students. They assist secondary schools in improving their quantitative and qualitative college admissions results among their vulnerable yet extremely talented students. High schools can leverage the expertise, resources, and networks of community-based and national CAOs to promote tangible gains in student achievement. Figure 5.1 illustrates key college access partnerships for secondary schools.

The aforementioned reforms sought to address how structural changes in the nation's high schools might help to advance higher education achievement and persistence for vulnerable students.

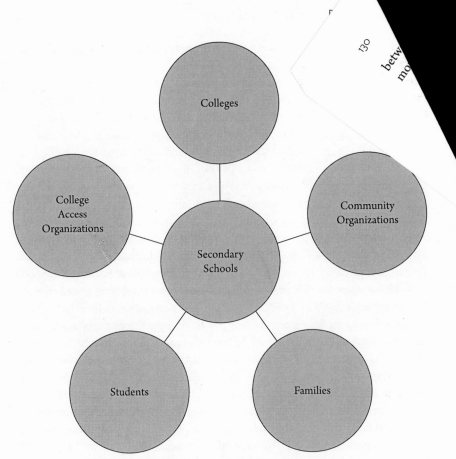

FIGURE 5.1. College-access partnerships for secondary schools

COLLEGE AFFORDABILITY

Making College Affordable

Making college more affordable is the best way to increase access. Governments and higher education institutions must make more need-based aid available to vulnerable students, and the proportion of grants to loans must improve. Both the actual and the perceived complexity of financial aid programs also presents challenges to effective implementation by low-socioeconomic-status (SES) families; the application process should be streamlined and simplified. In fact, the admissions and financial aid processes should be combined into one application. The rationale or justifications for keeping the status quo are unconvincing and outweighed by equity and efficiency gains

Ironically, compared to more affluent students, low-SES students have less access to valuable financial aid information. A recent study by the U.S. Consumer Financial Protection Bureau found that many students do not differentiate

een federal and private student loans or know that the former generally have
re consumer-friendly terms and protections.[51]

Research indicates that school counselors are ill equipped to advise students
about financial aid and do not typically receive training in this area.[52] Improving
knowledge of financial aid resources would at least reduce the number of students
who enroll in college but never apply for financial aid. A 2004 study found that
approximately 1.7 million low- and moderate-income students who enrolled in
colleges nationwide between 1999 and 2000 did not fill out the FAFSA form;
50 percent were probably eligible for Pell Grants.[53] FAFSA completion and college enrollment are strongly correlated, especially among low-SES populations.
A 2007 Chicago Public Schools study showed that students who complete the
FAFSA are twice as likely to enroll in college.[54] In response, the Department of
Education initiated a FAFSA Completion Project that ultimately would post
FAFSA completion rates online on a school-by-school basis. Former U.S. Secretary of Education Arne Duncan said, "if students don't think they can pay for college, they won't apply for college. Giving more young people access to the tools
they need to apply for federal student aid is a key part of our strategy to make
America number one in the world for college graduates by 2020."[55] Additionally,
the Obama administration spearheaded a number of innovations to assist families in their own assessment of college affordability: promoting colleges' use of
net-price calculators; allowing earlier FAFSA filing using prior-year tax data; and
publishing college-specific performance metrics, such as graduation rates, salaries, and average student debt loads. The status of and funding for these initiatives
remain uncertain under the Trump administration.

Despite these efforts, making higher education more affordable and attractive
to vulnerable students requires more audacious steps by federal and state governments, higher education institutions, and civil society. The rhetoric of "free college" has been gaining momentum in the popular press and with students, political candidates, and lawmakers. In 2018, the state of New York made college tuition
free for eligible students at in-state colleges and universities.[56] Without question,
the United States has the same ability as other developed countries to offer free
education, whether at community colleges, trade schools, minority-serving institutions, or four-year degree programs. As with many reforms, the major challenge is the degree of political will.

The Need for Government Intervention

Government intervention to stimulate demand in the higher education system
often occurs in two ways: public supply and public subsidy. Public supply, or the
provision of higher education by public institutions, is the most direct way to produce public benefits in areas where both student demand and provision by private nonprofit and for-profit institutions are low.[57] For example, public universities play a crucial role in training teachers for K–12 education. Higher tuition prices

at private nonprofit and for-profit institutions do not encourage students to pursue modestly paying K–12 teaching careers. Also, consider federal initiatives during the 1960s to integrate public education. Here, direct, deliberate government intervention was needed to effectuate broad social change because student, or so-called consumer, demand was insufficient to challenge access barriers resulting from racial segregation.[58]

In contrast to public supply, public subsidy occurs when governments increase demand by making resources available to pay college prices, usually student financial aid (demand-side subsidies) or institutional grants (supply-side subsidies).[59] Current federal financial aid loan and grant programs as well as the GI Bill are examples of successful demand-side public subsidies that produce significant public benefits.

Government intervention is also necessary to protect low-SES students from market volatility and exploitation. Students make postsecondary education choices based on perceived costs and benefits. These perceptions are inevitably influenced by contextual factors, that is, norms associated with a student's family and high school in addition to broader political, economic, and environmental forces.[60] Policies cannot simply assume the presence of rational market actors. Instead, they should consider differences in perception among groups and create incentives to encourage higher education institutions to address the needs of low-SES students. Government intervention in higher education is inevitably influenced by the ongoing debate over its status as a right or a privilege. This debate underlies a number of important policy discussions, such as the transition from grants to student loans and discharging student loans in bankruptcy.

Bolstering Need-Based Financial Aid Policies

Financial aid has four major components: source, form, goals, and eligibility criteria. It comes from an array of sources, including federal programs (65 percent), colleges and universities (21 percent), state governments (7 percent), and private organizations and employers (7 percent).[61] Its form varies among grants, loans, work-study programs, and tax credits and deductions. Aid policies reflect an assortment of goals, including rewarding achievement, encouraging human capital investment, promoting access for low-SES and other vulnerable students, improving affordability for middle-class students, and encouraging economic development.[62] Eligibility criteria generally fall into two categories: need based and not need based.

The discourse on financial aid reform at the federal, state, and institutional levels shows an interesting dichotomy between accessibility for low-SES students and affordability for middle-class students. Researchers at the Education Trust acknowledge that in federal budget debates, "most policymakers have focused on ways to control the 'unsustainable growth in the Pell Grant program.' . . . Meanwhile, the $19.4 billion spent on tuition tax credits and deductions in 2010—of which 61% and 91% of beneficiaries, respectively, were middle-income and upper-income families—have largely avoided scrutiny."[63] At the state level, "grants not based on need have grown at triple the rate of need-based grants over the past 10 years. These politically popular programs disproportionately benefit middle-income and upper-income students, who likely would go to college without the additional financial assistance. Such policies siphon funds away from low-income students and students of color." Over time, "the antipoverty origins of the 1965 Higher Education Act have faded into history as eligibility for federal student aid has been extended up the economic ladder."[64]

On the institutional level, "colleges and universities control more than a third of all funds available for student grants . . . . Yet these institutions [choose] to distribute this aid in a highly regressive manner." For example, "private nonprofit colleges and universities spent *almost twice as much* on students from families in the top quintile of family income as they did on those in the bottom quintile. Even public institutions spent *roughly the same amount* on students from the wealthiest families as they did on those from low-income backgrounds."[65] Low-SES and middle-class students inevitably compete for resources, but the latter often receive the political spoils. Lawmakers have struck a tacit bargain with middle- and upper-class voters that creates two parallel financial aid systems: a low-SES, need-based system characterized by grants, loans, and work-study; and a middle-class system characterized by merit-based aid, loans, tax credits, 529 plans, and subsidies.[66] The current balance between middle-class affordability concerns and reforms targeting low-SES students is distorted.

Higher education has become less affordable as a result of three trends: (1) tuition increases along with significant decreases in state education expenditures, (2) the growing proportion of low-income students, and (3) a movement away from need-based aid toward merit-based grants and scholarships.[67] The third trend is of particular importance. We must revert to need-based aid to promote a fair and efficient allocation of private and public resources and to further broad public goals.

The federal government does not set higher education prices but leaves pricing to the market. Nonetheless, the U.S. Department of Education spends approximately $155 billion per year in grants and loans, which account for roughly 15 percent of college revenues nationwide.[68] The provision of federal financial aid—grants, loans, and work-study—enables millions of low-SES students to attend college, yet the ratio among types of need-based aid has changed significantly over the years.[69]

Some observers argue that, in large part, the availability of federal loans contributed to increased college tuition costs. A *New York Times* article claimed that "expanding student loans enhances the ability of colleges to engage in a costly academic arms race that our nation increasingly cannot afford." According to Zumeta and colleagues, for states and institutions, "tuition increases become even easier to justify when they coincide with increases in federal funding for student financial aid, particularly when the aid programs are sensitive to tuition in calculating student eligibility for funds."[70] However, the empirical evidence does not fully support this conclusion. A 2008 analysis of a 2001 study found little connection between the availability of loan-based aid and tuition increases.[71] It indicated that tuition increases would have remained relatively steady had state investment in higher education continued at higher levels.[72] Tuition increases also result from costs shifting, rather than merely increasing. Reducing tuition generally occurs in two ways: college costs must decrease and/or subsidies from state and institutional sources must increase. Today, tuition levels are increasing faster than costs, while state and institutional subsidies from endowments are declining.[73] Consequently, students are bearing a higher proportion of overall costs.

Pell Grants are the most important support mechanism for low-SES students, but the program is often subject to cuts and projected to run deficits.[74] The federal government must place it on firmer financial footing, and the maximum grant amount must increase to keep up with rising tuition costs at public and private colleges. Pell Grants peaked in the mid- to late 1970s and have since been overtaken by a movement toward loan-based aid.[75] Their purchasing power toward a four-year college education in 2010 was less than half of what it was in 1979, when the maximum award covered 77 percent of the cost at a public four-year college and 36 percent at a private four-year college. By 2010–2011, these percentages had dropped to 36 percent and 15 percent, respectively. Another blow was the elimination, after only a single year of operation, of additional "year-round/summer" grants that supported study during the summer months, a cut at odds with increasing college completion rates. They should certainly be restored.[76] The reduction of Pell Grant purchasing power inevitably increases student reliance on loans, which, in turn, increases economic volatility.[77] For low-SES students, early debt and the burden of paying off loans have negative downstream effects on retirement savings, homeownership, and wealth building.

While the purchasing power of federal grant aid to low-SES students has declined in real terms, the eligibility requirements for loan-based aid have broadened to include more affluent students.[78] The shift began in 1978, when "the Middle Income Student Assistance Act (MISAA) . . . lifted the income ceiling for eligibility for guaranteed student loans." In 1992, amendments to the Higher Education Act created "the Parent Loan for Undergraduate Students (PLUS) program and an unsubsidized Stafford or guaranteed student loan (GSL) program, both without income caps for eligibility. . . . In particular, student loans became a way to help middle- and higher-income families finance college."[79] Today, more middle- and even upper-class students qualify for federal loans, thinly spreading financial resources at the expense of the needy. Making college affordable for middle-class families and students has, in essence, trumped access for lower- and working-class students. Popular tax credits, such as the American Opportunity

Tax Credit, and tax deductions also reflect this trend because they disproportion-
ately benefit more affluent households.[80]

Research shows the various effects of different types of aid on student enrollment. For example, grants have a more positive impact than loans. Low-SES students are more sensitive to borrowing than their middle-class counterparts.
Although loans certainly help to get students to and through college, the related
debt may skew future higher education, career, and professional choices.[81] Historically, policy makers have focused on the financial needs of students while they
are in college, ignoring what happens further down the road. The federal government now assists some borrowers after college, when loan payments are due,
through three income-driven repayment plans. One, the Income-Based Repayment (IBR) Plan, allows borrowers with low monthly incomes to make lower
monthly payments and have their remaining debt forgiven after twenty years.
However, this beneficial program is underused; out of the 37 million students who
had outstanding loan balances, only 1.1 million initially enrolled; notably, 5.4 million had a past-due student-loan account. Currently, borrowers must opt-in to the
program; instead, the IBR or a similar income-driven repayment plan should
become the default or primary means of loan repayment for all student borrowers.[82] The government must also step up efforts to educate students about their
income-driven repayment options.

In addition to increasing appropriations for need-based aid (e.g., raising current Pell Grant levels), the federal government must provide states with incentives to adopt aid policies that are more friendly to low-income students. Specifically, it should expand the modestly funded Leveraging Educational Assistance
Partnership (LEAP), which provides matching funds to encourage states to provide need-based aid to students, usually in the form of grants or work-study.[83] A
more expansive federal–state partnership based on the LEAP concept would
encourage states to increase appropriations for need-based aid over other types
of aid.

Although the U.S. Department of Education spends $155 billion per year on
financial aid, the accountability mechanisms are rather weak; to receive Title IV
student-aid funds, all higher education institutions—nonprofit, public, or for-
profit—must meet certain Cohort Default Rate thresholds. The Obama administration announced general plans to attach accountability mechanisms to federal
aid but did not unveil a detailed program. Any program should consider (1) some
form of performance-based funding to incentivize institutions to enroll and graduate greater numbers of low-SES students and (2) enhanced data collection and
reporting to evaluate qualitative concerns and the government's return on investment. Recent government attempts to heighten regulation of for-profit institutions, such as the Gainful Employment Rule (GER), seek to achieve greater
returns on government investment and to protect students.[84] Such accountability measures should, in some form, extend to all higher education programs. How-

ever, when crafting new accountability mechanisms, lawmakers must not encourage higher education institutions to abandon low-SES students, who are perceived as riskier.

In addition to increasing financial aid for students, the federal government can protect low-SES students and their families from market abuses and exploitation through a range of consumer-protection policies. Recent changes in the private student loan market are instructive. In the decade leading up to the financial crisis of 2008, the "private student loan market grew from less than $5 billion in 2001 to over $20 billion in 2008 before falling to less than $6 billion in 2010." During the growth period, lending standards were weak; lenders disbursed loans directly to students with limited school involvement or certification; and many low-SES students overborrowed and eventually defaulted on their private loans. After 2008, the federal government introduced a range of policy changes in the private student-loan market to curb abuses and default rates.[85] Following the passage of the Health Care and Education Reconciliation Act of 2010, the Federal Direct Loan Program eliminated the controversial role of private lenders and reduced costs.[86] Another example of enhanced consumer protections is the recent government effort to curb abuses by for-profit higher education providers. The Trump administration, however, has pursued a willfully blind approach to college affordability. In many instances, it has clawed back or, even worse, attempted to dismantle Obama administration advancements that still did not go far enough in addressing vulnerable student needs.

State Policies

State financial aid to students can take various forms, ranging from reduced tuition subsidies at state higher education institutions to portable grant programs. In the current economic climate, tuition has become an important source of revenue for public institutions. Public four-year colleges often rely on differential pricing for in- and out-of-state students to finance their programs. At many state flagship universities, in-state student tuition is subsidized by charging out-of-state students a premium. In theory, some public institutions could further exploit differential pricing by charging in-state students different prices based on their demonstrated financial need, for example, charging wealthier families more. These approaches present political and practical challenges. A growing number of citizens view higher education as a private good and support a rigid, market-based, consumer-driven approach. They seem reluctant to have their tax dollars and other payments subsidize low-SES groups.

State need-based and merit-based grants are another important source of support for students. The general state trend reflects a shift toward awarding more merit-based grants.[87] Programs like Georgia's HOPE Scholarships and Florida's Bright Futures are particularly popular among influential middle- and upper-class voters, which is "a side benefit for the governor and legislators." They are much more popular "than the targeted, need-based programs driven by concerns of effi-ciency and equity." In fact, the biggest problem may be that the public loves them too much. College officials and lawmakers alike complain that the scholarships are to middle-class parents what Social Security is to an older generation, and they are becoming impossible to change.[88] As a result, the proportion of available state need-based aid has declined. From 2001–2002 through 2010–2011, distributed state-level, need-based grant aid increased 84.8 percent, while distributed non-need-based grant aid increased 137.2 percent. From 2009–2010 through 2010–2011, when many states were experiencing a budget crisis, their need-based grant aid increased 1.5 percent, and non-need-based grant aid increased 11 percent. Dur-ing this period, 19 states cut non-need-based grant aid, but 23 cut need-based grant aid.[89] Today's large-scale state budget shortfalls threaten the viability of even the popular merit-based programs.

Beyond financial aid, states can play an important consumer protection role. Through enhanced licensing requirements for higher education institutions, state governments can help to prevent the issuance of bogus degrees and abuses by "degree mills."[90] State attorney generals' offices should investigate and prosecute predatory practices and abuses in the higher education sector.

Institutional Practices

Private and public higher education institutions can help to propel low-SES stu-dents toward degree attainment through an assortment of need-based aid poli-cies. The overwhelming majority of U.S. colleges and universities subsidize their students' education; that is, tuition does not cover the total cost of services. How-ever, their means and methods differ. For example, public institutions tend to rely on federal, state, and local appropriations, while private institutions rely on endowment earnings, gifts, and grants. At most public institutions, nearly 90 percent of total subsidies are given to all students in the form of across-the-board reductions to in-state tuition. This general approach often leaves fewer resources for more discretionary individual aid. Alternatively, private institutions often subsidize through individual aid given to "different students in different amounts for different reasons," such as financial need, athletic prowess, and aca-demic ability. While their tuition may be much higher than that of public institu-tions, their overall individual subsidies are also higher, nearly 30 percent of total subsidies.[91] Institutions make strategic choices regarding the type of subsidies they provide—individual, general, or a combination. On average, private institutions provide a high-cost education at a high price, and public institutions provide a lower-cost education at a lower price.

Although they enroll very small numbers of low-SES students, well-endowed private institutions have a financial advantage in being less tuition-dependent and more able to provide larger individual subsidies to students. Of course, endow-ments face restrictions. Moreover, high costs do not necessarily deter many targeted applicants. A high-priced private college education is a "positional good": its standing relative to other institutions enhances its attractiveness to families. It also resembles an "associative good," where its attractiveness is tied to the personal characteristics of its students.

Public universities, particularly state flagships, compete with private universities for students and attempt to prevent brain drain by offering merit-based scholarships to high-achieving in-state students, a practice that has undercut need-based aid.[92] The economic downturn also made full-paying out-of-state students a very attractive option. Some selective public flagship and private colleges cater to relatively indistinguishable socioeconomic demographics. In a 2013 Inside Higher Ed survey of college-admissions directors, over half of respondents indicated that they had consciously stepped up efforts to recruit "full pay" students in recent years. These efforts to attract affluent students include generous merit-based aid packages and auxiliary spending on campus amenities.[93] Within this context, the financial needs of low-SES students are subverted, but the threat or nudge of federal and state action might prompt all types of institutions to adjust their policies to become more hospitable to low- and moderate-income students.

Optimistically, various private and public colleges have instituted progressive aid policies that cap student loans or offer free tuition for low- and moderate-income students.[94] These policies, especially at public universities, may have far-reaching impact. They reflect the important "social contract" public institutions should have with citizens. Beyond providing direct support, they may have an indirect motivational or signaling impact on low-SES students' higher education aspirations.[95]

College affordability profoundly impacts student higher education choices. It has both systemic and individual dimensions. Serious reform efforts must target both of these dimensions.

COLLEGE-LEVEL REFORMS

The Importance of Diversity and Inclusion at Academic Institutions

College access and completion efforts will have limited impact without the commitment and sustained effort of higher education institutions. The cultivation of dynamic and diverse learning communities that prepare future leaders is a vital societal function academic institutions serve. Outreach to secondary schools and partnerships with college access organizations are imperative, yet the commitment and social responsibility of academic institutions extend well beyond admissions. Academic institutions must make considerable efforts to improve the day-to-day environment and academic success of vulnerable students. Diversity and inclusion efforts must yield real, not symbolic, fruit. Without truly inclusionary college environments characterized by consistent cross-cultural dialogue and participation, the benefits of diversity and inclusion are not realized. Some schools have taken a more targeted approach, specifically designing programming to address the needs of vulnerable students, such as first-generation students. Diversity and inclusion must also extend beyond students to all facets of university life and stakeholders: faculty, staff, administrators, alumni, and community partners.

For example, too many institutions ignore or fail to adequately address an obvious problem: the dearth of tenured professors of color. Institutional efforts that narrowly focus on administrative hiring to achieve diversity are insufficient. In 2015, minorities constituted only 17 percent of full-time professors at postsecondary degree-granting institutions nationwide.[96] The number is even smaller for selective institutions. Improvements in the hiring, promotion, and retention of minority faculty across disciplines are needed for an assortment of reasons. Tenured faculty are a permanent fixture and set the character of academic institutions. The faculty can voice valid concerns that other employees are reluctant to raise in fear for their job security or some form of retaliation. Tenure decisions bind institutions in many ways beyond salaries and benefit packages. The demographic composition of an institution's tenured faculty inevitably sends signals to various constituencies, especially the entire student body.

Admissions Practices That Accurately Reflect Student Potential

Admissions practices can advance higher education attainment among vulnerable students. A number of colleges adopt need-blind practices that do not consider an applicant's ability to pay when deciding to accept, but upon acceptance, they may not meet that student's demonstrated financial need. Only a handful of schools can live up to such a commitment. The popularity of need-blind admissions has declined in an economic climate that pressures institutions to be more "need-aware" or "need-sensitive." While most public institutions are need-blind, private institutions, which must use a larger proportion of institutional funds to meet financial needs, remain conscious of students' financial circumstances when managing enrollment.

Professor Lani Guinier argues that admissions decisions at selective higher education institutions constitute political decisions that have broad consequences for American society: "The task of constituting each class is a political act because it implicates the institution's sense of itself as a community, as well as the larger society's sense of itself as a democracy." She cites upward mobility and individualism as core values that "[legitimize] our democratic ideal of equal opportunity for all." Higher education promotes upward mobility because it functions as a "status marker," not simply enhancing learning by matching skills with the appropriate learning environment. However, of the three types of upward mobility—contest, sponsored, and structural—admissions officers are most likely to support the first two. Contest mobility is "achieved through competitive success on standardized tests" or "the candidate's own efforts in an open contest"; sponsored mobility occurs when people in influential positions "hand-pick a few candidates to ascend the ladder of higher education"; and structural mobility is the role that colleges and universities play when they craft admissions policies around "the greater role of higher education in the political, economic, and social structure of community"[97]

Selection systems tend to perpetuate structural inequality and inherited privilege. Middle- and upper-income families can afford SAT preparation, which raises test scores, and college counseling, which enhances admission prospects. Students from families with low and modest incomes often lack these resources.[98] This criticism, in part, prompted the College Board to modify the SAT, acknowledging that it had "become disconnected from the work of our high schools" and that "only 20 percent" of classroom teachers "see college-admission tests as a fair measure of the work their students have done."[99] Ongoing debate concerning the SAT's efficacy has prompted a number of schools to drop it as a requirement for admission. A study conducted with over 3,500 participants found that "follow-through in high school was a better predictor than all other measured variables, including SAT scores and high school rank, of leadership and accomplishment in college."[100] Although the SAT-optional or "fair test" movement is growing, Wake Forest University is the only top-25 national university, as ranked by *U.S. News & World Report*, to have dropped it as an admission requirement, with no corresponding drop in national ranking or student selectivity and performance. According to the dean of admissions, after dropping the SAT requirement, "The number of students who had graduated in the top 10% of their class rose substantially. We doubled the number of international students, and 23% of our enrolling freshmen were students of color, up from 18% the previous year. More than 10% of the entering class was first-generation college students."[101]

Some of the most selective private institutions in the country are SAT-optional. Ironically, prior to adopting the SAT, the University of California system functioned more equitably than it does now: "Before 1960 . . . the University of California admitted approximately the top 15% of all state high school graduates. After the implementation of the 1960 Master Plan for Higher Education, that figure was reduced to the top 12.5%." Again, "prior to 1960, UC had admissions policies that allowed for approximately 10% of all admissions to be Special Action, precisely in recognition of the varying quality of high schools and the adverse circumstances faced by many students who are from poor and underrepresented groups."[102]

Implementing alternative selection methods is often prevented by resource restraints and narrow, overly deterministic estimates of student potential. The Wake Forest dean of admissions acknowledged, "In retrospect, we could not have anticipated the dramatic increase in workload, the labor-intensiveness of the process, the challenge of attempting to interview the entire applicant pool, the technical challenges of written online interview options." Another analyst explains that "for larger universities, which might receive 10,000 or more applications each year, the shift would be more complicated. Additional, trained file readers would be needed to ensure that each student's credentials are carefully reviewed."[103]

Overly deterministic perspectives on vulnerable student potential are often incomplete and lack a sound empirical foundation. For example, Charles Murray argues that society harbors unrealistic ambitions for low-income students with lower standardized admission test scores, who attend schools that are too intellectually demanding for them and drop out.[104] Extensive research by Bowen, McPherson, and Chingos and the SMF experience debunk this view: low-SES students generally do not overreach when selecting colleges; in fact, many attend schools well below those for which their GPAs and standardized test scores qualify them.[105] The authors also found that the most accurate predictor of college completion was not standardized admission tests like the SAT or ACT but students' high school GPA, irrespective of where they attended. Only marginal differences in graduation rates distinguish students from low- and high-quality secondary schools.[106]

Even "[a] principled commitment to merit selection can perpetuate ascribed identities and experiences of those in a position to define merit."[107] No matter which selection system is used, some degree of gaming may be unavoidable. We must develop, constantly reassess, and diversify admissions practices to better reflect student potential than SES. Guinier observes a disturbing correlation between the SAT and SES: "the relationship between test scores and status markers such as parents' education, grandparents' socioeconomic status, racial identity, and geographic location is very strong. The correlation between test scores and SES indicators is even stronger than the correlation between test scores and future academic performance."[108] Sternberg explains that "school assessments, like standardized tests, often emphasize analytical and memory-based skills. . . . These memory and analytical skills are precisely the abilities in which many children of the middle and upper middle classes excel, resulting in a fairly substantial correlation between test scores and socioeconomic class."[109]

To address these problems, experts suggest adopting selection systems that promote "structural mobility" by crafting admissions policies around "the greater role of higher education in the political, economic, and social structure of community."[110] They cite the GI Bill and the Texas Ten Percent Plan as policies that promoted structural mobility and student diversity across class, geographic and racial lines.[111] However, even strict adherence to such approaches can have limitations or negative consequences.[112]

With the ambiguity surrounding the Supreme Court's decision in *Fisher v. Texas*, some higher education observers began to consider using class as an alternative to race in college admissions.[113] At the time, some observers questioned the efficacy of so-called race-neutral means to promote racial diversity, recognizing the "unavoidable reality" that no race-neutral proxy will work as well as a race-conscious means of promoting racial diversity, and that all proxies impose costs.[114] An exclusively class-based approach would dilute the number of Hispanic and African American students in certain regions because, among other factors, they constitute a smaller proportion of the population. A study shows that a group-based affirmative action policy in the United States would make 27.3 million black and Hispanic households, or 24 percent of all U.S. households, eligible, while under a class-based policy, at the same 24 percent cutoff, 63 percent of black households and 70 percent of Hispanic households would lose eligibility, to be replaced by 18 percent of Asian households and 20 percent of white households.[115] Policy makers should not pit various types of diversity—race and class—against one another; inclusion requires simultaneous and consistent attention to both. While *Fisher v. University of Texas* established that affirmative action would continue as a routine college admissions practice,[116] the Supreme Court's shifting composition threatens a fragile status quo and the discretion afforded to higher education institutions in promoting diversity.

Tapping Additional Pathways: Community Colleges and Beyond

Even if the proposed integrated and complementary modes of college counseling were made widely available to public high school students nationwide, incrementally enhancing college attendance rates may not be enough for the United States to maintain the international advantage that accrues from a college-educated workforce. Bold steps are needed to meet the demand for college-educated workers. Lawmakers as well as colleges and universities should consider improving college access for additional segments of the population—adults, nontraditional students, community college students, veterans, and immigrants. One longitudinal study showed that low-income community college transfer students had a better chance of completing a four-year degree than their low-income peers who started at four-year colleges across all institutional selectivity levels. Notwithstanding, low-income community college students are highly unlikely to transfer to selective colleges and universities.[117]

Forging Key Partnerships with College Access Organizations

In addition to building stronger relationships with vulnerable students, postsecondary institutions should pursue partnerships with CAOs that function as nontraditional college-feeder organizations. CAOs help to bridge gaps between public schools, students, and colleges. Despite the identification of certain organizational best practices and the popularity of certain organizations, no particular CAO is the archetype. Therefore, partnering with a range of CAOs, large and small, regional and national, is a prudent approach. These collaborations are mutually beneficial. From the college perspective, CAO partnerships bring together talented public school students and dynamic universities. At virtually no cost to colleges, they identify a talented group of students from vulnerable and

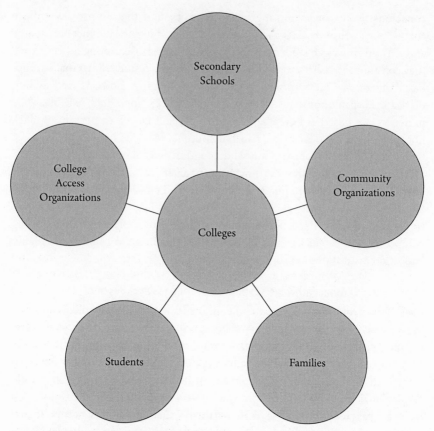

FIGURE 5.2. College-access partnerships for colleges

underrepresented demographics, providing a recruiting mechanism that is less biased than traditional methods and practices criticized for their class, racial, and geographic biases. A growing number of college admissions departments are establishing outreach programs and community partnerships that target CAOs. Figure 5.2 illustrates the key college access partnerships for colleges.

The aforementioned reforms promoting college access and opportunity would, if properly implemented, substantially improve the plight of vulnerable students in this country. Improving upon existing policies and practices requires significant political will, which may or may not exist. The next chapter offers parting thoughts on the future of SMF and college access in this country.

6 · PARTING THOUGHTS

Potential is simply not enough, and even the best students need a helping hand.

—Pamela

The previous chapters captured the vexing problem of a broken K–16 bridge for vulnerable students that contributes to disparate higher education trajectories. The higher education achievement gap is multifaceted, with systemic and individual dimensions. Extending beyond acquiring academic skills or information, it includes, among other things, social capital acquisition and survival skills, which SMF's programming targets. A significant body of research analyzes the efficacy of college access interventions and, in many cases, provides significant support for the activities, tactics, and approaches SMF has employed for over two decades.

In sum, SMF aims to open one door—opportunity. The SMF experience illustrates how civil society, against a backdrop of policy gaps and structural obstacles, can perform a "gap filling" role. The interviews with former participants demonstrate how interventions targeting the college selection process can alter the higher education, career, and life trajectories of vulnerable students. The educational and career achievements of the SMF students are impressive, but what conclusions or inferences can be drawn? Although the findings are not generalizable, they confirm and extend current knowledge about vulnerable students' access to college. SMF's success illustrates what is possible through college access interventions, sustained effort, and a relatively small financial investment. From another angle, its success holds a mirror up to society, exposing critical and reparable reform gaps that remain unaddressed.

JUSTIFICATIONS FOR COLLEGE ACCESS REFORMS

Before providing a summary of potential reforms, I want to articulate the strong justifications for them. Higher education benefits are often underestimated or misunderstood in academic and political debates. The justifications for comprehensive reform are not simply the oft-mentioned gains in individual earnings, jobs, or broader economic growth. They also include long-term, individual, nonmarket, and societal benefits. Higher education is a dynamic process with short- and long-term consequences that defy prediction. Its total impact cannot be reduced to numbers; its value accrues to intellect, personality, civic responsibility, and other intangible characteristics.

> College does produce, on the average, certain clearly identifiable effects on its students. . . . On the average, college education significantly raises the level of knowledge, the intellectual disposition, and the cognitive powers of its students. It produces a large increase in substantive knowledge; moderate increases in verbal skills, intellectual tolerance, esthetic sensibility, and lifelong cognitive development; and small increases in mathematical skills, rationality, and creativity.[1]

The tendency to focus narrowly on the economic benefits of higher education significantly underestimates equally important individual, social, and political factors and benefits that remain invisible until decades later. This underestimation may lead to unfair evaluations of the efficacy of college access programming and underinvestment in worthy initiatives.

Individual

From an individual standpoint, higher education does much more than contribute to income; it is linked to an important array of benefits that are not always easily measured: better personal, spousal, and child health outcomes; children's educational gains; greater longevity and even happiness. At the individual level, educational attainment correlates with the ability to sell our labor in the marketplace for a premium. The correlation between formal education and higher occupational status has been asserted since at least 1927, and today, according to David Bills, it "may be the firmest empirical finding in the sociology of education."[2] Pitirim Sorokin further asserts that "schools represent one of the most important channels of vertical circulation [and social mobility] . . . a graduate is often paid better than a non-graduate at the same position." Graduates of elite institutions earn about $2 million more over a lifetime.[3]

College education helps students to discover their true interests and to secure careers commensurate with those interests.[4] College-educated people have higher incomes, experience less unemployment, work longer hours, and "have greater 'allocative ability,' that is, ability to adjust promptly and appropriately to changing economic demands, technologies, and resource supplies."[5] Notably, "far fewer people without, at least, a college education are represented in the highest income brackets"; 70 percent of "top income earners have at least a bachelor's degree," while only 12 percent in the bottom third of the income bracket graduated from college.[6]

Higher education influences individual behavior, values, and attitudes, thereby spontaneously changing society, particularly where college-educated persons engage socially as voters, consumers, workers, family members, and organizational leaders.[7]

Societal

While some assert that most higher education benefits are individual,[8] a significant portion are societal and ignored by policy makers at their peril. These benefits include reduction of poverty and inequality, greater participation in democratic processes that influence political stability and human rights, lower criminal justice costs and crime rates, lower health care costs, lower public assistance and transfer payments, diffusion of new knowledge, environmental sustainability, higher levels of volunteerism, and greater social cohesion.[9] In light of these benefits, current levels of investment in higher education are too low, especially for vulnerable students, where they can make a transformative difference. For example, a recent study finds that "an additional year of average university level education in a country raises national output by a remarkable 19 percent."[10] Indeed, extending higher education has benefits superior to, and distinct from, those that accrue from extending other social benefits, such as transfer payments, distribution of goods in kind, and progressive taxation, because "it not only changes what people get but also what they can contribute and what they are."[11] Beyond economic necessity and enlightened self-interest, the failure to expand access to the vulnerable frustrates the American Dream, particularly the egalitarian notion of attaining equality through education.[12] Higher education attainment for vulnerable students is essential to achieving democratic norms of inclusion and greater social cohesion.

Despite these compelling societal justifications for expanding higher education attainment for vulnerable populations, the political discourse is often characterized by divisive rhetoric. Examining broader questions of democracy, economic growth, and social justice carries implications for the future of *all* Americans by prompting them to think about fulfilling the nation's potential. The expansion of higher education access among vulnerable students illustrates how individual, group, and societal interests ultimately converge. Addressing these broader questions related to the public good will reorient the college access debate away from a narrow, market-based paradigm and build common ground among legal observers, policy makers, and the public. The costs associated with the broken K–16 bridge for vulnerable students are vast and merit an aggressive reform response.

SUMMARY OF REFORMS

The search for the single magic solution to the elusive achievement gap is unrealistic. To better address higher education access for vulnerable students, reforms must target all phases of the K–16 continuum: K–12 academic preparation; transitional assistance between secondary school and higher education; and college-level achievement and persistence. This book focuses on the middle phase, which is often underappreciated, yet this critical component affects the entire education continuum. College access reforms must be comprehensive and address emerging demographics, quality, stratification, and market failures, such as information asymmetries. Tackling such a meta-problem requires broad stakeholder engagement: federal, state, and local government actors as well as higher education institutions, private actors, and civil society must pool their collective knowledge and resources to enhance their impact.

The list that follows summarizes reforms and recommendations highlighted in the preceding chapters. This list, although not exhaustive, captures key college access–related reforms targeting high school level, affordability, and college level challenges.

HIGH SCHOOL LEVEL
- Enhance college-counseling capabilities in public high schools nationwide.
- Collect and report college access data.
- Supplement college advising through college access organizations' complementary services.
- Establish partnerships among college access organizations and high schools.
- Create a national online course on college admissions designed by experts and make it available to public schools nationwide.
- Move toward the consolidation of college and financial aid applications to streamline admissions and financial aid processes.

COLLEGE AFFORDABILITY
- Bolster need-based financial aid policies at the federal, state, and institutional levels.

Federal
  o Increase Pell Grant amounts and purchasing power.
  o Make income-based repayment the default plan for all student borrowers.
  o Match funds to encourage states to provide need-based aid to students.
  o Establish accountability mechanisms that should include (1) some performance-based funding to incentivize institutions to enroll and graduate greater numbers of low-socioeconomic-status students; and (2) enhanced data collection and reporting to evaluate qualitative concerns and the federal government's return on investment.
  o Develop a range of consumer-protection policies to prevent market abuses, predatory institutions, and exploitation.

State
  o Differentiate tuition pricing at public institutions charging in-state students different prices based on their demonstrated financial need; for example, charging wealthier students more.

o Reverse state trends away from politically popular merit-based aid toward need-based aid.
o Protect against abuses by "degree mills" by enhancing licensing requirements and state attorney general investigations and prosecutions.

Institutional
o Implement progressive student-aid policies capping student loans.
o Establish free or significantly reduced tuition for low- to moderate-income students.

COLLEGE LEVEL
- Develop admissions practices that better reflect student potential rather than serving as a proxy for socioeconomic status.
- Establish partnerships among college access organizations and colleges.
- Create college access pathways for additional segments of the U.S. population, including community college students, adults, and veterans.
- Create diverse and inclusionary higher education environments.

The Emerging College Access Movement

Nearly two decades ago, when SMF was founded, *college access* was not a widely used term of art, yet many organizations were engaged in what is now called college access programming. Recently, it was an integral part of the Obama administration's higher education agenda, particularly the 2020 goal to reclaim the nation's position as the world's top producer of college graduates. The U.S. Department of Education's College Access Initiative, under the direction of senior adviser Gregory Darneider, raised the profile of the field's contributions. In 2015, the president and first lady issued a call to action, drawing attention to *Increasing College Opportunity for Low-Income Students*.[13] Notably, former first lady Michelle Obama is a first-generation college student who grew up in a working-class household on Chicago's South Side. She attended both Princeton University and Harvard Law School. Her personal higher education narrative does not differ from those of many students served by SMF and other college access organizations across the country. She is an excellent ambassador for college access, especially in launching her own Reach Higher Initiative, which aims to expand opportunities by making sure "all students understand what they need to complete their education, including,

- exposing students to college and career opportunities,
- understanding financial aid eligibility that can make college affordability a reality,
- encouraging academic planning and summer learning opportunities,
- supporting high school counselors who can help more kids get into college."[14]

A national organization called the National Consortium for School Counseling and Postsecondary Success grew out of the former first lady's Reach Higher Initiative.[15]

As mentioned, the Obama administration made concrete improvements to alleviate the plight of vulnerable students. These measures demonstrate a better understanding of the ground-level challenges these students face. Future administrations must build on this legacy. Unfortunately, the Trump administration's positions, or lack thereof, threaten the momentum of prior college access efforts. The present political context is a cause for alarm, but it should not dampen enthusiasm for expanding college access. It is a wake-up call: a reminder to double down on efforts to achieve greater equity and a call to action for greater civil society interventions.

THE FUTURE OF SMF AND IMPROVEMENTS

Before discussing SMF's future and possible improvements, let us summarize the features of successful college access programs discussed in the preceding chapters. This nonexhaustive list of features generated from two decades of organizational experiences, our interview responses, and academic literature may assist practitioners, policy makers, and program evaluators. This list may have relevance to all college access organizations; however, these variables are perhaps most useful for smaller, boutique programs like SMF with less than a hundred students.

Features of Successful College Access Programs
- Secondary school outreach
- Grassroots community partner outreach (e.g., organizations and individuals)
- College admissions office outreach along with informal and formal partnerships
- Tracking of student college admissions milestones and progress (e.g., applications submitted, Free Application for Federal Student Aid [FAFSA] completion)
- Program evaluation capabilities
- Various program elements (e.g., seminars, college visitations, scholarships)
- Programming synched with college admissions calendar
- College visitation opportunities that reflect diverse institutional environments (e.g., public, private, liberal arts, technical, selective, urban, rural, and minority serving institutions);
- Strong mentoring components (e.g., one-on-one, group, professional, and near-peer)
- Alumni network cultivated and leveraged to assist current students

- Informal and/or formal mechanisms for continued college and career guidance after high school
- Access to local college and university resources through formal or informal partnerships
- Parental and caregiver engagement
- Safe environment for discussion and guidance
- Strong program leadership, preferably by individuals with extensive higher education and professional networks

Future Improvements

SMF's current organizational life-cycle is well beyond the start-up phase, and it must identify creative new ways to sustain and deepen its programmatic impact. Student respondents were asked how SMF could improve its services. Recognizing that they might be reluctant to offer direct criticism, the question was posed as an opportunity to provide feedback that would help SMF improve. A common theme in the responses reflected a desire for more communication, including more frequent face-to-face interaction with SMF mentors. In an age of virtual social media relationships, student respondents still clamored for and valued more traditional modes of communication. Responses made clear that students valued the close-knit feel of the program.

Other suggestions called for more "straight talk" about the implications of selectivity and school brand; raising SMF's profile at more local high schools and organizations; and more contact with near-peer college students. A key area of growth and improvement is to keep mentoring long after high school; that is, extending the duration of participant engagement. Such mentoring often occurs but informally. Formalizing and strengthening this mentoring network after high school, even if it must be online, would support more SMF alumni as they navigate college, career, and beyond.

In terms of self-assessment, SMF, like other organizations, is limited by finite resources, namely, time and money. In a perfect world, we would offer more seminars developing critical thinking, more robust standardized test preparation, more scholarship assistance, more data tracking, and more formalized mentoring as participants go on to college and beyond. Key challenges for grassroots organizations like SMF include (1) developing and disseminating robust evidence of program success and (2) sustained leadership.[16]

In the first case, small-scale programs have greater difficulty demonstrating their impact for several reasons, such as (1) limited resources for data collection and student tracking, (2) lack of in-house evaluation expertise, and (3) limited access to venues where they can communicate findings to a broad array of stakeholders. The evaluation of program effectiveness is certainly important for sustaining and improving college access programming. In the present accountability

environment, metrics for donors, lawmakers, and other stakeholders are necessary. However, the collection of "data for data's sake" can harm organizational
missions by syphoning off key resources from effective programming. A rule of
reason or appropriate balance should apply to data collection.

We have also considered what would happen if the loss of a sustained leader
should threaten the organization's continuity and viability. A succession plan is
needed to avoid the mistake made by many now-extinct organizations and
programs.

Despite these challenges, SMF is poised to deliver strong programming at its
current scale and scope. Scaling up the SMF program too fast brings the risk of
eliminating its close-knit feel and would require more resources. At the moment
and into the foreseeable future, SMF can serve as a resource and model for other
organizations.

A Stronger K–16 Bridge: The Challenge Ahead

Today, our nation stands at a crucial juncture where the expansion of higher education access to vulnerable populations will determine our future economic,
social, and civic vitality. As approximately 70 million baby boomers retire, if current trends continue, the nation will face a shortage of 14 million college-educated
workers in 2020. At the same time, six out of ten jobs will require highly trained
personnel with college degrees.[17] Meeting future workforce demand requires
expanding college access for vulnerable students.

Policy makers have explored K–12 academic achievement and the admissions
practices at higher education institutions, but they have largely neglected the transitional phase, when students and their families select higher education options.
Even with the mountain of problems that plague K–12 education, if college counseling for vulnerable students does not remain a meaningful part of the overall
education reform debate, investments in K–12 and postsecondary reform efforts
will not yield significant returns. Earnestly addressing vulnerable student needs
will require a more expansive vision of K–12 schools as social networking stations,
where students receive ancillary services, such as quality college counseling, alongside academic instruction. Although college information can be disseminated
online and through other indirect formats, direct student-to-counselor interactions are extremely valuable. Both the creation of an integrated college counseling function in the nation's high schools and data collection to invest resources
strategically have significant empirical and anecdotal support. If properly implemented alongside other reforms, we will see a stronger K–16 bridge; vulnerable
students will be able to convert their academic achievement into college enrollment and completion.

Higher education access is not solely a class-based or minority concern; it is
inextricably linked to the nation's need for "all the trained talent it can marshal."[18]
Nearly a century ago, John Dewey observed the dangers of social stratification that

could prevent interaction between groups, stifle diversity of thought, and thwart social advancement; he highlighted the role of schools in countering this tendency and promoting social advancement. He realized that society "must see to it that intellectual opportunities are accessible to all on equable and easy terms."[19] SMF student success and the impact of SMF's interventions capture the essence of Dewey's observations: the nation's need to develop the potential on the periphery. We should not tolerate disparities when promising solutions and tools exist.

PARTING THOUGHTS

Despite being an established academic, I never intended to research and write a book on college access. I feel incredibly uncomfortable studying a program and, most of all, people whom I admire greatly and may have helped or mentored over the past two decades. SMF's activities were never carried out with any thought about future research. We focused on executing and improving programming for students. Having said that, completing the study, maintaining a critical distance, and analyzing the interviews have clarified for me why a broader audience must engage with this important subject. The book captures unfiltered and complex narratives that are often overlooked or not adequately understood in educational discourse. The topic of higher education for vulnerable students often prompts skepticism and a sense of futility. Problems are conceived as intractable. This book offers a counternarrative. It provides sobering descriptive insights alongside forward-looking, pragmatic proposals. It frames the problem and offers constructive avenues to eradicate it.

Due to diverse personal and professional experiences, I have had the luxury of developing a panoramic view of opportunity and possibility. In leading SMF, I attempt to share this panoramic view with young people and their families. At the same time, these experiences have shown me the complex challenges students face. They explain why interventions by SMF and other college access organizations are necessary to the nation's higher education mission. My hope is that this book will inform practitioners, administrators, teachers, counselors, policy makers, and academics that small investments in college access programming for vulnerable students can yield exponential returns that often defy prediction. Our best prospects for advancing our common interests as a nation may rest in the hands of people very different from ourselves. Whittling down the student narratives into a single descriptive statistic, classification, or theoretical frame is perhaps impossible. For many students, the pursuit of higher education is chaos, and they must somehow, often with assistance, create their own agency and their own sense of order.

Serving young people through SMF has been the highlight of my professional career. Nothing else comes close. SMF was and remains a grassroots effort, not for recognition or monetary compensation, but simply to make a positive impact on the lives of young people. We have certainly made mistakes along the way, but we have always given our best effort with the resources available. Interviewing former students, some of whom I had not heard from in over a decade, was a once-in-a-lifetime experience: remarkable, rare, and unbelievably rewarding. I am extremely proud of my former students' educational and career trajectories and even prouder of the people they have become: purposeful leaders in their chosen communities. My life has been enriched by my association with SMF students much more than I could have enriched theirs. They bring out the best in me. At many junctures in my own professional and personal journey, I could have gracefully abandoned the college access efforts I started in my twenties, but random calls, emails, and visits from former students, relaying their achievements and gratitude, motivate me to continue. The more SMF students achieve, the more my resolve to help grows.

Tackling the challenges that thwart college access requires a multifaceted response by many stakeholders and constituencies. It calls for looking beyond ourselves. I often convey this call to action to SMF students: "We know, without question, you will be successful, but we expect more from you. We ask that wherever you go, and no matter how far you travel, you take others with you." This call extends to every person, group, or entity in a position of privilege to promote college access for vulnerable students: bring others with you, connect with them, and develop potential on the periphery.

ACKNOWLEDGMENTS

This book is dedicated to my daughters, Sydney and Zoe. It honors the memory and legacy of my family heroines and heroes: Cynthia Treco Simmons, Nathaniel (Nat) Preston Simmons Jr., Nathaniel (Nate) Preston Simmons III, Lillie Belle Simmons, Amelia Treco, Coretha Knowles, and Robert W. Saunders Sr. I want to give special thanks to my extended family, friends, and mentors, who have provided support, guidance, inspiration, and wisdom through the years. Your generosity, kindness, and thoughtfulness have profoundly influenced my personal and professional journey.

I wish to thank Wake Forest University School of Law for its generous research support. I wish to thank Sally Irvin, Elizabeth Johnson, and the entire Wake Law Library and Information Technology staff for their valuable assistance through various phases of this book project. I want to thank Julie Edelson for her valuable editorial insights. I also want to recognize and thank Timothy Davis, Freddye Hill, Willie Pearson, Andrew Smiler, Sarah Watts, and Ronald Wright, who provided valuable insights at various stages of this endeavor.

I relied on the hard work and dedication of my student research assistants at Wake Forest University School of Law: Taylor Anderson, Charity Barger, Alina Bosanac, Amanda Byrnes, Jason Chung, Jenna Coogle, Tyler Gardner, Elizabeth Grindell, Nicholas Illuminati, Afzul Karim, Matthew Lewis, Christopher Salera, Kristin Smith, Lanie Summerlin, Samantha Tracy, and Justine Wright. Without your many contributions this project would not have been possible. I extend my deepest thanks and gratitude to all of you.

I want to thank Rutgers University Press, especially Lisa Banning and Kimberly Guinta, for their tremendous support of this book project.

Finally, a heartfelt thank you to all members of the SMF family. Your contributions—to me and to society generally—make this book our collective achievement. But our connection and friendship go far beyond the four corners of any book. We are all part of an esteemed SMF legacy and *family* that continue to grow. Knowing you is an enduring privilege, honor, and source of inspiration!

NOTES

INTRODUCTION

1. Ralph Ellison, *Going to the Territory* (New York: Random House, 1986), 66.
2. Omari Scott Simmons, "Class Dismissed: Rethinking Socio-Economic Status and Higher Education Attainment," *Arizona State Law Journal* 46, no. 1 (2014): 234.
3. Ronald J. Daniels, Phillip M. Spector, and Rebecca Goetz, "Fault Lines in the Compact: Higher Education and the Public Interest in the United States," *Carnegie Reporter* (Winter 2014), https://higheredreporter.carnegie.org/wp-content/uploads/2014/02/Daniels_Spector _Goetz_Fault-Lines.pdf.
4. Simmons, "Class Dismissed," 238. Low socioeconomic status students are particularly vulnerable to choices over whether and where to attend college.
5. Ibid., 234.
6. Ibid., 259.
7. Ibid., 292–296. A student's higher socioeconomic status can be a proxy for so-called merit-based college selection, reflecting the need for more diversified admissions processes.
8. Simmons, "Lost in Transition: The Implications of Social Capital for Higher Education Access," *Notre Dame Law Review* 87, no. 1 (2011): 220; William G. Bowen, Matthew M. Chingos, and Michael S. McPherson, *Crossing the Finish Line: Completing College at America's Public Universities* (Princeton, NJ: Princeton University Press, 2009), 103.
9. Simmons, "Class Dismissed," 270; Claire Gilbert and Donald Heller, "The Truman Commission and Its Impact on Federal Higher Education Policy from 1947 to 2010," Working Paper 9 (Pennsylvania State University, 2010), https://ed.psu.edu/cshe/working-papers/wp-9.
10. See Glenn Loury, "A Dynamic Theory of Racial Income Differences," in *Women, Minorities, and Employment Discrimination*, ed. Phyllis A. Wallace and Annette M. LaMond (Lexington, MA: Lexington Books, 1977), 176. Due to differences in social capital, "absolute equality of opportunity . . . is an ideal that cannot be achieved."
11. Simmons, "Lost in Transition," 229, quoting Loury, "Dynamic Theory," 176.
12. Simmons, "Class Dismissed," 241.
13. See Drew Desilver, "U.S. Income Inequality, on Rise for Decades, Is Now Highest Since 1928," *Pew Research Center*, December 5, 2013, http://www.pewresearch.org/fact-tank/2013/12 /05/u-s-income-inequality-on-rise-for-decades-is-now-highest-since-1928/.
14. Steve Suitts, "A New Majority Update: Low Income Students in the South and Nation," *Southern Education Foundation* (October 2013), http://www.southerneducation.org/News-and -Events/posts/April-2014/Juvenile-Justice-Education-Programs-in-the-United-aspx.aspx.
15. Ibid.
16. The Great Recession exacerbated decreases in household wealth as well as intra- and intergroup wealth gaps. Between 2005 and 2009, U.S. household wealth fell 28 percent. Compared to the 16 percent decrease for white households, household wealth fell 66 percent for Hispanics and 53 percent for blacks. Kochhar et al., "Wealth Gaps Rise to Record Highs between Whites, Blacks and Hispanics," *Pew Research Center*, July 26, 2011, 13–14, http:// www.pewsocialtrends.org/files/2011/07/SDT-Wealth-Report_7-26-11_FINAL.pdf.
17. Steve Suitts, "A New Diverse Majority: Students of Color in the South's Public Schools," (Atlanta: Southern Education Foundation, October 2010).

18. Bowen et al., *Crossing the Finish Line*, 8–9.

19. Suitts, "New Majority Update."

20. Bowen et al., *Crossing the Finish Line*, 9. Upper-class white students already have a higher rate of educational attainment than most other students.

21. Mitchell L. Stevens, *Creating a Class: College Admissions and the Education of Elites* (Cambridge, MA: Harvard University Press, 2007), 14. "My research suggests that one profound result of higher education's expansion has been the entrenchment of a complicated, publicly palatable, and elaborately costly machinery through which wealthy parents hand privilege down to their children."

22. Many parents see elite college degrees as "guaranteed access to the nation's top corporations as well as graduate and professional schools." Simmons, "Class Dismissed," 252; Jacques Steinberg, *The Gatekeepers: Inside the Admissions Process of a Premier College* (London: Penguin Books, 2003), xiv.

23. Simmons, "Class Dismissed," 257; Brian Pusser, "Higher Education, Markets, and the Preservation of the Public Good," in *Earnings from Learning: The Rise of For-Profit Universities*, eds. David W. Breneman, et al. (Albany: State University of New York Press, 2006), 23, 26–27.

24. See the National Association for College Admission Counseling website, http://www.nacacnet.org/Pages/default.aspx; the National College Access Network website, http://www.collegeaccess.org/; the College Board website, https://www.collegeboard.org; and the Obama White House Archives website, https://obamawhitehouse.archives.gov/issues/education/k-12.

CHAPTER 1   ORIGINS

1. Omari Scott Simmons, "Lost in Transition: The Implications of Social Capital for Higher Education Access." *Notre Dame Law Review* 87, no. 1 (2012): 216.

2. Mitchell L. Stevens, *Creating a Class: College Admissions and the Education of Elites* (Cambridge. MA: Harvard University Press, 2009), 15, describes the significant advantages that high-SES parents, "keenly aware of the terms of elite college admission," can provide to mold their children into "ideal [college] applicants."

3. Jandhyala B.G. Tilak, "Higher Education: A Public Good or a Commodity? Commitment *to* Higher Education or Commitment *of* Higher Education to Trade," *Prospects* 38, no. 4 (December 2008): 454.

4. Ibid., 453.

5. Tomiko Brown-Nagin, "Rethinking Proxies for Disadvantage in Higher Education: A First Generation Student's Project," *University of Chicago Legal Forum* 2014, no. 1 (2014): 40, http://chicagounbound.uchicago.edu/uclf/vol2014/iss1/8.

6. Ibid., 252; John Dewey, *Democracy and Education* (London: Macmillan, 1996), 101, 114; Martha Minow, *In Brown's Wake: Legacies of America's Educational Landmark* (Oxford: Oxford University Press, 2010), 159–162.

7. James Forman Jr., "The Rise and Fall of School Vouchers: A Story of Religion, Race, and Politics," *UCLA Law Review* 54, no. 3 (2007): 547.

8. Critics of affirmative action in these discussions usually assert that reverse discrimination and affirmative action hurt "economic productivity" and "academic standards in higher education"; that they are "inconsistent with the antidiscrimination provisions of VII of the Civil Rights Act of 1964," violate "American ideals of fairness and meritocracy," and are unnecessary because discrimination is no longer a problem; that they cause political divisiveness and hurt African Americans and other beneficiaries. Fred L. Pincus, *Reverse Discrimination: Dismantling the Myth* (Boulder: Lynne Rienner Publishers, Inc., 2003), 35.

9. See *Hopwood v. Texas*, 236 F.3d 256 (US 5th Cir. Ct. App. 2000); *Regents of the University of California v. Bakke*, 438 U.S. 265 (1978).

10. See *Grutter v. Bollinger*, 539 U.S. 306 (2003).

11. William G. Bowen and Derek Bok, *The Shape of the River* (Princeton: Princeton University Press, 1998), 128–129.

12. Ibid.

13. Jeremy Ashkenas, Haeyoun Park, and Adam Pearce, "Even with Affirmative Action, Blacks and Hispanics Are More Underrepresented at Top Colleges Than 35 Years Ago," *New York Times*, August 24, 2017, https://www.nytimes.com/interactive/2017/08/24/us/affirmative-action.html?mcubz=0.

14. Geoffrey Canada's Harlem Children's Zone project implemented an integrated college-counseling function and data tracking that may provide a template for other jurisdictions. Simmons, "Lost in Transition," 213.

15. Magnus Nilsson and Jannika Mattes, "The Spatiality of Trust: Factors Influencing the Creation of Trust and the Role of Face-to-Face Contact," *European Management Journal* 33, no. 4 (2015): 230.

16. See McCabe Scholars, http://www.swarthmore.edu/mccabe-scholars, detailing the components of the scholarship at Swarthmore College, including a link to more information on Thomas B. McCabe's life and accomplishments.

17. For details about John Hollis's public service, see Press Release, Connecting Generations, The Robert A. Kasey, Jr. Lifetime Achievement Award, http://www.connecting-generations.org/john-hollis-award.

18. Jacques Steinberg, "Graduates Fault Advice of Guidance Counselors," *New York Times*, March 3, 2010, A20.

19. Jacques Steinberg, *The Gatekeepers: Inside the Admissions Process of a Premier College* (New York: Viking, 2002).

20. Henry M. Levin, "Education as a Public and Private Good," *Journal of Policy Analysis and Management* 6, no. 4 (1987): 629–630.

21. William C. Kidder and Jay Rosner, "How the SAT Creates Built-in-Headwinds: An Educational and Legal Analysis of Disparate Impact," *Santa Clara Law Review* 43, no. 1 (2002–2003): 133. Rosner argues that the "process of selecting and developing SAT questions" actually "unfairly exacerbates the test's already significant disparate impact on African American and Chicano test-takers."

22. Simmons, "Lost in Transition," 222. See also "Measuring Up 2008: The National Report Card on Higher Education," *National Center for Public Policy and Higher Education* (2008): 5–6, http://measuringup2008.highereducation.org/print/NCPPHEMUNationalRpt.pdf.

23. Simmons, "Lost in Transition," 222.

24. Ibid. See also Jenny Nagaoka, Melissa Roderick, and Vanessa Coca, "Barriers to College Attainment: Lessons from Chicago," *Center for American Progress* (2009): 4, https://www.americanprogress.org/issues/higher-education/report/2009/01/27/5432/barriers-to-college-attainment-lessons-from-chicago.

25. Simmons, "Lost in Transition," 222.

26. Simmons, "Class Dismissed: Rethinking Socio-economic Status and Higher Education Attainment." *Arizona State Law Journal* 46, no. 1 (2014): 246.

27. Ibid. See also William G. Bowen, Derek Bok, Matthew M. Chingos, and Michael S. McPherson, *Crossing the Finish Line: Completing College at America's Public Universities* (Princeton: Princeton University Press, 2009), 9–10.

28. Simmons, "Lost in Transition," 209.

29. Ibid., 244.

30. Ibid., 221. See also Bowen et al., *Crossing the Finish Line*, 104–105: Effective guidance is the key to "increasing social mobility and augmenting the nation's human capital."

31. Caroline Hoxby and Christopher Avery, "The Missing 'One-Offs': The Hidden Supply of High-Achieving, Low-Income Students," *Brookings Papers on Economic Activity* (Spring 2013): 23–24.

32. Ibid., 30.

33. Ibid., 24.

34. Ibid., 26.

35. Ibid., 25–26.

36. Ibid., 31, 25.

37. Ibid., 30–31.

38. Ibid., 26.

39. Ibid., 28.

40. Ibid.

41. Students from families with low and modest incomes often lack these resources. Robert Schaeffer, "Test Scores Do Not Equal Merit," in *SAT Wars: The Case for Test-Optional College Admissions*, ed. Joseph A. Soares (New York: Teachers College Press, 2012), 157.

42. Guinier, *The Tyranny of the Meritocracy: Democratizing Higher Education in America* (Boston: Beacon Press, 2015).

43. Simmons, "Lost in Transition," 215.

44. Melissa Roderick, Jenny Nagaoka, Vanessa Coca, and Eliza Moeller, "From High School to the Future: Potholes on the Road to College," *University of Chicago, Consortium on Chicago School Research* (March 2008), 5, http://consortium.uchicago.edu/publications/high-school -future-potholes-road-college.

45. Simmons, "Lost in Transition," 215.

46. See Sigal Alon and Marta Tienda, "Assessing the 'Mismatch' Hypothesis: Differences in College Graduation Rates by Institutional Selectivity," *Society for Education* 78 (October 2005): 305, 309; and Roderick, Nagaoka, Coca, and Moeller, "From High School to the Future: Making Hard Work Pay Off," *Consortium on Chicago School Research* (2009), 53, http://consortium .uchicago.edu/publications/high-school-future-making-hard-work-pay.

47. Simmons, "Lost in Transition," 215–216. See also Bowen and Bok, *Shape of the River*, 129.

48. Dominic J. Brewer, Eric Eide, and Ronald G. Ehrenberg, "Does It Pay to Attend an Elite Private College? Cross-Cohort Evidence on the Effects of College Type on Earnings," *Journal of Human Resources* 34, no. 1 (Winter 1999): 114; Eric R. Eide, Dominic J. Brewer, and Ronald G. Ehrenberg, "Does It Pay to Attend an Elite Private College? Evidence on the Effects of Under-graduate College Quality on Graduate School Attendance," *Economics of Education Review* 17, no. 4 (October 1998): 371–372.

49. Simmons, "Lost in Transition," 216; Bowen and Bok, *Shape of the River*, 128.

50. Stacy Berg Dale and Alan B. Krueger, "Estimating the Payoff to Attending a More Selec-tive College: An Application of Selection on Observables and Unobservables," *Quarterly Jour-nal of Economics* 117, no. 4 (November 2002): 1524–1525.

51. See Roderick et al., "From High School to the Future: Potholes," 2; on AP and IB classes, see Diane Ravitch, *EdSpeak: A Glossary of Education Terms, Phrases, Buzzwords, and Jargon* (Alexandria, VA: Association for Supervision and Curriculum Development, 2007), 14, 124.

52. Simmons, "Lost in Transition," 216–217; Roderick et al., "From High School to the Future: Potholes," 10.

53. Simmons, "Lost in Transition," 217.

54. Ibid; Roderick et al., "From High School to the Future: Potholes," 3.

55. Ibid., 3, 32.

56. Simmons, "Lost in Transition," 218.

57. Ibid.

58. Roderick et al., "From High School to the Future: Potholes," 32.

59. Ibid., 107; see Roderick et al., "From High School to the Future: Potholes," 52–54, for various studies assessing the effect of college matching on graduation rates.

60. Bowen et al., *Crossing the Finish Line*, 105.

61. Simmons, "Lost in Transition," 221; Bowen et al., *Crossing the Finish Line*, 104.

62. Simmons, "Lost in Transition," 221.

63. See William C. Symonds, Robert B. Schwartz, and Ronald Ferguson, "Pathways to Prosperity: Meeting the Challenge of Preparing Young Americans for the 21st Century," *Harvard Graduate School of Education* (February 2011), https://www.gse.harvard.edu/sites/default/files/documents/Pathways_to_Prosperity_Feb2011-1.pdf.

64. Simmons, "Lost in Transition," 221; Bowen et al., *Crossing the Finish Line*, 101, 110.

65. Bowen et al., *Crossing the Finish Line*, 101.

CHAPTER 2   THE SMF COLLEGE ACCESS PROGRAM

1. See National College Access Network, Members, http://www.collegeaccess.org/Our_Members.

2. National College Access Network, Target Populations: Adult Learners, http://www.collegeaccess.org/Target_Populations.

3. See the National College Access Network website, which generated reports from NCAN's program directory, http://www.collegeaccess.org/accessprogramdirectory/reports.aspx.

4. These goals were largely carried over from the earlier Delaware program. See *supra*, 35–42.

5. See W.K. Kellogg Foundation, http://wkkf.org/.

6. See James A. Michener, *Chesapeake* (New York: Random House, 1978).

7. Delaware Department of Education, "Delaware Public Education at a Glance: 2014–15," *Rodel Foundation of Delaware*: 30.

8. *Plessy v. Ferguson*, 16 U.S. 537 (1896); Robert L. Hayman Jr., "A History of Race in Delaware: 1639–1950," in *Choosing Equality: Essays and Narratives on the Desegregation Experience.*, eds. Robert L. Hayman Jr. and Leland Ware (University Park: The Pennsylvania State University Press, 2009), 21–68.

9. Ibid., 61.

10. Ibid.

11. *Brown v. Board of Education*, 347 U.S. 483 (1954); *Bulah v. Gebhart*, 33 Del.Ch. 144 (Del. 1952); *Belton v. Gebhart*, 33 Del.Ch. 144 (Del. 1952); Robert L. Hayman Jr. and Leland Ware eds., *Choosing Equality: Essays and Narratives on the Desegregation Experience* (University Park: The Pennsylvania State University Press, 2009), 3–4.

12. A judge for over fifty years, Collins Seitz was known professionally for his *Belton v. Gebhart* decision, which required certain segregated Delaware schools to admit black children and played "a persuasive role" in *Brown v. Board of Education*. He was personally known for his "enthusiasm for the law and his patience with human beings and their frailties." Dolores K. Sloviter, "Tribute to Collins J. Seitz: A Kind Man," *Villanova Law Review* 40, no. 3 (1995): 553–54, 557.

13. On Redding's legacy, see Hayman, "A History of Race in Delaware," 59–61; Eric Pace, "L.L. Redding, 96, Desegregation Lawyer, Dies," *New York Times*, October 2, 1998, http://www.nytimes.com/1998/10/02/us/l-l-redding-96-desegregation-lawyer-dies.html.

14. Hayman, "A History of Race in Delaware," 62.

15. Ibid.

16. *Parker v. Univ. of Delaware*, 31 Del. Ch. 381 (Del. 1950).

17. "The Greensboro Sit-In," History Channel, http://www.history.com/topics/black-history/the-greensboro-sit-in.

18. Omari Scott Simmons, "Lost in Transition: The Implications of Social Capital for Higher Education Access." *Notre Dame Law Review* 87, no. 1 (2012): 215.

19. See William G. Bowen, Derek Bok, Matthew M. Chingos, and Michael S. McPherson, *Crossing the Finish Line: Completing College at America's Public Universities* (Princeton: Princeton University Press, 2009). Using a data pool of 60,000 seniors who attended more than 300 schools, the research analyzed application and college enrollment trends among North Carolina public high school seniors in 1999.

20. James J. Johnson Jr. and William Rand Kenan Jr., "Major Trends Facing North Carolina: Implications for Our State and the University of North Carolina," The University of North Carolina Tomorrow Commission, https://old.northcarolina.edu/nctomorrow/Johnson_-_Demographics_Brief-Final1.pdf.

21. See Camila Domonoske, "Supreme Court Declines Republican Bid to Revive North Carolina Voter ID Law," National Public Radio (Washington, D.C.), May 15, 2017, https://www.npr.org/sections/thetwo-way/2017/05/15/528457693/supreme-court-declines-republican-bid-to-revive-north-carolina-voter-id-law; Richard Fausset, "Bathroom Law Repeal Leaves Few Pleased in North Carolina," *New York Times*, March 30, 2017, https://www.nytimes.com/2017/03/30/us/north-carolina-senate-acts-to-repeal-restrictive-bathroom-law.html; Christopher A. Cooper and H. Gibbs Knotts, *The New Politics of North Carolina* (Chapel Hill: The University of North Carolina Press, 2012), 289.

22. See Anselm Strauss and Juliet Corbin, "Grounded Theory Methodology," in *Handbook of Qualitative Research*, eds. Norman K. Denzin and Yvonna S. Lincoln (Thousand Oaks, CA: Sage Publications, 1994), 273–285.

23. Emily Springfield, Anne Gwozdek, and Andrew P. Smiler, "Transformation Rubric for Engaged Learning: A Tool and Method for Measuring Life-Changing Experiences," *International Journal of ePortfolio*, 5, no. 1 (2015): 63–74.

24. See W. Edwards Deming, "On Errors in Surveys," *American Sociological Review*, 9, no. 4 (August 1994): 359–360, 367. It identifies 13 factors that may contribute to errors in survey research, including personal bias created by "differences in education, experience, and environment."

25. Harvey S. James Jr., "Self-Selection Bias in Business Ethics Research," *Business Ethics Quarterly*, 16, no. 4 (October 2006): 559, 561: "Self-selection is based on the idea that individuals have some control over what they do."; see also Gregory T. Sica, "Bias in Research Studies," *RSNA Radiology*, 238, no. 3 (March 2006), doi: http://dx.doi.org/10.1148/radiol.2383041109: "Selection bias can exist when procedures for subject or case selection or factors that influence a subject's participation affect the study's outcome"; and Kristen Olson, "Survey Participation, Nonresponse Bias, Measurement Error Bias, and Total Bias," *Public Opinion Quarterly*, 70, no. 5 (2006): 737.

26. See Joshua Klayman, "Varieties of Confirmation Bias," in *Decision Making from a Cognitive Perspective*, ed. Jerome Busemeyer, Reid Hastie, and Douglas L. Medin (San Diego: Academic Press, 1995), 386: "[T]he confirmation bias label . . . refer[s] to an inclination to retain, or a disinclination to abandon, a currently favored hypothesis." See also Barbara Koslowski and Mariano Maqueda, "What Is Confirmation Bias and When Do People Actually Have It?" *Merril-Palmer Quarterly*, 39, no. 1 (January 1993): 104.

27. See Scott E. Carrell and Bruce Sacerdote, "Late Interventions Matter Too: The Case of College Coaching in New Hampshire," National Bureau of Economic Research, Working Paper

no. 19031 (2012); Eric P. Bettinger, Bridget Terry Long, Phillip Oreopoulos, and Lisa Sanbonmatsu, "The Role of Application Assistance and Information in College Decisions: Results from the H&R Block FASFA Experiment," *Quarterly Journal of Economics,* 1277, no. 3 (2012): 1205–1242; George Bulman, "The Effect of Access to College Assessments on Enrollment and Attainment," *American Economic Journal: Applied Economics,* 7, no. 4 (2015): 1–36.

28. Historically black colleges and universities (HBCUs), both private and public, are among the top universities in the country. Private HBCUs include Fisk University, Hampton University, Howard University, and Spelman College. Public HBCUs include Florida A&M University, Jackson State University, and North Carolina A&T State University.

CHAPTER 3   CHALLENGES IN COLLEGE ACCESS

1. Ralph Ellison, "That Same Pain, That Same Pleasure," in *The Collected Essays Ralph Ellison,* ed. John F. Callahan (New York: The Modern Library, 2003), 78.

2. See Scott E. Carrell and Bruce Sacerdote, "Late Interventions Matter Too: The Case of College Coaching in New Hampshire," Working Paper no. 19031 (Washington, DC: National Bureau of Economic Research, 2012); Eric P. Bettinger, Bridget Terry Long, Phillip Oreopoulos, and Lisa Sanbonmatsu, "The Role of Application Assistance and Information in College Decisions: Results from the H&R Block FASFA Experiment." *Quarterly Journal of Economics* 1277, no. 3 (2012): 1205–1242; George Bulman, "The Effect of Access to College Assessments on Enrollment and Attainment," *American Economic Journal: Applied Economics* 7, no. 4 (2015): 1–36.

3. Zoe Blumberg Corwin and William G. Tierney, *Getting There–and Beyond: Building a Culture of College-Going in High Schools* (Los Angeles: University of Southern California Center for Higher Education Policy Analysis, 2007), http://files.eric.ed.gov/fulltext/ED498731.pdf.

4. "Increasing College Opportunity for Low-Income Students: Promising Models and a Call to Action" (Washington, DC: Executive Office of the President, January 2014), 7, https://obamawhitehouse.archives.gov/sites/default/files/docs/increasing_college_opportunity_for_low-income_students_report.pdf.

5. Anthony G. Greenwald and Linda Hamilton Kreiger, "Implicit Bias: Scientific Foundations," *California Law Review* 94, no. 4 (July 2006): 957–958.

6. Ibid., 946.

7. Ibid., 956, 957–958.

8. Derald Wing Sue, Annie I. Lin, Gina C. Torino, Christina M. Capodilupo, and David P. Rivera, "Racial Microaggressions and Difficult Dialogues on Race in the Classroom," *Cultural Diversity and Ethnic Minority Psychology* 15, no. 2 (April 2009): 183–190, doi: http://dx.doi.org/10.1037/a0014191; Derald Wing Sue, *Microaggressions in Everyday Life: Race, Gender, and Sexual Orientation* (New York: John Wiley & Sons, Inc., 2010); Derald Wing Sue, Kevin L. Nadal, Christina M. Capodilupo, Annie I. Lin, Gina C. Torino, and David P. Rivera, "Racial Microaggressions against Black Americans: Implications for Counseling," *Journal of Counseling and Development* 86, no. 3 (Summer 2008): 330–38.

9. Alexis de Tocqueville, *Democracy in America* (Indianapolis: Liberty Fund, Inc., 1835), 595–599.

10. Nan Lin, *Social Capital: A Theory of Social Structure and Action* (Cambridge, UK: Cambridge University Press, 2001), 19.

11. Robert D. Putnam, *Bowling Alone* (New York: Simon & Schuster, 2000), 296.

12. Pierre Bourdieu, "The Forms of Capital," in *Handbook of Theory and Research for the Sociology of Education,* ed. J. E. Richardson (New York: Greenwood, 1986), 248–249.

13. Alejandro Portes, "Social Capital: Its Origins and Applications in Modern Sociology," *Annual Review of Sociology* 24, no. 1 (August 1998): 6, 9.

14. Ibid., 3.

15. Ibid., 12, 15.

16. Omari Scott Simmons, "Lost in Transition: The Implications of Social Capital for Higher Education Access." *Notre Dame Law Review* 87, no. 1 (2012): 225–226; Portes, "Social Capital," 11; James S. Coleman, "Social Capital in the Creation of Human Capital," *American Journal of Sociology* 94, Supplement: Organizations and Institutions: Sociological and Economic Approaches to the Analysis of Social Structure (1988): S110–111.

17. Portes, "Social Capital," 14.

18. Ibid.

19. Ibid., 12.

20. Ibid., 13–14.

21. Ibid., 14; Loïc J. D. Wacquant, and William Julius Wilson, "The Cost of Racial and Class Exclusion in the Inner City," *Annals of the American Academy of Political and Social Science* 501 (January 1989): 22–23, http://www.jstor.org/stable/1045646?seq=1#page_scan_tab_contents.

22. Portes, "Social Capital," 13.

23. See Simmons, "Lost in Transition," 227, for a list of factors that encumber academic attainment in rural populations. See also Rachel E. Durham and P. Johnelle Smith, "Nonmetropolitan Status and Kindergarteners' Early Literacy Skills: Is There a Rural Disadvantage?" *Rural Sociology,* 71, no. 4 (2006): 633.

24. Durham and Smith, "Nonmetropolitan Status," 628.

25. Simmons, "Lost in Transition," 227.

26. Lin, *Social Capital,* 99–102.

27. Ibid., 101–102.

28. Ibid., 40.

29. Ibid., 95–96.

30. Ibid.

31. Ibid., 44–45.

32. Douglas S. Massey, Camille Z. Charles, Garvey F. Lundy, and Mary J. Fischer, *The Source of the River: The Social Origins of Freshmen at America's Selective Colleges and Universities* (Princeton: Princeton University Press, 2006), 5.

33. Ibid., 6.

34. Lin, *Social Capital,* 97.

35. Simmons, "Lost in Transition," 228.

36. Howard Gardner, "Paroxysms of Choice," *New York Review of Books,* October 19, 2000, 44, 49, http://www.nybooks.com/articles/archives/2000/oct/19/paroxysms-of-choice. See also William G. Bowen, Martin A. Kurzweil, and Eugene M. Tobin, *Equity and Excellence in American Higher Education* (Charlottesville: University of Virginia Press, 2005), 73–94; Anthony P. Carnevale and Stephen J. Rose, "Socioeconomic Status, Race/Ethnicity, and Selective College Admissions," in *America's Untapped Resource: Low-Income Students in Higher Education,* ed. Richard D. Kahlenberg (New York: Century Foundation Press, 2004), 101, 106; Mitchell L. Stevens, *Creating a Class: College Admissions and the Education of Elites* (Cambridge, MA: Harvard University Press, 2009), 15; Richard H. Sander, "Class in American Legal Education," *Denver University Law Review* 88, no. 4 (2011): 632–633.

37. Laura W. Perna, "Toward a More Complete Understanding of the Role of Financial Aid in Promoting College Enrollment: The Importance of Context," in *Higher Education: Handbook of Theory and Research,* ed. John C. Smart (Houten: Springer Netherlands, 2010), 25, 131.

38. See Sandy Baum, Jennifer Ma, and Kathleen Payea, "Education Pays 2010: The Benefits of Higher Education for Individuals and Society," College Board Advocacy and Policy Center (2010): 34–35, http://trends.collegeboard.org/sites/default/files/education-pays-2010-full -report.pdf.

39. See William G. Bowen, Derek Bok, Matthew M. Chingos, and Michael S. McPherson, *Crossing the Finish Line: Completing College at America's Public Universities* (Princeton: Princeton University Press, 2009), 73. The demographic breakdown for recipients of Pell Grants, the federal government's primary form of assistance for low-income students, follows a similar pattern.

40. "A New Majority: Low Income Students Now a Majority in the Nation's Public Schools," *Southern Education Foundation* (2007): 3–6, http://www.southerneducation.org/getattachment /4ac62e27-5260-47a5-9d02-14896ec3a531/A-New-Majority-2015-Update-Low-Income -Students-Now.aspx.

41. Ibid., 6.

42. Perna, "Toward a More Complete Understanding," 131–132.

43. Rakesh Kochhar, Richard Fry, Gabriel Velasco, and Seth Motel, "Wealth Gaps Rise to Record Highs between Whites, Blacks and Hispanics" (Washington, DC: Pew Research Center, 26 July 2011) 1, 13–14, http://www.pewsocialtrends.org/files/2011/07/SDT-Wealth-Report_7 -26-11_FINAL.pdf.

44. Lani Guinier (comment), "Admissions Rituals as Political Acts: Guardians at the Gates of Our Democratic Ideals," *Harvard Law Review* 117, no. 1 (November 2003): 113, 129–130.; Michael Hout, "More Universalism, Less Structural Mobility: The American Occupational Structure in the 1980s," *American Journal of Sociology* 93, no. 6 (May 1988): 1358, 1392. See also Diane Ravitch, *The Death and Life of the Great American School System: How Testing and Choice Are Undermining Education* (New York: Basic Books, 2011), 226–228, 241.

45. Omari Scott Simmons, "For-Profits and the Market Paradox," *Wake Forest Law Review* 48, no. 2 (2013): 334–335.

46. Jenny Nagaoka, Melissa Roderick, and Vanessa Coca, "Barriers to College Attainment: Lessons from Chicago" (Washington, DC: Center for American Progress, 2009), 6, https://www .americanprogress.org/issues/higher-education/report/2009/01/27/5432/barriers-to -college-attainment-lessons-from-chicago.

47. Josephs Neff, Ann Doss Helms, and David Raynor. "Counted Out," *Raleigh News & Observer*, n.d., http://www.newsobserver.com/news/local/education/article149459574.html.

48. Tomiko Brown-Nagin, "Rethinking Proxies for Disadvantage in Higher Education: A First Generation Student's Project," *University of Chicago Legal Forum* 2014, no. 1 (2014): 472, http:// chicagounbound.uchicago.edu/uclf/vol2014/iss1/8.

49. Kevin Eagan, Ellen Bara Stolzenberg, Joseph J. Ramirez, Melissa C. Aragon, Maria Ramirez Suchard, and Sylvia Hurtado, *The American Freshman: National Norms Fall 2014* (Los Angeles: Higher Education Research Institute at UCLA, 2014), 2–3.

50. Lin, *Social Capital*, 53.

51. Simmons, "Lost in Transition," 220–221.

52. Horace, "Adversity," in Tryon Edwards, comp., *A Dictionary of Thoughts: Being a Cyclopedia of Laconic Quotations from the Best Authors of the World, Both Ancient and Modern* (1897; Detroit: F.B. Dickerson Company, 1908).

53. Angela L. Duckworth, Christopher Peterson, Michael D. Matthews, and Dennis R. Kelly, "Grit: Perseverance and Passion for Long-Term Goals," *Journal of Personality and Social Psychology* 92, no. 6 (2007): 1087–1088.

54. Ibid., 1099, 1100, and 1088.

55. Marcus Credé, Michael C. Tynan, and Peter D. Hams, "Much Ado about Grit: A Meta-Analytic Synthesis of the Grit Literature," *Journal of Personality and Social Psychology* 113, no. 3 (2017): 504.

CHAPTER 4   THE ROLE OF SMF INTERVENTION

1. See Kevin O'Neill and Marlene Scardamalia, "Mentoring in the Open: A Strategy for Supporting Human Development in the Knowledge Society," *International Conference on the Learning Sciences* (2000), http://www.ikit.org/fulltext/2000_Mentoring.pdf.

2. Marcus Aurelius, *Meditations*, trans. Gregory Hays (New York: Modern Library, 1997), see especially Book 1, 11.

3. Cindy Buell, "Models of Mentoring in Communication," *Communication Education* 53, no. 1 (2004): 56–73.

4. David L. DuBois, Nelson Portillo, Jean E. Rhodes, Naida Silverthorn, and Jeffrey C. Valentine, "How Effective Are Mentoring Programs for Youth? A Systematic Assessment of the Evidence," Association for Psychological Science (2011): 66, https://teammates.org/wp-content/uploads/2011/01/DuBoisetalMeta.pdf.

5. Ibid., 58.

6. Ibid., 57–58.

7. Ibid., 37.

8. Ibid., 55.

9. Ibid., 58.

10. Ibid., 62, 63–66.

11. Ibid., 78.

12. Ibid., 77–78.

13. Alejandro Portes, "Social Capital: Its Origins and Applications in Modern Sociology," *Annual Review of Sociology*, 24, no. 1 (August 1998), 14.

14. Nan Lin, *Social Capital: A Theory of Social Structure and Action* (Cambridge, UK: Cambridge University Press, 2001), 229–230; Laura W. Perna, "Studying College Access and Choice: A Proposed Conceptual Model," in *Higher Education: Handbook of Theory and Research*, ed. John C. Smart (Houten: Springer Netherlands, 2006), 21, 112.

15. DuBois et al., "How Effective Are Mentoring Programs for Youth?" 68–69.

16. Ibid.

17. Ibid., 79.

18. See *supra* chap. 2, 69, 75.

19. Stacy Berg Dale and Alan B. Krueger, "Estimating the Payoff to Attending a More Selective College: An Application of Selection on Observables and Unobservables," *Quarterly Journal of Economics*, 117, no. 4 (2002), 1524–1525; William G. Bowen and Derek Bok, *The Shape of the River* (Princeton: Princeton University Press, 1998), 128.

20. Scholarships, Simmons Memorial Foundation, http://www.smfnonprofit.org/what-we-do/scholarships/.

21. Bowen and Bok, *Shape of the River*, 128.

22. Program Overview, Wake Forest Magnolia Scholars, http://college.wfu.edu/magnolia/program-overview.

23. The expression comes from a novel by Catherine Ryan Hyde, *Pay It Forward* (New York: Simon & Schuster, 1999).

CHAPTER 5   REFORMS

1. Michelle Obama, "This Issue Is Personal for Me," http://edition.cnn.com/2016/10/11/opinions/cnn-films-we-will-rise-michelle-obama.

2. See Scott E. Carrell and Bruce Sacerdote, "Late Interventions Matter Too: The Case of College Coaching in New Hampshire." Working Paper no. 19031. (Washington, DC: National Bureau of Economic Research, 2012); Eric P. Bettinger, Bridget Terry Long, Phillip Oreopoulos, and Lisa Sanbonmatsu, "The Role of Application Assistance and Information in College Decisions: Results from the H&R Block FASFA Experiment," *Quarterly Journal of Economics* 1277, no. 3 (2012): 1205–1242; George Bulman, "The Effect of Access to College Assessments on Enrollment and Attainment," *American Economic Journal: Applied Economics* 7, no. 4 (2015): 1–36.

3. Kenneth I. Maton, Freeman A. Hrabowski III, and Carol L. Schmitt, "African-American College Students Excelling in the Sciences: College and Postcollege Outcomes in the Meyerhoff Scholars Program," *Journal of Research in Science Teaching*, 37, no. 7 (2000): 629–654; http://cssiacyberwars.org/pdf/20000255-AfricanAmericanCollegeStudentsExcellingintheSciences-CollegeandPost-CollegeOutcomesintheMeyerhoffScholarsProgram.pdf.

4. Hautahi Kingi, "The Āwhina Effect," *Reducing Achievement Gaps in STEM: Promising International Research, Policies and Practices Conference*, May 22, 2017, http://achievestem.hsoc.gatech.edu/wp-content/uploads/sites/587/2017/03/Hautahi_AwhinaPresentation.pdf.

5. See Melissa Roderick, Jenny Nagaoka, Vanessa Coca, and Eliza Moeller, "From High School to the Future: Making Hard Work Pay Off," Chicago: Urban Education Institute, UChicago Consortium on Chicago School Research, April 2009, 3.

6. Ibid., 103; Steinberg, "Graduates Fault Advice of Guidance Counselors," *New York Times*, March 3, 2010, A20.

7. Jenny Nagaoka, Melissa Roderick, and Vanessa Coca, *Barriers to College Attainment: Lessons from Chicago* (Washington, DC: Center for American Progress, 2009), 11, https://www.americanprogress.org/issues/higher-education/report/2009/01/27/5432/barriers-to-college-attainment-lessons-from-chicago.

8. See Julie Hartline and Debra C. Cobia, "School Counselors: Closing Achievement Gaps and Writing Results Reports," *Professional School Counseling* 16, no. 1 (October 2012): 77; Robert Evans, "Reframing the Achievement Gap," *Phi Delta Kappa* 86, no. 8 (April 2005): 585.

9. Diane Ravitch, *The Death and Life of the Great American School System* (New York: Basic Books, 2010), 166–167.

10. See Patricia M. McDonough, *Choosing Colleges: How Social Class and Schools Structure Opportunity* (Albany: State University of New York Press, 1997), 4; Patricia M. McDonough, "Counseling Matters: Knowledge, Assistance, and Organizational Commitment in College Preparation," in *Preparing for College: Nine Elements of Effective Outreach*, eds. William G. Tierney, Zoe B. Corwin, and Julia E. Colyar (Albany: State University of New York Press, 2004), 69; Patricia Gándara and Deborah Bial, "Paving the Way to Postsecondary Education: K–12 Intervention Programs for Underrepresented Youth," National Postsecondary Education Cooperative (2001), http://nces.ed.gov/pubs2001/2001205.pdf; Jacqueline E. King, "The Decision to Go to College," College Board (1996), http://files.eric.ed.gov/fulltext/ED398775.pdf; Andrea Venezia, Michael W. Kirst, and Anthony L. Antonio, "Betraying the Dream: How Disconnected K–12 and Postsecondary Education Systems Undermine Student Aspirations," Stanford University Bridge Project (2002), https://web.stanford.edu/group/bridgeproject/betrayingthecollegedream.pdf; Stephen B. Plank and Will J. Jordan, "Effects of Information, Guidance, and Actions on Postsecondary Destinations: A Study of Talent Loss," *American Educational Research Journal* 38, no. 4 (2001): 947; James E. Rosenbaum, Shazia Rafiullah Miller,

and Melinda Scott Krei, "Gatekeeping in an Era of More Open Gates: High School Counselors' Views of Their Influence on Students' College Plans," *American Journal of Education* 104, no. 4 (1996): 257.

11. See Patrick O'Connor, "Inadequate Counsel," *Diverse: Issues in Higher Education* 27, no. 23 (2010): 17.

12. Jean Johnson and Jon Rochkind with Amber Ott and Samantha duPont, "Can I Get a Little Advice Here? How an Overstretched High School Guidance System Is Undermining Students' College Aspirations," *Public Agenda* (2010): 3, https://www.publicagenda.org/files/can-i-get -a-little-advice-here.pdf.

13. See also Patricia M. McDonough, "Counseling and College Counseling in America's High Schools," National Association for College Admission Counseling (January 2005): 10, http://citeseerx.ist.psu.edu/viewdoc/download?doi=10.1.1.543.5670&rep=rep1&type=pdf.

14. Laura W. Perna, Heather T. Rowan-Kenyon, Scott Loring Thomas, Angela Bell, Robert Anderson, and Chunyan Li, "The Role of College Counseling: Variations across High Schools," *Review of Higher Education* 31, no. 2 (2008): 131, 134.

15. Ibid.

16. McDonough, "Counseling and College Counseling," 14.

17. Thomas Nachazel and Gretchen Hannes, eds., "The Condition of Education 2010," National Center for Education Statistics, US Department of Education, 262, http://nces.ed.gov /pubsearch/pubsinfo.asp?pubid=2010028.

18. Ibid., 154.

19. Laura W. Perna et al., "Role of College Counseling in Shaping College Opportunity: Variations across High Schools." *Review of Higher Education* 31, no. 2 (2008), 133.

20. Ibid., 143, 154.

21. Ibid., 140.

22. McDonough, "Counseling and College Counseling," 7–8.

23. Perna et al., "Role of College Counseling," 133, 143.

24. McDonough, "Counseling and College Counseling," 6–8.

25. Ibid.

26. O'Connor, "Inadequate Counsel," 17.

27. Ibid.

28. Perna et al., "Role of College Counseling," 148.

29. Ibid., 133.

30. McDonough, "Counseling and College Counseling," 7.

31. Johnson et al., "Can I Get a Little Advice Here?" 9.

32. Perna et al., "Role of College Counseling," 153.

33. David A. Hawkins and Melissa Clinedinst, "State of College Admission 2006," National Association for College Admissions Counseling (2006), 55, https://www.immagic.com /eLibrary/ARCHIVES/GENERAL/NACAC_US/N060508H.pdf.

34. Perna et al., "Role of College Counseling," 152.

35. Hawkins and Clinedinst, "State of College Admission 2006," 51; McDonough, "Counseling and College Counseling," 4, 7–8, 13.

36. Perna et al., "Role of College Counseling," 143.

37. Ibid., 148.

38. McDonough, "Counseling and College Counseling," 4.

39. See, e.g., Chicago Public Schools, "Choose Your Future," https://chooseyourfuture .cps.edu; Colorado Department of Higher Education, "College in Colorado," http://collegein colorado.org.

40. College Scorecard, U.S. Department of Education, https://collegescorecard.ed.gov/.

41. U.S. Department of Education, "Race to the Top Program Executive Summary" (2009); http://www2.ed.gov/programs/racetothetop/executive-summary.pdf.

42. Perna et al., "Role of College Counseling," 150, 154.

43. Under the Elementary and Secondary Education Act, states need only report on the academic achievement standards and graduation rates at their secondary schools; see 20 U.S.C. § 6311 (2006); and U.S. Department of Education, "A Blueprint for Reform: The Reauthorization of the Elementary and Secondary Education Act" (2001): 8–9, http://www2.ed.gov/policy/elsec/leg/blueprint/blueprint.pdf.

44. US Department of Education, "College- and Career-Ready Students" (2010): 4, http://www2.ed.gov/policy/elsec/leg/blueprint/college-career-ready.pdf.

45. James E. Ryan, "The Perverse Incentives of the No Child Left Behind Act," *NYU Law Review* 79, no. 3 (June 2004): 934–936; Lawyers Committee for Civil Rights Under Law, "Framework for Providing All Students an Opportunity to Learn through Reauthorization of the Elementary and Secondary Education Act," National Association for the Advancement of Colored People (2010), 3–5, http://www.naacpldf.org/files/case_issue/Framework%20for%20Providing%20All%20Students%20an%20Opportunity%20to%20Learn%202.pdf.

46. See Memorandum from the NAACP Legal Defense and Education Fund, Inc., to the Senate Committee on Health, Education, Labor, and Pensions (May 7, 2010) (on file with author).

47. "Core Principles for New Accountability in Education," Aspen Institute, Education & Society Program (November 2009): 8, http://www.aspeninstitute.org/sites/default/files/content/docs/pubs/Core_Principles_April2010.pdf.

48. Ryan, "Perverse Incentives." A similar construct could apply to a measurement of higher education outcomes focused on achievement gains over time for individuals or groups of students.

49. For example, the Family Education Rights and Privacy Act, 20 U.S.C. § 1232(g); Family Educational Rights and Privacy, 34 C.F.R. § 99 (2002).

50. Ryan, "Perverse Incentives," 955–956.

51. Consumer Financial Protection Bureau, "Private Student Loans" (29 August 2012), 3, 11–13, http://files.consumerfinance.gov/f/201207_cfpb_Reports_Private-Student-Loans.pdf.

52. Brian Pusser, "Higher Education, Markets, and the Preservation of the Public Good" in *Earnings from Learning: The Rise of For-Profit Universities*, eds. David W. Breneman, Brian Pusser, and Sarah E. Turner (Albany: State University of New York Press, 2006), 39; Perna et al., "Role of College Counseling," 147–149.

53. Perna et al., "Role of College Counseling," 156.

54. Roderick et al., "From High School to the Future," 4.

55. Todd May, "ED Announces FAFSA Completion Project Expansion," *Official Blog of the US Department of Education*, May 31, 2012, https://blog.ed.gov/2012/05/ed-announces-fafsa-completion-project-expansion/; Constancia Warren, Leslie Rennie-Hill, and Jay Jordon Pfeiffer, "From Information to Action: A Guide to Using Postsecondary Data to Improve Students' Chances for Postsecondary Success" US Department of Education (2012), 3, https://www2.ed.gov/programs/slcp/information-to-action.pdf; "FAFSA Completion by High School and Public School District," *Federal Student Aid: An Office of the US Department of Education*, https://studentaid.ed.gov/sa/about/data-center/student/application-volume/fafsa-completion-high-school.

56. Tuition-Free Degree Program: The Excelsior Scholarship, https://www.ny.gov/programs/tuition-free-degree-program-excelsior-scholarship.

57. Pusser, "Higher Education," 34–36.

58. Ibid., 35.

59. Ibid., 34–36.

60. Perna et al., "Role of College Counseling," 145.

61. Ibid., 134.

62. Ibid., 134–136.

63. Mamie Lynch, Jennifer Engle, and José L. Cruz, "Priced Out: How the Wrong Financial-Aid Policies Hurt Low-Income Students," Educational Trust (June 1, 2011): 2, https://edtrust .org/resource/priced-out-how-the-wrong-financial-aid-policies-hurt-low-income-students/.

64. Lawrence Gladieux, "Low-Income Students and the Affordability of Higher Education," in *America's Untapped Resource: Low-Income Students in Higher Education*, ed. Richard D. Kahlenberg (New York: Century Foundation Press, 2004), 32–34.

65. Lynch, Engle, and Cruz, "Priced Out," 2, emphasis original; see also Lynch, Engle, and Cruz, "Lifting the Fog on Inequitable Financial-Aid Policies," Education Trust (2011): 7, Figs. 7, 8, https://edtrust.org/resource/lifting-the-fog-on-inequitable-financial-aid-policies/.

66. See William Zumeta, David W. Breneman, Patrick M. Callan, and Joni E. Finney, *Financing American Higher Education in the Era of Globalization* (Cambridge, MA: Harvard Education Press, 2012), 164–165; Edward P. St. John, *Refinancing the College Dream: Access, Equal Opportunity, and Justice for Taxpayers* (Baltimore: Johns Hopkins University Press, 2003), 2–4; Gladieux, "Low-Income Students," 39, Fig. 1.10.

67. Zumeta et al., *Financing American Higher Education*, 16–28; Gladieux, "Low-Income Students," 28–34.

68. Gladieux, "Low-Income Students," 38.

69. Zumeta et al., *Financing American Higher Education*, 92–94, Tables 4.3. 4.4.

70. Richard Vedder, "Loans Are Part of the Problem Not the Solution," *New York Times*, May 12, 2012, http://www.nytimes.com/roomfordebate/2012/05/12/easing-the-pain-of-student-loans /loans-are-part-of-the-problem-not-the-solution; Zumeta et al., *Financing American Higher Education*, 166; see also Dylan Matthews, "The Tuition Is Too Damn High, Part VII—Is Government Aid Actually Making College More Expensive?" *Washington Post*, September 3, 2013, http://www.washingtonpost.com/blogs/wonkblog/wp/2013/09/03/the-tuition-is-too -damn-high-part-vii-is-government-aid-actually-making-college-more-expensive; William J. Bennett, "Our Greedy Colleges," *New York Times*, February 18, 1987, http://www.nytimes.com /1987/02/18/opinion/our-greedy-colleges.html?pagewanted=all&src=pm.

71. Alisa F. Cunningham, "Study of College Costs and Prices, 1988–89 to 1997–98" U.S. Department of Education, National Center for Education Statistics (2008), http://nces.ed.gov /pubs2002/2002157.pdf.

72. St. John, *Refinancing the College Dream*, 105.

73. "Issue Brief #1: Who Pays for Higher Education? Changing Patterns in Cost, Price, and Subsidies," *Delta Project on Postsecondary Education Costs, Productivity, and Accountability* (November 29, 2010), http://eric.ed.gov/?id=ED535368.

74. "Increasing Return on Investment from Federal Student Aid," National College Access Network (2012): 4, http://www.collegeaccess.org/images/documents/ROIfromFSAExecSum.pdf.

75. Gladieux, "Low-Income Students," 33–34.

76. Shannon M. Mahan, "Federal Pell Grant Program of the Higher Education Act: Background, Recent Changes, and Current Legislative Issues," Congressional Research Service (2011): 25–26, Fig.6, http://cdn.cnsnews.com/documents/FEDERAL%20PELL%20GRANT% 20PROGRAM-CRS-MAY-12-2011.pdf; "Increasing Return on Investment," 4.

77. Caroline Ratcliffe and Signe-Mary McKernan, "Forever in Your Debt: Who Has Student Loan Debt, and Who's Worried?" Urban Institute (June 26, 2013): 7, https://www.urban.org /sites/default/files/publication/23736/412849-Forever-in-Your-Debt-Who-Has-Student -Loan-Debt-and-Who-s-Worried-.PDF.,

78. Pusser, "Higher Education, Markets, and the Preservation of the Public Good," 32–34.

79. Zumeta et al., *Financing American Higher Education*, 70–76.

80. "Increasing Return on Investment," 5.

81. Ibid., 33–34; Gladieux, "Low-Income Students," 24.

82. "Increasing Return on Investment," 5–6.

83. Zumeta et al., *Financing American Higher Education*, 168.

84. Amanda Harmon Cooley, "The Need for Legal Reform of the For-Profit Educational Industry," *Tennessee Law Review* 79, no. 3 (Spring 2012): 515.

85. Consumer Financial Protection Bureau, "Private Student Loans," 3, 21–24, 27–29.

86. David M. Herszenhorn, "Student Loan Bill Poised to Pass in Health Vote," *New York Times*, March 21, 2010, http://www.nytimes.com/2010/03/22/education/22pell.html.

87. Daniel de Vise, "State Grant Aid Goes Increasingly to the Wealthy," *Washington Post*, May 15, 2012, http://www.washingtonpost.com/blogs/college-inc/post/state-grant-aid-goes-increasingly-to-the-wealthy/2012/05/15/gIQARIvHRU_blog.html; Baum et al., "Beyond Need and Merit: Strengthening State Grant Programs," Brookings Institution (2012), http://www.brookings.edu/research/reports/2012/05/08-grants-chingos-whitehurst.

88. Zumeta et al., *Financing American Higher Education*, 76; Carl Vinson Institute of Government, "HOPE Scholarship Joint Study Commission Report" (2003): 15–16. For a discussion of the popularity of state merit-based scholarship programs, including Georgia HOPE and Florida Bright Futures, see Jeffrey Selingo, "Questioning the Merit of Merit Scholarships," *Chronicle of Higher Education*, January 9, 2001, A20; http://chronicle.com/article/Questioning-the-Merit-of-Merit/15616.

89. National Association of State Student Grant & Aid Programs, "42nd Annual Survey Report on State-Sponsored Student Financial Aid 2010–2011" (2012): 9–10, http://www.nassgap.org/viewrepository.aspx?categoryID=3#.

90. Robert H. Reid, *American Degree Mills: A Study of Their Operations and of Existing and Potential Ways to Control Them* (Whitefish, MT: Literacy Licensing LLC, 2012).

91. Michael McPherson, Morton Schapiro, and Gordon Winston, "The Economic Analogy," Williams Project on the Economics of Higher Education Discussion Paper No. 37 (1996): 2–13.

92. Stephen Burd, "Undermining Pell, Volume II: How Colleges' Pursuit of Prestige and Revenue is Hurting Low-Income Students," New America Foundation (2013): 3–4.

93. Scott Jaschik and Doug Lederman, "The 2013 Inside Higher Ed Survey of College & University Admissions Directors," Washington, DC: Inside Higher Ed and Gallup, Inc., 2013, https://sparkroom.com/wp-content/uploads/2013/09/IHE_2013AdmissionsSurvey-final.pdf.; Matthews, "Tuition Is Too Damn High."

94. Douglass, *The Conditions for Admission: Access, Equity, and the Social Contract of Public Universities* (Palo Alto: Stanford University Press, 2007).

95. Perna et al., "Role of College Counseling," 138–139.

96. G. Kena, W. Hussar, J. McFarland, C. de Brey, L. Musu-Gillette, X. Wang, J. Zhang, A. Rathbun, S. Wilkinson-Flicker, M. Diliberti, A. Barmer, F. Bullock Mann, and E. Dunlop Velez, "Characteristics of Postsecondary Faculty," in *The Condition of Education 2016* (NCES 2016-144) (Washington, DC: U.S. Department of Education, National Center for Education Statistics, 2016), https://nces.ed.gov/pubsearch/pubsinfo.asp?pubid=2016144.

97. Lani Guinier, "Admissions Rituals as Political Acts: Guardians at the Gates of Our Democratic Ideals," *Harvard Law Review* 117 (2003): 135–138, 143–144, 151, 159.

98. Robert Schaeffer, "Test Scores Do Not Equal Merit," in *SAT Wars: The Case for Test-Optional College Admissions*, ed. Joseph A. Soares (New York: Teachers College Press, 2012), 153, 157.

99. Tamar Lewin, "A New SAT Aims to Realign with Schoolwork," *New York Times*, March 5, 2014, http://www.nytimes.com/2014/03/06/education/major-changes-in-sat-announced-by-college-board.html?_r=.

100. See also Claire Robertson-Kraft and Angela L. Duckworth, "True Grit: Trait-Level Perseverance and Passion for Long-Term Goals Predicts Effectiveness and Retention among Novice Teachers," *Teachers College Record* 116, no. 3 (2014): 16, https://www.ncbi.nlm.nih.gov/pmc/articles/PMC4211426.

101. Martha Allman, "Going Test Optional," in *SAT Wars: The Case for Test-Optional College Admissions*, ed. Joseph A. Soares (New York: Teacher's College Press, 2012), 169, 175.

102. John Aubrey Douglass, "SAT Wars at the University of California," in ibid., 50, 52, 61–62. See also *Association of Christian Schools International v. Stearns, et al.*, "Expert Report of John Aubrey Douglass Regarding the History of UC Admissions," 3–4, http://ncse.com/files/pub/legal/stearns/expert_witness_douglass.pdf.

103. Allman, "Going Test Optional," 175; Schaeffer, "Test Scores Do Not Equal Merit," 165.

104. Richard J. Herrnstein and Charles Murray, *Bell Curve: Intelligence and Class Structure in American Life* (Detroit: Free Press, 1994); Richard Sander, "The Consideration of Race in UCLA Undergraduate Admissions," UCLA School of Law (October 20, 2012), http://www.seaphe.org/pdf/uclaadmissions.pdf.

105. William G. Bowen. Matthew M. Chingos, and Michael S. McPherson, *Crossing the Finish Line: Completing College at America's Public Universities* (Princeton: Princeton University Press, 2009), 101–108; Anthony P. Carnevale and Jeff Strohl, *Separate and Unequal: How Higher Education Reinforces the Intergenerational Reproduction of White Racial Privilege* (Washington, DC: Georgetown Center on Education and the Workforce, 2013), 29–31.

106. Paul Tough, *How Children Succeed: Grit, Curiosity, and the Hidden Power of Character* (New York: Mariner Books, 2013), 150–154.

107. Guinier, "Admissions Rituals," 142.

108. Ibid. 146–147.

109. Robert J. Sternberg, "College Admissions Assessments: New Techniques for a New Millennium," in *SAT Wars*, ed. Soares (2012), 85, 87.

110. Guinier, "Admissions Rituals," 159.

111. Ibid., 161–162; Danielle Holley and Delia Spencer, "The Texas Ten Percent Plan," *Harvard Civil Rights-Civil Liberties Law Review* 34, no. 1 (1999): 245.

112. See, e.g., Michelle Adams, "Isn't It Ironic? The Central Paradox at the Heart of 'Percentage Plans,'" *Ohio State Law Journal* 62, no. 6 (2001): 1729, 1735; Omari Scott Simmons, "For-Profits and the Market Paradox," *Wake Forest Law Review* 48, no. 2 (2013): 333.

113. *Fisher v. University of Texas at Austin*, 645 F. Supp. 2d 587 (W.D. Tex. 2009), *aff'd* 631 F.3d 213 (5th Cir. 2011), *rev'd* 133 S. Ct. 2411 (2013). See also Eric Hoover, "Colleges Contemplate a 'Race Neutral' Future," *Chronicle of Higher Education* (October 14, 2013), http://chronicle.com/article/Colleges-Contemplate-a/142291/.

114. Thomas J. Kane, and James E. Ryan, "Why 'Fisher' Means More Work for Colleges," *Chronicle of Higher Education* (July 29, 2013), http://chronicle.com/article/Why-Fisher-Means-More-Work/140567/.

115. William Darity Jr., Ashwini Deshpande, and Thomas Weisskopf, "Who Is Eligible? Should Affirmative Action be Group- or Class-Based?" *American Journal of Economics and Sociology* 70, no. 1 (2011): 245–246, doi: 10.1111/j.1536-7150.2010.00770.x.

116. Michael Barone, "After *Fisher v. University of Texas*, colleges can use race as part of a 'holistic' admissions process," *National Review* (July 6, 2016), http://www.nationalreview.com/article/437500/supreme-court-fisher-v-university-texas-affirmative-action-case-preserves-race. See *Fisher v. University of Texas at Austin*, 136 S. Ct. 2198 (2016).

117. See Alicia C. Dowd, John J. Cheslock, and Tatiana Melguizo, "Transfer Access from Community Colleges and the Distribution of Elite Higher Education," *Journal of Higher Education* 79, no. 4 (2008): 459–460; Tatiana Melguizo and Alicia C. Dowd, "The Study of Economic, Informational, and Cultural Barriers to Community College Student Transfer Access at Selective Institutions," (2008): 36–37, http://citeseerx.ist.psu.edu/viewdoc/download?rep=rep1&type=pdf&doi=10.1.1.205.9468.

CHAPTER 6   PARTING THOUGHTS

1. William G. Bowen, Derek Bok, Matthew M. Chingos, and Michael S. McPherson, *Crossing the Finish Line: Completing College at America's Public Universities* (Princeton: Princeton University Press, 2009), 432–433; see also 22, 447–448.

2. David B. Bills, "Credentials, Signals, and Screens: Explaining the Relationship between Schooling and Job Assignment," *Review of Educational Research* 73, no. 4 (Winter 2003): 441.

3. Pitirim A. Sorokin, *Social and Cultural Mobility* (Detroit: Free Press, 1959), 170–171; Anthony P. Carnevale and Jeff Strohl, *Separate and Unequal: How Higher Education Reinforces the Intergenerational Reproduction of White Racial Privilege* (Washington, DC: Georgetown Public Policy Institute, 2013), 29–31, https://cew.georgetown.edu/wp-content/uploads/2014/11/SeparateUnequal.FR_.pdf.

4. Bowen et al., *Crossing the Finish Line*, 434.

5. Ibid.

6. Byron G. Auguste, Bryan Hancock, and Martha Laboissiere, "The Economic Cost of the US Education Gap," *McKinsey & Co.* (2009): 99; http://mckinseyonsociety.com/the-economic-impact-of-the-achievement-gap-in-americas-schools/.

7. Bowen et al., *Crossing the Finish Line*, 263. For an additional list of benefits, see Brian Pusser, "Higher Education, Markets, and the Preservation of the Public Good," in *Earnings from Learning: The Rise of For-Profit Universities*, eds. David W. Breneman, Brian Pusser, and Sarah E. Turner (Albany: State University of New York Press, 2006), 36–38.

8. Henry Hansmann, "The Evolving Economic Structure of Higher Education," *University of Chicago Law Review* 79, no. 1 (Winter 2012): 159.

9. Walter McMahon, *Higher Learning, Greater Good: The Private and Social Benefits of Higher Education* (Baltimore: Johns Hopkins University Press), 326, asserting that most higher education benefits are individual.

10. Ronald J. Daniels, Phillip M. Spector, and Rebecca Goetz, "Fault Lines in the Compact: Higher Education and the Public Interest in the United States," *Carnegie Reporter* (2014): 73–74, http://higheredreporter.carnegie.org/wpcontent/uploads/2014/02/Daniels_Spector_Goetz_Fault-Lines.pdf.

11. Bowen et al., *Crossing the Finish Line*, 358.

12. Ibid., 342.

13. White House, Office of the Press Secretary, "FACT SHEET: The President and First Lady's Call to Action on College Opportunity," https://www.whitehouse.gov/the-press-office/2014/01/16/fact-sheet-president-and-first-lady-s-call-action-college-opportunity.

14. White House, The Reach Higher Initiative, https://www.whitehouse.gov/reach-higher.

15. National Consortium for School Counseling and Postsecondary Success, http://www.ncscps.org.

16. Lee Staples, *Roots to Power: A Manual for Grassroots Organizing* (Santa Barbara: Praeger Publishers, 2004), 62, 226, 295.

17. Anthony P. Carnevale, Nicole Smith, and Jeff Strohl, "Help Wanted: Projections of Jobs and Education Requirements through 2018," *Georgetown University Center on Education and the Workforce* (June 2010): 25, 1, https://cew.georgetown.edu/wp-content/uploads/2014/12/fullreport.pdf.

18. Bowen et al., *Crossing the Finish Line*, 161–162.

19. John Dewey, *Democracy and Education* (Detroit: Free Press, 1916), 101–102, 114; see also Martha Minow, in Brown's *Wake: Legacies of America's Educational Landmark* (London: Oxford University Press, 2010), 138.

BIBLIOGRAPHY

Adams, Michelle. "Isn't It Ironic? The Central Paradox at the Heart of 'Percentage Plans.'" *Ohio State Law Journal* 62 (2001): 1729–1780.

Allman, Martha. "Going Test Optional." In *SAT Wars: The Case for Test-Optional College Admissions*, edited by Joseph A. Soares. New York: Teacher's College Press, 2012, 169–176.

Alon, Sigal, and Marta Tienda. "Assessing the 'Mismatch' Hypothesis: Differences in College Graduation Rates by Institutional Selectivity." *Sociology of Education* 78, no. 4 (2005): 294–315.

Ashkenas, Jeremy, Haeyoun Park, and Adam Pearce. "Even with Affirmative Action, Blacks and Hispanics Are More Underrepresented at Top Colleges Than 35 Years Ago." *New York Times*, 24 August 2017. https://www.nytimes.com/interactive/2017/08/24/us/affirmative-action .html?mcubz=0.

Aspen Institute. "Core Principles for New Accountability in Education." Aspen, CO: Aspen Institute Education & Society Program, November 2009. http://www.aspeninstitute.org /sites/default/files/content/docs/pubs/Core_Principles_April2010.pdf.

Association of Christian Schools International v. Stearns, et al. "Expert Report of John Aubrey Douglass Regarding the History of UC Admissions." http://ncse.com/files/pub/legal/stearns /expert_witness_douglass.pdf.

Auguste, Byron G., Bryan Hancock, and Martha Laboissiere. "The Economic Cost of the US Education Gap." McKinsey & Co., 2009. http://mckinseyonsociety.com/the-economic -impact-of-the-achievement-gap-in-americas-schools/.

Aurelius, Marcus. *Meditations*. Translated by Gregory Hays. New York: Modern Library, 1997.

Barone, Michael. "After *Fisher v. University of Texas*, Colleges Can Use Race as Part of a 'Holistic' Admissions Process." *National Review* (July 6, 2016). http://www.nationalreview.com /article/437500/supreme-court-fisher-v-university-texas-affirmative-action-case-preser ves-race.

Baum, Sandy, Jennifer Ma, and Kathleen Payea. "Education Pays 2010: The Benefits of Higher Education for Individuals and Society." Washington, DC: College Board Advocacy and Policy Center, 2010. http://trends.collegeboard.org/sites/default/files/education-pays -2010-full-report.pdf.

Belton v. Gebhart, 33 Del. Ch. 144 (Del. 1952).

Bennett, William J. "Our Greedy Colleges." *New York Times*, February 18, 1987. http://www .nytimes.com/1987/02/18/opinion/our-greedy-colleges.html?pagewanted=all&src=pm.

Bettinger, Eric P., Bridget Terry Long, Phillip Oreopoulos, and Lisa Sanbonmatsu. "The Role of Application Assistance and Information in College Decisions: Results from the H&R Block FASFA Experiment." *Quarterly Journal of Economics* 1277, no. 3 (2012): 1205–1242.

Bills, David B. "Credentials, Signals, and Screens: Explaining the Relationship between Schooling and Job Assignment." *Review of Educational Research* 73, no. 4 (Winter 2003): 441–449.

Bourdieu, Pierre. "The Forms of Capital." In *Handbook of Theory and Research for the Sociology of Education*, edited by John G. Richardson, 241–258. New York: Greenwood Press, 1986.

Bowen, William G., and Derek Bok. *The Shape of the River*. Princeton: Princeton University Press, 1998.

Bowen, William G., Matthew M. Chingos, and Michael S. McPherson. *Crossing the Finish Line: Completing College at America's Public Universities.* Princeton: Princeton University Press, 2009.

Bowen, William G., Martin A. Kurzweil, and Eugene M. Tobin. *Equity and Excellence in American Higher Education.* Charlottesville: University of Virginia Press, 2005.

Brewer, Dominic J., Eric R. Eide, and Ronald G. Ehrenberg. "Does It Pay to Attend an Elite Private College? Cross-Cohort Evidence on the Effects of College Type on Earnings." *Journal of Human Resources* 34, no. 1 (1999): 104–123.

Brown Center on Education Policy at Brookings. "Beyond Need and Merit: Strengthening State Grant Programs." Washington, DC: Brookings Institution, May 8, 2012. http://www .brookings.edu/research/reports/2012/05/08-grants-chingos-whitehurst.

Brown v. Board of Education, 75 S.Ct 753 (1955).

Brown-Nagin, Tomiko. "Rethinking Proxies for Disadvantage in Higher Education: A First Generation Student's Project." *University of Chicago Legal Forum* (2014): 40. http:// chicagounbound.uchicago.edu/uclf/vol2014/iss1/8.

Buell, Cindy. "Models of Mentoring in Communication." *Communication Education* 53, no. 1 (2004): 56–73.

Bulah v. Gebhart, 33 Del.Ch. 144 (Del. 1952).

Bulman, George. "The Effect of Access to College Assessments on Enrollment and Attainment." *American Economic Journal: Applied Economics* 7, no. 4 (2015): 1–36.

Burd, Stephen. "Undermining Pell, Volume II: How Colleges' Pursuit of Prestige and Revenue is Hurting Low-Income Students." Washington, DC: New America Foundation, 2014, 3–4. https://www.luminafoundation.org/files/resources/undermining-pell-vol2.pdf.

Carnevale, Anthony P., and Stephen J. Rose. "Socioeconomic Status, Race/Ethnicity, and Selective College Admissions." In *America's Untapped Resource: Low-Income Students in Higher Education,* edited by Richard D. Kahlenberg, 101–156. New York: Century Foundation Press, 2004.

Carnevale, Anthony P., and Jeff Strohl. *Separate and Unequal: How Higher Education Reinforces the Intergenerational Reproduction of White Racial Privilege.* Washington, DC: Georgetown Public Policy Institute. 2013. https://cew.georgetown.edu/wp-content/uploads/2014/11 /SeparateUnequal.FR_.pdf.

Carnevale, Anthony P., Nicole Smith, and Jeff Strohl. "Help Wanted: Projections of Jobs and Education Requirements through 2018: Executive Summary." Washington, DC: Georgetown University Center on Education and the Workforce, June 2010. https://cew.georgetown.edu /wp-content/uploads/2014/12/HelpWanted.ExecutiveSummary.pdf.

Carrell, Scott E., and Bruce Sacerdote. "Late Interventions Matter Too: The Case of College Coaching in New Hampshire." Working Paper no. 19031. Washington, DC: National Bureau of Economic Research, 2012.

Chicago Public Schools. "Choose Your Future." https://chooseyourfuture.cps.edu.

Coleman, James S. "Social Capital in the Creation of Human Capital." *American Journal of Sociology* 94, Supplement: Organizations and Institutions: Sociological and Economic Approaches to the Analysis of Social Structure (1988): S110–111.

Colorado Department of Higher Education. "College in Colorado." http://collegeincolorado.org.

Connecting Generations. "The Robert A. Kasey, Jr. Lifetime Achievement Award." http://www .connecting-generations.org/john-hollis-award/.

Consumer Financial Protection Bureau. "Private Student Loans." Washington, DC: CFPB, August 29, 2012. http://files.consumerfinance.gov/f/201207_cfpb_Reports_Private -Student-Loans.

Cooley, Amanda Harmon. "The Need for Legal Reform of the For-Profit Educational Industry." *Tennessee Law Review* 79, no. 515 (2012): 515–571.

Cooper, Christopher A., and H. Gibbs Knotts. *The New Politics of North Carolina.* Chapel Hill: University of North Carolina Press, 2012.

Corwin, Zoe Blumberg, and William G. Tierney. *Getting There–and Beyond: Building a Culture of College-Going in High Schools.* Los Angeles: University of Southern California Center for Higher Education Policy Analysis, 2007. http://files.eric.ed.gov/fulltext/ED498731.pdf.

Credé, Marcus, Michael C. Tynan, and Peter D. Hams. "Much Ado about Grit: A Meta-Analytic Synthesis of the Grit Literature." *Journal of Personality and Social Psychology* 113, no. 3 (2017): 492–511.

Cunningham, Alisa F. "Study of College Costs and Prices, 1988–89 to 1997–98." Washington, DC: National Center for Education Statistics, 2008. http://nces.ed.gov/pubs2002/2002157.pdf.

Dale, Stacy Berg, and Alan B. Krueger. "Estimating the Payoff to Attending a More Selective College: An Application of Selection on Observables and Unobservables." *Quarterly Journal of Economics* 117, no. 4 (2002): 1491–1527.

Daniels, Ronald J., Phillip M. Spector, and Rebecca Goetz. "Fault Lines in the Compact: Higher Education and the Public Interest in the United States." *Carnegie Reporter* (2014): 73–74. http://higheredreporter.carnegie.org/wpcontent/uploads/2014/02/Daniels_Spector_Goetz_Fault-Lines.pdf.

Darity, Jr., William, Ashwini Deshpande, and Thomas Weisskopf. "Who Is Eligible? Should Affirmative Action Be Group- or Class-Based?" *American Journal of Economics and Sociology* 70 (2011): 238–268.

de Vise, Daniel. "State Grant Aid Goes Increasingly to the Wealthy." *Washington Post,* May 15, 2012. http://www.washingtonpost.com/blogs/college-inc/post/state-grant-aid-goes-increasingly-to-the-wealthy/2012/05/15/gIQARIvHRU_blog.html.

Delaware Department of Education. "Delaware Public Education at a Glance: 2014–15." Wilmingon, DE: Rodel Foundation of Delaware, 2015.

Delta Project on Postsecondary Education Costs, Productivity, and Accountability. "Issue Brief #1: Who Pays for Higher Education: Changing Patterns in Cost, Price, and Subsidies." Washington, DC: Delta Project, November 29, 2010. http://eric.ed.gov/?id=ED535368.

Deming, W. Edwards. "On Errors in Surveys." *American Sociological Review,* 9, no. 4 (August 1994): 359–369.

Denzin, Norman K., and Yvonna S. Lincoln, eds. *Handbook of Qualitative Research.* Thousand Oaks, CA: Sage Publications, 1994.

Desilver, Drew. "U.S. Income Inequality, on Rise for Decades, Is Now Highest since 1928." Washington, DC: Pew Research Center, December 5, 2013. http://www.pewresearch.org/fact-tank/2013/12/05/u-s-income-inequality-on-rise-for-decades-is-now-highest-since-1928/.

Dewey, John. *Democracy and Education; An Introduction to the Philosophy of Education.* New York: Macmillan, 1916, 2016.

———. *Experience and Education.* New York: Free Press, 1938, 1997.

Domonoske, Camila. "Supreme Court Declines Republican Bid to Revive North Carolina Voter ID Law." National Public Radio, May 15, 2017. https://www.npr.org/sections/thetwo-way/2017/05/15/528457693/supreme-court-declines-republican-bid-to-revive-north-carolina-voter-id-law.

Douglass, John Aubrey. *The Conditions for Admission: Access, Equity, and the Social Contract of Public Universities.* Stanford, CA: Stanford University Press, 2007.

———. "SAT Wars at the University of California." In *SAT Wars: The Case for Test-Optional College Admissions,* edited by Joseph A. Soares. New York: Teacher's College Press, 2012, 50–68.

Dowd, Alicia C., John J. Cheslock, and Tatiana Melguizo, "Transfer Access from Community Colleges and the Distribution of Elite Higher Education." *Journal of Higher Education* 79, no. 4 (2008): 442–472.

Dubois, David L., Nelson Portillo, Jean E. Rhodes, Naida Silverthorn, and Jeffrey C. Valentine. "How Effective Are Mentoring Programs for Youth? A Systematic Assessment of the Evidence." *Psychological Science in the Public Interest* 12, no. 2 (2011): 57–91. https://teammates .org/wp-content/uploads/2011/01/DuBoisetalMeta.pdf.

Duckworth, Angela L., Christopher Peterson, Michael D. Matthews, and Dennis R. Kelly. "Grit: Perseverance and Passion for Long-Term Goals." *Journal of Personality and Social Psychology* 92, no. 6 (2007): 1087–1101.

Durham, Rachel E., and P. Johnelle Smith. "Nonmetropolitan Status and Kindergarteners' Early Literacy Skills: Is There a Rural Disadvantage?" *Rural Sociology* 71, no. 4 (2006): 625–661.

Eagan, Kevin, Ellen Bara Stolzenberg, Joseph J. Ramirez, Melissa C. Aragon, Maria Ramirez Suchard, and Sylvia Hurtado. *The American Freshman: National Norms Fall 2014*. Los Angeles: Higher Education Research Institute at UCLA, 2014 (2014).

Eide, Eric R., Dominic J. Brewer, and Ronald G. Ehrenberg. "Does It Pay to Attend an Elite Private College? Evidence on the Effects of Undergraduate College Quality on Graduate School Attendance." *Economics of Education Review* 17, no. 4 (1998): 371–376.

Ellison, Ralph. *Going to the Territory*. New York: Random House, 1986.

———. "That Same Pain, That Same Pleasure: *An Interview*." In *The Collected Essays of Ralph Ellison*, edited by John F. Callahan. New York: Modern Library, 1995, 63–81.

Evans, Robert. "Reframing the Achievement Gap." *Phi Delta Kappa* 86, no. 8 (April 2005): 582–589.

Family Education Rights and Privacy Act, 20 U.S.C. § 1232(g).

Family Educational Rights and Privacy, 34 C.F.R. § 99 (2002).

Fausset, Richard. "Bathroom Law Repeal Leaves Few Pleased in North Carolina." *New York Times*, March 30, 2017. https://www.nytimes.com/2017/03/30/us/north-carolina-senate -acts-to-repeal-restrictive-bathroom-law.html.

Federal Student Aid Office. "FAFSA Completion by High School and Public School District." Washington, DC: US Department of Education, n.d. https://studentaid.ed.gov/sa/about /data-center/student/application-volume/fafsa-completion-high-school.

Fisher v. University of Texas at Austin. 645 F. Supp. 2d 587 (W.D. Tex. 2009). Affirmed 631 F.3d 213 (5th Cir. 2011). Reversed 133 S. Ct. 2411 (2013).

Forman, Jr., James. "The Rise and Fall of School Vouchers: A Story of Religion, Race, and Politics." *UCLA Law Review* 54, no. 547 (2007): 547–604.

Gándara, Patricia, and Deborah Bial. "Paving the Way to Postsecondary Education: K–12 Intervention Programs for Underrepresented Youth." Washington, DC: National Postsecondary Education Cooperative, 2001. http://nces.ed.gov/pubs2001/2001205.PDF.

Gardner, Howard. "Paroxysms of Choice." *New York Review of Books,* October 19, 2000. http:// www.nybooks.com/articles/archives/2000/oct/19/paroxysms-of-choice/.

Gilbert, Claire, and Donald Heller. "The Truman Commission and Its Impact on Federal Higher Education Policy from 1947 to 2010." Working Paper 9. University Park: Pennsylvania State University, 2010. https://ed.psu.edu/cshe/working-papers/wp-9.

Gladieux, Lawrence. "Low Income Students and the Affordability of Higher Education." In *America's Untapped Resource: Low-Income Students in Higher Education*, edited by Richard D. Kahlenberg, 32–34. New York: The Century Foundation, 2004.

"Greensboro Sit-In." History Channel. http://www.history.com/topics/black-history/the -greensboro-sit-in.

Greenwald, Anthony, and Linda Hamilton Krieger. "Implicit Bias: Scientific Foundations." *California Law Review* 94, no. 4 (July 2006): 957–958.

Grutter v. Bollinger, 123 S.Ct 2325 (2003).

Guinier, Lani. "Admissions Rituals as Political Acts: Guardians at the Gates of Our Democratic Ideals." *Harvard Law Review* 117 (2003): 125–221.

———. *The Tyranny of the Meritocracy: Democratizing Higher Education in America*. Boston: Beacon Press, 2015.

Hansmann, Henry. "The Evolving Economic Structure of Higher Education." *University of Chicago Law Review* 79, no. 1 (Winter 2012): 159–183.

Hartline, Julie, and Debra C. Cobia. "School Counselors: Closing Achievement Gaps and Writing Results Reports." *Professional School Counseling* 16, no. 1 (October 2012): 71–79.

Hawkins, David A., and Melissa Clinedinst. "State of College Admission 2006." Alexandria, VA: National Association for College Admissions Counseling, 2006. https://www.immagic.com/eLibrary/ARCHIVES/GENERAL/NACAC_US/N060508H.pdf.

Hayman, Jr., Robert L. "A History of Race in Delaware: 1639–1950." In *Choosing Equality: Essays and Narratives on the Desegregation Experience*, edited by Robert L. Hayman Jr. and Leland Ware, 21–68. University Park: Pennsylvania State University Press, 2009.

———, and Leland Ware, eds. *Choosing Equality: Essays and Narratives on the Desegregation Experience*. University Park: Pennsylvania State University Press, 2009.

Herrnstein, Richard J., and Charles Murray. *The Bell Curve: Intelligence and Class Structure in American Life*. New York: Free Press, 1994.

Herszenhorn, David M. "Student Loan Bill Poised to Pass in Health Vote." *New York Times*, March 21, 2010. http://www.nytimes.com/2010/03/22/education/22pell.html?_r=0.

Holley, Danielle, and Delia Spencer. "The Texas Ten Percent Plan." *Harvard Civil Rights-Civil Liberties Law Review* 34, no. 245 (1999): 245–278.

Hoover, Eric. "Colleges Contemplate a 'Race Neutral' Future." *Chronicle of Higher Education*, October 14, 2013. http://chronicle.com/article/Colleges-Contemplate-a/142291/.

Hopwood v. Texas. 236 F.3d 256 (5th Cir. 2000).

Horace. "Adversity." In *A Dictionary of Thoughts: Being a Cyclopedia of Laconic Quotations from the Best Authors of the World, Both Ancient and Modern*, compiled by Tryon Edwards. Detroit: F.B. Dickerson Company, 1897, 1908.

Hout, Michael. "More Universalism, Less Structural Mobility: The American Occupational Structure in the 1980s." *American Journal of Sociology* 93, no. 6 (May 1988): 1358–1400.

Hoxby, Caroline, and Christopher Avery. "The Missing 'One-Offs': The Hidden Supply of High-Achieving, Low-Income Students." *Brookings Papers on Economic Activity* (Spring 2013): 1–66. http://www.brookings.edu/~/media/projects/bpea/ spring%202013/2013a_hoxby.pdf.

Hyde, Catherine Ryan. *Pay It Forward*. New York: Simon & Schuster, 1999.

James, Jr., Harvey S. "Self-Selection Bias in Business Ethics Research." *Business Ethics Quarterly* 16, no. 4 (October 2006): 559–577.

Jaschik, Scott, and Doug Lederman, "The 2013 Inside Higher Ed Survey of College & University Admissions Directors." Washington, DC: Inside Higher Ed and Gallup, Inc., 2013. https://sparkroom.com/wp-content/uploads/2013/09/IHE_2013AdmissionsSurvey-final.pdf.

Johnson, Jr., James J., and William Rand Kenan, Jr. "Major Trends Facing North Carolina: Implications for Our State and the University of North Carolina." Chapel Hill: University of North Carolina Tomorrow Commission, n.d. https://old.northcarolina.edu/nctomorrow/Johnson_-_Demographics_Brief-Final1.pdf.

Johnson, Jean, and Jon Rochkind with Amber Ott and Samantha duPont. "Can I Get a Little Advice Here? How an Overstretched High School Guidance System Is Undermining Students' College Aspiration." *Public Agenda* (2010). https://www.publicagenda.org/files /pdf/can-i-get-a-little-advice-here.pdf.

Kane, Thomas J., and James E. Ryan. "Why 'Fisher' Means More Work for Colleges." *Chronicle of Higher Education*, July 29, 2013. http://chronicle.com/article/Why-Fisher-Means -More-Work/140567/.

Kena, G., W. Hussar, J. McFarland, C. de Brey, L. Musu-Gillette, X. Wang, J. Zhang, A. Rathbun, S. Wilkinson-Flicker, M. Diliberti, A. Barmer, F. Bullock Mann, and E. Dunlop Velez. "Characteristics of Postsecondary Faculty." In *The Condition of Education 2016*. Washington, DC: US Department of Education, National Center for Education Statistics, 2016. https:// nces.ed.gov/pubsearch/pubsinfo.asp?pubid=2016144.

Kidder, William C., and Jay Rosner. "How the SAT Creates Built-in-Headwinds: An Educational and Legal Analysis of Disparate Impact." *Santa Clara Law Review* 43, no. 1 (2002): 131–212.

King, Jacqueline E. "The Decision to Go to College: Attitudes and Experiences Associated with College Attendance among Low-Income Students." Washington, DC: College Board, 1996. http://files.eric.ed.gov/fulltext/ED398775.pdf.

Kingi, Hautahi. "The Āwhina Effect." Reducing Achievement Gaps in STEM: Promising International Research, Policies and Practices Conference, May 22, 2017. http://achievestem .hsoc.gatech.edu/wp-content/uploads/sites/587/2017/03/Hautahi_AwhinaPresentation .pdf.

Klayman, Joshua. "Varieties of Confirmation Bias." In *Decision Making from a Cognitive Perspective*, edited by Jerome Busemeyer, Reid Hastie, and Douglas L. Medin. San Diego: Academic Press, 1995, 385–418.

Kochhar, Rakesh. Richard Fry, Gabriel Velasco, and Seth Motel. "Wealth Gaps Rise to Record Highs between Whites, Blacks and Hispanics." Washington, DC: Pew Research Center, July 26, 2011. http://www.pewsocialtrends.org/files/2011/07/SDT-Wealth-Report_7-26-11 _FINAL.pdf.

Koslowski, Barbara, and Mariano Maqueda. "What Is Confirmation Bias and When Do People Actually Have It?" *Merril-Palmer Quarterly* 39, no. 1 (January 1993): 104–130.

Lawyers Committee for Civil Rights Under Law. "Framework for Providing All Students an Opportunity to Learn through Reauthorization of the Elementary and Secondary Education Act." Washington, DC: Lawyers Committee for Civil Rights Under Law, 2010. https:// lawyerscommittee.org/wp-content/uploads/2015/07/Framework-for-Providing-All -Students-an-Opportunity-to-Learn.pdf.

Levin, Henry M. "Education as a Public and Private Good." *Journal of Policy Analysis and Management* 6, no. 4 (1987): 629–630.

Lewin, Tamar. "A New SAT Aims to Realign with Schoolwork." *New York Times*, March 5, 2014. http://www.nytimes.com/2014/03/06/education/major-changes-in-sat-announced-by -college-board.html?_r=.

Lin, Nan. *Social Capital: A Theory of Social Structure and Action*. Cambridge, UK: Cambridge University Press, 2001.

Loury, Glenn. "A Dynamic Theory of Racial Income Differences." In *Women, Minorities, and Employment Discrimination*, edited by Phyllis A. Wallace and Annette M. LaMond. Lexington, MA: Lexington Books, 1977, 153–186.

Lynch, Mamie, Jennifer Engle, and Jose L. Cruz. "Lifting the Fog on Inequitable Financial Aid Policies." Washington, DC: Education Trust, November 2014. https://edtrust.org/resource /lifting-the-fog-on-inequitable-financial-aid-policies/.

————. "Priced Out: How the Wrong Financial-Aid Policies Hurt Low-Income Students." Washington DC: Education Trust, June 1, 2011. https://edtrust.org/resource/priced-out -how-the-wrong-financial-aid-policies-hurt-low-income-students/.

Mahan, Shannon M. "Federal Pell Grant Program of the Higher Education Act: Background, Recent Changes, and Current Legislative Issues." CRS Report No. R41437. Washington, DC: Congressional Research Service, 2011. https://www.cnsnews.com/sites/default/files /documents/FEDERAL%20PELL%20GRANT%20PROGRAM-CRS-MAY-12-2011.pdf.

Massey, Douglas S., Camille Z. Charles, Garvey F. Lundy, and Mary J. Fischer, *The Source of the River: The Social Origins of Freshmen at America's Selective Colleges and Universities*. Princeton: Princeton University Press, 2006.

Maton, Kenneth I., Freeman A. Hrabowski III, and Carol L. Schmitt, "African-American College Students Excelling in the Sciences: College and Postcollege Outcomes in the Meyerhoff Scholars Program." *Journal of Research in Science Teaching* 37, no. 7 (2000): 629–654. http://cssiacyberwars.org/pdf/20000255-AfricanAmericanCollegeStudentsExcellingint heSciences-CollegeandPost-CollegeOutcomesintheMeyerhoffScholarsProgram.pdf.

Matthews, Dylan. "The Tuition Is Too Damn High, Part VIII: Is This All Rich Kids' Fault?" *Washington Post*, September 4, 2013. http://www.washingtonpost.com/blogs/wonkblog /wp/2013/09/03/the-tuition-is-too-damn-high-part-vii-is-government-aid-actually -making-college-more-expensive.

May, Todd. "ED Announces FAFSA Completion Project Expansion." *Official Blog of the US Department of Education*, May 31, 2012. http://www.ed.gov/blog/2012/05/ed-announces -fafsa-completion-project-expansion/.

McDonough, Patricia M. *Choosing Colleges: How Social Class and Schools Structure Opportunity*. Albany: State University of New York Press, 1997.

————. "Counseling and College Counseling in America's High Schools." Alexandria, VA: National Association for College Admission Counseling, 2004. http://inpathways.net /McDonough%20Report.pdf.

————. "Counseling Matters: Knowledge, Assistance, and Organizational Commitment in College Preparation." In *Preparing for College: Nine Elements of Effective Outreach*, edited by William G. Tierney, Zoe B. Corwin, and Julia E. Colyar. Albany: State University of New York Press, 2004, 69–88.

McMahon, Walter. *Higher Learning, Greater Good: The Private and Social Benefits of Higher Education*. Baltimore: Johns Hopkins University Press, 2009.

McPherson, Michael, Morton Owen Schapiro, and Gordon Winston. "The Economic Analogy." Discussion Paper No. 37. Williamstown, MA: Williams Project on the Economics of Higher Education, June 1996. http://sites.williams.edu/wpehe/files/2011/06/DP -37.pdf.

Melguizo, Tatiana, and Alicia C. Dowd. "The Study of Economic, Informational, and Cultural Barriers to Community College Student Transfer Access at Selective Institutions." Los Angeles: Center for Urban Education, University of Southern California, 2008. http://www .jkcf.org/assets /files/0000/0196/Section_I.pdf.

Michener, James A. *Chesapeake*. New York: Random House, 1978.

Minow, Martha. In Brown's *Wake: Legacies of America's Educational Landmark*. London: Oxford University Press, 2010.

Nachazel, Thomas, and Gretchen Hannes, eds. "The Condition of Education 2010." Washington, DC: National Center for Education Statistics, U.S. Department of Education. http:// nces.ed.gov/pubsearch/pubsinfo.asp?pubid=2010028.

Nagaoka, Jenny, Melissa Roderick, and Vanessa Coca. *Barriers to College Attainment: Lessons from Chicago*. Washington, DC: Center for American Progress, 2009. https://www

.americanprogress.org/issues/higher-education/report/2009/01/27/5432/barriers-to
-college-attainment-lessons-from-chicago.

National Association of State Student Grant and Aid Programs. "42nd Annual Survey Report
on State-Sponsored Student Financial Aid: 2010–2011 Academic Year." 2012. http://www
.nassgap.org/viewrepository.aspx?categoryID=3#.

National Center for Public Policy and Higher Education. *Measuring Up 2008: The National
Report Card on Higher Education.* San Jose: NCPPHE, 2008. http://measuringup2008
.highereducation.org /print/NCPPHEMUNationalRpt.pdf.

National College Access Network. "Increasing Return on Investment from Federal Student
Aid." Washington, DC: NCAN, 2012. https://www.collegeaccess.org/roifromfsa.

Neff, Joseph, Ann Doss Helms, and David Raynor. "Counted Out." *Raleigh News and Observer*,
n.d. http://www.newsobserver.com/news/local/education/article149459574.html.

New York State, Tuition-Free Degree Program: The Excelsior Scholarship. https://www.ny.gov
/programs/tuition-free-degree-program-excelsior-scholarship.

Nilsson, Magnus, and Jannika Mattes. "The Spatiality of Trust: Factors Influencing the Creation of Trust and the Role of Face-to-Face Contact." *European Management Journal* 33,
no. 4 (2015): 230–244.

Obama, Michelle. "This Issue Is Personal for Me." CNN, October 13, 2016. http://edition.cnn
.com/2016/10/11/opinions/cnn-films-we-will-rise-michelle-obama.

O'Connor, Patrick. "Inadequate Counsel." *Diverse Issues in Higher Education* 27, no. 23 (2010):
17.

Olson, Kristen. "Survey Participation, Nonresponse Bias, Measurement Error Bias, and Total
Bias." *Public Opinion Quarterly* 70, no. 5 (2006): 737–758.

O'Neill, D. Kevin, and Marlene Scardamalia. "Mentoring in the Open: A Strategy for Supporting Human Development in the Knowledge Society." In *Proceedings of the Fourth International Conference of the Learning Sciences,* edited by B. Fishman and S. O'Connor-Divelbiss,
326–333. Mahwah, NJ: Erlbaum, 2000. http://www.ikit.org/fulltext/2000_Mentoring.pdf.

Pace, Eric. "L.L. Redding, 96, Desegregation Lawyer, Dies." *New York Times,* October 2, 1998.
Parker v. Univ. of Delaware, 31 Del. Ch. 381 (Del. 1950).

Perna, Laura W. "Studying College Access and Choice: A Proposed Conceptual Model." In
Higher Education: Handbook of Theory and Research, edited by John L. Smart. New York:
Springer, 2006, 99–157.

———. "Toward a More Complete Understanding of the Role of Financial Aid in Promoting
College Enrollment: The Importance of Context." In *Higher Education: Handbook of Theory and Research,* edited by John C. Smart. Houten: Springer Netherlands, 2010, 129–179.

———, Heather T. Rowan-Kenyon, Scott L. Thomas, Angela Bell, Robert Anderson, and
Chunyan Li. "The Role of College Counseling in Shaping College Opportunity: Variations
across High Schools." *Review of Higher Education* 31, no. 2 (2008): 131–159.

Pincus, Fred L. *Reverse Discrimination: Dismantling the Myth.* Colorado: Lynne Rienner
Publishers, 2003.

Plank, Stephen B., and Will J. Jordan. "Effects of Information, Guidance, and Actions on Postsecondary Destinations: A Study of Talent Loss." *American Educational Research Journal* 38,
no. 4 (2001): 947–979

Plessy v. Ferguson, 16 S.Ct 1138 (1896).

Portes, Alejandro. "Social Capital: Its Origins and Applications in Modern Sociology." *Annual
Review of Sociology,* 24, no. 1 (August 1998): 1–24.

Pusser, Brian. "Higher Education, Markets, and the Preservation of the Public Good." In *Earnings from Learning: The Rise of For-Profit Universities,* edited by David W. Breneman, Brian
Pusser, and Sarah E. Turner. Albany: State University of New York Press, 2006, 23–50.

Putnam, Robert D. *Bowling Alone*. New York: Simon & Schuster, 2000.

Ratcliffe, Caroline, and Signe-Mary McKernan. "Forever in Your Debt: Who Has Student Loan Debt, and Who's Worried?" Urban Institute (June 26, 2013): 7. https://www.urban.org /research/publication/forever-your-debt-who-has-student-loan-debt-and-whos -worried.

Ravitch, Diane. *The Death and Life of the Great American School System*. New York: Basic Books, 2010.

———. *Edspeak: A Glossary of Education Terms, Phrases, Buzzwords, and Jargon*. Alexandria, VA: Association for Supervision and Curriculum Development, 2007.

Regents of the University of California v. Bakke, 438 U.S. 265 (1978).

Reid, Robert H. *American Degree Mills: A Study of Their Operations and of Potential Ways to Control Them*. Whitefish, MT: Literary Licensing, LLC, 2012.

Robertson-Kraft, Claire, and Angela L. Duckworth. "True Grit: Trait-level Perseverance and Passion for Long-term Goals Predicts Effectiveness and Retention among Novice Teachers." *Teachers College Record* 116, no. 3 (2014): 16. https://www.ncbi.nlm.nih.gov/pmc /articles/PMC4211426.

Roderick, Melissa, Jenny Nagaoka, Vanessa Coca, and Eliza Moeller. "From High School to the Future: Making Hard Work Pay Off." Chicago: Urban Education Institute, UChicago Consortium on Chicago School Research, April 2009. http://consortium.uchicago.edu /publications/high-school-future-making-hard-work-pay.

———. "From High School to the Future: Potholes on the Road to College." Chicago: Urban Education Institute, UChicago Consortium on Chicago School Research, March 2008. http://consortium.uchicago.edu/publications/high-school-future-potholes-road -college.

Rosenbaum, James E., Shazia Rafiullah Miller, and Melinda Scott Krei. "Gatekeeping in an Era of More Open Gates: High School Counselors' Views of their Influence on Students' College Plans." *American Journal of Education* 104, no. 4 (1996): 257–279.

Ryan, James E. "The Perverse Incentives of the No Child Left Behind Act." *NYU Law Review* 79, no. 3 (2004): 934–936.

Sander, Richard H. "Class in American Legal Education." *Denver University Law Review* 88, no. 4 (2011): 632–633.

———. "The Consideration of Race in UCLA Undergraduate Admissions." Los Angeles: Project SEAPHE, UCLA School of Law, October 20, 2012. http://www.seaphe.org/pdf /uclaadmissions.pdf.

Schaeffer, Robert. "Test Scores Do Not Equal Merit." In *SAT Wars: The Case for Test-Optional College Admissions*, edited by Joseph A. Soares. New York: Teachers College Press, 2012, 153–168.

Seligman, Jason, Richard Milford, John O'Looney, and Jim Ledbetter. *HOPE Scholarship Joint Study Commission Report*. Athens, GA: Carl Vinson Institute of Government, University of Georgia, 2004.

Selingo, Jeffrey. "Questioning the Merit of Merit Scholarships." *Chronicle of Higher Education*, January 19, 2001. http://chronicle.com/article/Questioning-the-Merit-of-Merit/15616/.

Sica, Gregory T. "Bias in Research Studies." *RSNA Radiology* 238, no. 3 (March 2006): 780–789.

Simmons, Omari Scott. "Class Dismissed: Rethinking Socio-economic Status and Higher Education Attainment." *Arizona State Law Journal* 46, no. 1 (2014): 231–298.

———. "For-Profits and the Market Paradox." *Wake Forest Law Review* 48, no. 2 (2013): 333–360.

———. "Lost in Transition: The Implications of Social Capital for Higher Education Access." *Notre Dame Law Review* 87, no. 1 (2012): 205–252.

Sloviter, Dolores K. "Tribute to Collins J. Seitz: A Kind Man." *Villanova Law Review* 40, no. 3 (1995): 553–558.

Soares, Joseph A., ed. *SAT Wars: The Case for Test-Optional College Admissions.* New York: Teacher's College Press, 2012.

Sorokin, Pitirim A. *Social and Cultural Mobility.* Glencoe, IL: Free Press, 1959.

Southern Education Foundation. "A New Majority: Low Income Students Now a Majority in the Nation's Public Schools." *Research Bulletin* (January 2015). http://www.southerneducation .org/getattachment/b1995557-faec-42a1-a951-5fad5491b9e4/Publications/A-New-Majority -Low-Income-Students-in-the-South-s.aspx.

Springfield, Emily, Anne Gwozdek, and Andrew P. Smiler. "Transformation Rubric for Engaged Learning: A Tool and Method for Measuring Life-Changing Experiences." *International Journal of ePortfolio* 5, no. 1 (2015): 63–74.

St. John, Edward P. *Refinancing the College Dream: Access, Equal Opportunity, and Justice for Taxpayers.* Baltimore: Johns Hopkins University Press, 2003.

Staples, Lee. *Roots to Power: A Manual for Grassroots Organizing.* Santa Barbara: Praeger Publishers, 2004.

Steinberg, Jacques. *The Gatekeepers: Inside the Admissions Process of a Premier College.* New York: Viking, 2002.

———. "Graduates Fault Advice of Guidance Counselors." *New York Times,* March 3, 2010, A20.

Sternberg, Robert J. "College Admissions Assessments: New Techniques for a New Millennium." In *SAT Wars: The Case for Test-Optional College Admissions,* edited by Joseph A. Soares. New York: Teacher's College Press, 2012: 85–103.

Stevens, Mitchell L. *Creating a Class: College Admissions and the Education of Elites.* Cambridge, MA: Harvard University Press, 2009.

Strauss, Anselm, and Juliet Corbin. "Grounded Theory Methodology." In *Handbook of Qualitative Research,* edited by Norman K. Denzin and Yvonna S. Lincoln, 273–285. Thousand Oaks, CA: Sage Publications, 1994.

Sue, Derald Wing. *Microaggressions in Everyday Life: Race, Gender, and Sexual Orientation.* Hoboken, NJ: John Wiley & Sons, 2010.

———, Annie I. Lin, Gina C. Torino, Christina M. Capodilupo, and David P. Rivera. "Racial Microaggressions and Difficult Dialogues on Race in the Classroom." *American Psychological Association* 15, no. 2 (2009): 183–190.

———, Kevin L. Nadal, Christina M. Capodilupo, Annie I. Lin, Gina C. Torino, and David P. Rivera. "Racial Microaggressions against Black Americans: Implications for Counseling." *Journal of Counseling and Development* (Summer 2008): 330–338.

Suitts, Steve. "A New Diverse Majority: Students of Color in the South's Public Schools." Atlanta: Southern Education Foundation, October 2010.

———. "A New Majority Update: Low Income Students in the South and Nation." Atlanta: Southern Education Foundation, 2013. http://www.southerneducation.org/News-and -Events/posts/April-2014/Juvenile-Justice-Education-Programs-in-the-United-aspx.

Symonds, William C., Robert B. Schwartz, and Ronald Ferguson. "Pathways to Prosperity: Meeting the Challenge of Preparing Young Americans for the 21st Century." Cambridge, MA: Pathways to Prosperity Project, Harvard University Graduate School of Education. February 2011. http://www.gse.harvard.edu /news_events/features/2011/Pathways_to_ Prosperity_Feb2011.pdf.

Tilak, Jandhyala B. G. "Higher Education: A Public Good or a Commodity? Commitment to Higher Education or Commitment of Higher Education to Trade." *Prospects* 38, no. 4 (December 2008): 449–466.

Tocqueville, Alexis de. *Democracy in America.* Indianapolis: Liberty Fund, Inc., 1835.

Tough, Paul. *How Children Succeed: Grit, Curiosity, and the Hidden Power of Character*. New York: Houghton Mifflin Harcourt, 2012.

United States Department of Education. "A Blueprint for Reform." March 2010. http://www2 .ed.gov/policy/elsec/leg/blueprint/blueprint.pdf.

———. "College- and Career-Ready Students." 2010. http://www2.ed.gov/policy/elsec/leg /blueprint/college-career-ready.pdf.

———. "College Scorecard." https://collegescorecard.ed.gov/.

———. "Race to the Top Program Executive Summary." November 2009. http://www2.ed .gov/programs/racetothetop/executive-summary.pdf.

Vedder, Richard. "Loans Are Part of the Problem Not the Solution." *New York Times*, May 12, 2012. http://www.nytimes.com/roomfordebate/2012/05/12/easing-the-pain-of-student -loans/loans-are-part-of-the-problem-not-the-solution.

Venezia, Andrea, Michael W. Kirst, and Anthony L. Antonio. "Betraying the Dream: How Disconnected K–12 and Postsecondary Education Systems Undermine Student Aspirations." Stanford, CA: Stanford University's Bridge Project, 2002. https://web.stanford.edu/group /bridgeproject/betrayingthecollegedream.pdf.

Wacquant, Loïc J. D., and William Julius Wilson. "The Cost of Racial and Class Exclusion in the Inner City." *Annals of the American Academy of Political and Social Science* 501 (January 1989). http://www.jstor.org/stable/1045646?seq=1#page_scan_tab_contents.

Warren, Constancia, Leslie Rennie-Hill, and Jay Jordon Pfeiffer. "From Information to Action: A Guide to Using Postsecondary Data to Improve Students' Chances for Postsecondary Success." Washington, DC: US Department of Education, 2012. http://www2.ed.gov /programs/slcp/information-to-action.pdf.

White House. "Reach Higher." n.d. https://www.whitehouse.gov/reach-higher.

White House. Executive Office of the President. "Increasing College Opportunity for Low-Income Students: Promising Models and a Call to Action." January 2014. https://permanent .access.gpo.gov/gpo45359/white_house_report_on_increasing_college_opportunity _for_low-income_students_1-16-2014_final.pdf.

White House. Office of the Press Secretary. "FACT SHEET: The President and First Lady's Call to Action on College Opportunity." January 16, 2014. https://www.whitehouse.gov/the -press-office/2014/01/16/fact-sheet-president-and-first-lady-s-call-action-college -opportunity.

Zumeta, William, David W. Breneman, Patrick M. Callan, and Joni E. Finney. *Financing American Higher Education in the Era of Globalization*. Cambridge, MA: Harvard Education Press, 2012.

INDEX

Page numbers in *italics* represent tables and figures.

ABOUT THE AUTHOR

OMARI SCOTT SIMMONS is the Howard L. Oleck Professor of Business Law and director of the Business Law Program at Wake Forest University School of Law. He is a recognized expert on college access as well as corporate governance. He has written numerous publications and frequently lectures on these topics to academic and nonacademic audiences across the country and abroad. He is a member of the American Law Institute.

Professor Simmons is the co-founder and executive director of the Simmons Memorial Foundation (SMF), a grassroots nonprofit organization that promotes higher education access for vulnerable students in North Carolina and Delaware. Over the past two decades, he and other SMF volunteers have helped hundreds of talented students attain their higher education goals.

Before entering academia, Professor Simmons practiced law in Washington, D.C. He received his undergraduate education at Wake Forest University; his juris doctorate from the University of Pennsylvania Law School; and a master of laws from the University of Cambridge. At the University of Pennsylvania, he received the Thouron Award and the Fontaine Fellowship. The many honors recognizing his efforts in promoting higher education opportunity include the 2016 *Winston-Salem Chronicle* Community Service Award; the 2015 MERIT Hall of Fame Award; the 2004 Dr. Sadie T.M. Alexander Distinguished Graduate Award for Outstanding Service from the Black Law Students Association of the University of Pennsylvania Law School; and the 2002 MBNA Foundation's Best Practices in Education Award.